# EX AUDITU

Volume II 1986

CONTENTS

# Introduction

*

Thomas W. Gillespie

The first annual Frederick Neumann Symposium on the Theological Interpretation of Scripture was held at Princeton Theological Seminary in August 1986. Scholars from diverse disciplines, nations, and confessions assembled in Adams House (the Center of Continuing Education) for four days of presenting, hearing, and discussing invitational papers, enjoying informal conversations, and joining together in worship. The Symposium was graced by the presence of Dr. Edith Neumann, widow of the pastor, missionary, and scholar whose name the Symposium proudly bears.

The essays published in this second volume of *Ex Auditu* represent the papers presented at the initial Symposium. The broad theme which unites them is the issue of church and state as attested in various ways by a diversity of biblical texts. Dr. Richard K. Fenn's essay focuses more specifically upon the nature of spiritual authority in primitive Christianity from the perspective of modern sociology. As such, it introduces a method of interpretation which transcends both historical and theological hermeneutics. Moreover, it reminds us that the theological interpretation of scripture does not and cannot take place in isolation from other disciplines. One of the positive characteristics of the Symposium was its openness to the multi-dimensional nature of biblical interpretation.

The second Frederick Neumann Symposium will be held on the campus of Princeton Seminary October 16–19, 1987.

# EX AUDITU AND THE THEOLOGICAL INTERPRETATION OF HOLY SCRIPTURE

PETER STUHLMACHER

## I

THE ANNUAL OF THE FREDERICK NEUMANN Symposium on Theological Interpretation of Scripture bears the title EX AUDITU, which is derived from the Vulgate translation of Rom 10:17. As Thomas W. Gillespie established in his "Introduction" to the first edition of the journal, this title involves a program and an obligation at the same time: theological interpretation of Holy Scripture grows out of the patient, open and obedient hearing of the Word of God, which is testified to by the Scripture; if this theological interpretation proceeds otherwise, it does not deserve its name.

The editor and associate editor, the annual's editorial board, its contributors and the participants of our first symposium come from various churches and have enjoyed varied theological training. When they nonetheless come together under the motto EX AUDITU, they acknowledge that Holy Scripture (consisting of Old and New Testaments) is a given for us as ecclesiastical canon and that we perceive God's Word nowhere more originally and clearly than through the witness of the Bible.

To the extent that this persuasion unifies us, it makes sense to consider at the beginning of our cooperation what rules and standards are given to us by Holy Scripture itself for interpreting the Bible. Theological interpretation of Scripture stands commissioned by and in service to the Church. Since its beginning in the second and third centuries, it has always made use of the best and most modern philological methods in order to determine the content of biblical texts for the Church's teaching and life. But it could and can only succeed in its exegetical work when, in using these methods, it remains conscious of doing justice to the biblical texts and their special claim. When we remind ourselves of the hermeneutical standards which are given by Holy Scripture itself, we in no way have to renounce modern, scientifically confirmed methods of interpretation in favor of biblical rules of interpretation. Such a renunciation would not be in accordance with the history of biblical exegesis. But we do have to relate critically the biblical rules to our contemporary methods of interpretation. As clearly as exegetical methods of the twentieth century transcend the boundaries of ancient philology and allegorizing, so we clearly must stand ready to transcend these modern methods at the point where they set the limits for the truth claim of Holy Scripture. The hearing which is raised to a standard of theological interpretation by the motto EX AUDITU includes the obligation not simply to push the hermeneutical rules and the hermeneutical experience of the Bible aside as obsolete, but rather carefully to examine how and where we have to be in accordance with them.

Since most interpretations of the Bible do not reach a decision in light of the texts, but decisions are made already at the preliminary stage of interpretation, the following methodo-

[1]I want to express my thanks to Stephen J. Amador (Tübingen) and Dr. Robert Guelich (Edina) for their help in translating the German manuscript into readable English. For further information and details concerning the parameters of biblical hermeneutics cf. my book: *Vom Verstehen des Neuen Testaments. Eine Hermeneutik*, Grundrisse zum Neuen Testament 6, Göttingen (Vandenhoeck & Ruprecht) Second revised Edition 1986.

logical reflections concerning the exegetical procedure we choose gain some significance, even when (as in the present) hermeneutical reflections are not too highly valued.

## II

Rom 10:17 represents, in Rabbinic-hermeneutical terms, a *k*$^{e}$*lāl*, i.e. a short summary, in which Paul sums up his exegetical argument up to that point: faith comes from hearing the message (=*akoē*), but the message goes back to the Word of Christ (=*rhēma Christoy*). The "Word of Christ" is, in accordance with Rom 10:5–8, the word preached by Paul (and other apostles), in which Christ himself is present. According to Paul Dt 30:11–14 speaks concerning this word. It summons first and foremost to faith in and the confession of Jesus Christ, and not to doing of righteousness which Moses teaches. The Word of Christ is conveyed by the spiritual presence of the Christ who became human, was crucified, descended into the abyss, and was resurrected by God. The "message" which grows out of this word is, according to Rom 10:16, the message of ("the servant of the Lord") Jesus Christ (cf. the citation of Is 53:1 in Rom 10:16), which the apostles proclaim as eschatological "evangelists" (10:13–15). "Faith" confesses Jesus as the Lord and Reconciler whom God resurrected, and precisely therefore will not be put to shame (at the Final Judgment; cf. Rom 10:9,11). In terms of content, therefore, the summary of Rom 10:17 carries the greatest possible amount of weight. It does not involve a marginal note (="Randbemerkung . . . eines Glossators") which wound up at a wrong place in the text, as R. Bultmann thought, but rather was intended by Paul himself. Faith depends on the proclamation of Jesus (as "servant of the Lord"), whom God made Lord and Christ through the resurrection (Acts 2:36). Following the basic level of Paul's argument, we can add: This proclamation is authorized by the missionary commission of the Resurrected One, who is present with his apostolic messengers through the Spirit and initiates faith in the hearers of their message. The *k*$^{e}$*lāl* indicates the enormous significance that the proclamation conveyed by the Spirit of Christ has for faith and likewise the significance of faith itself, which results from this proclamation.

In view of this, Rom 10:17 is very significant for the theological interpretation of Scripture. Theological exegesis as such is still not the preaching of faith. But it should interpret Scripture in such a way that the biblical texts come thereby to their own expression. If these texts, in the course of interpretation, transform themselves from historical sources that we analyze into testimonies that in turn interpret the interpreter and demand an answer from the interpreter, then the interpretation of Scripture must not prevent this role-reversal between text and exegete. Rather it should prepare and promote this.

## III

Paul himself had to deal with the question of how understanding the gospel comes about. This question was forced upon him for two reasons. First, as a persecutor of the church, he had rejected and stood opposed to the missionary gospel of Christians, only later to recognize its truth. Second, as an apostle, he had constantly to stand up for an appropriate understanding of his own gospel against a false understanding. In the Corinthian Letters he deals with both of these grounds.

The gospel was revealed to Paul by revelation (Gal 1:12,16). He does not have it at his disposal, but must preach it for better or for worse (1 Cor 9:16f.). With respect to content, the gospel concerns Christ who was crucified and resurrected by God and through whom God reconciled himself to the world. It is, as the "word of the cross" (1 Cor 1:18), the "word of reconciliation" (2 Cor 5:19). Paul did not of himself gain this recognition of Christ which leads him to proclaim the gospel, rather God endowed him with this recognition. God, the Creator of Eternal Light, illuminated his heart with the recognition that the divine glory rests on the face of the (crucified and) resurrected Christ (2 Cor 4:6).

This recognition entered into the Pauline gospel. But it also is and remains here the precious gift of God! The one to whom Paul's gospel of Christ remains dark and hidden is, according to Paul, "lost"; the mind of such a person has been blinded by "the god of this age", i.e. Satan (2 Cor 4:3f.). But those who experience the illuminating recognition of Christ as the likeness of God by the power of the gospel cannot attribute this recognition to themselves, but rather to the Holy Spirit, who comes through the message (and is powerful in baptized Christians).

The Spirit is received in the hearing of the "message of faith" (Gal 3:2); the Spirit enables the gospel to enlighten as the power of God (1 Cor 1:18,24); the Spirit alone leads to the recognition of God's gift of grace in Christ (1 Cor 2:10–12). As it was for Paul, so also for the persons to whom he proclaims God's gospel, the message of Christ is the revelation to which they must open themselves in faith. Neither Paul nor the hearers of his preaching have the right to change this gospel (Gal 1:6–9). Promulgated in human speech, the gospel wishes to be received and accepted as the Word of God, which becomes effective in those who believe (1 Thess 2:9,13).

For theological interpretation of Scripture which stands under the motto EX AUDITU, these statements of the apostle have again foundational significance. They mean that biblical interpretation in keeping with Paul must accept the gospel as a given and as a standard, and must carefully consider how spiritual and exegetical understanding of the gospel relate to one another. If the apostle is correct, then biblical exegisis does not have the purpose of critically analyzing the gospel in order to relativize it (e.g. as time-conditioned). Exegetical investigation has as its primary goal to lead one intelligibly into the gospel, to grasp all of its dimensions and to make it accessible to the reader. A hermeneutic principally of critical suspicion comes, in view of Paul's statements on understanding the gospel, under the judgment that the "Word of the Cross" appears to the wise of the world as "foolishness" (cf. 1 Cor 1:18–20). By contrast, the "spiritual" epistemology of the apostle invites one to a hermeneutic of openness and hearing and rejects all human critique of the gospel as a sign of blindness which is set against God.

The consent at which the gospel aims is faith. According to Paul, faith expresses itself in confession, in participation in the life of the church, in day-to-day service for righteousness and in the hope of the ultimate deliverance of the world through Christ's coming again. Faith in the gospel is lived-out fear of God that comes from Christ and leads back to Christ. Just as the fear of God is the beginning of all wisdom for the Old Testament (cf. Prov 1:7; 9:10; 15:33; Ps 111:10; Job 28:28), so the obedience of faith is for Paul and the New Testament the basic condition for comprehending the wisdom of God as it reveals itself in Christ (1 Cor 1:30; 2:6ff.; Col. 1:15–20; 2:3; Jn 1:1–18).

The hermeneutical problem in this association of wisdom and fear of God, faith and revelation, is that both the gospel and faith as the fear of God which is lived in Christ elude the methodological grasp of theological exegesis. Theological exegesis has to allow the gospel to be a given of the Scriptures; it can of itself neither produce faith as the condition of true understanding of the gospel, nor raise it to methodological presuppostion; it can only aim at avoiding hindering the gospel and faith by its particular methods and general procedure.

Accordingly one measures the scientific nature of biblical exegesis not only on the basis that its methods and procedures are rationally sensible and critically verifiable, but also to the extent, that it is able to transcend the limits of rational criticism and methodological doubt for the benefit of the gospel and faith as fear of God in Jesus Christ. If it proceeds otherwise, it does not do justice to its texts, which contain a special claim of revelation.

## IV

For Paul, his students, and all those who risk using him for their hermeneutic orientation, the gospel is a revelation for whose truth one must contend. When the gospel's truth was at stake, the apostle did not shrink from a confrontation even with Peter (cf. Gal 2:11ff.). For a theological interpretation of Scripture which seeks to follow Rom 10:17, this insight is important. Theological exegesis of the Bible and critique according to the standard of the Bible do not exclude one another. They complement one another! A theological interpretation of Scripture which places without differentiation one word of Holy Scripture next to another, and does not dare to judge on the basis of the gospel what is central and what is peripheral, neglects its duty to judge theologically.

This duty to judge critically pertains to each level of theological interpretation of the Bible. For example: at the level of the historical origin of the texts, one must decide how Paul relates to his critics (in Galatians or 2 Corinthians), how the critique of Paul's theses by the Letter of James (cf. Jas 2:24 with Rom 3:28) relates to Paul himself, or how Paul relates to Peter (cf. Gal 2:11ff. and 1 Cor 1:12; 9:3ff.; 15:9–11). At the level of the biblical canon, in which the four Gospels stand next to Paul's Letters, Paul's Letters next to the Catholic Letters, and the Letter to the Hebrews next to the Revelation of John, theological judgment has to be more comprehensive. Here it is necessary to ask (with respect to the truth of the gospel) about the relationship between Jesus and Paul, John and the Synoptics, 1 Jn 1:8f; 2:1f. and Heb 6:4ff.; 10:26f., etc. But above all it is necessary to decide how the Old and New Testaments belong to one another and whether the (Pauline) gospel really represents the center of Scripture. When theological exegesis of the Bible then ultimately advances to the level of interpretation of Scripture for today, it must itself be in possession of a standard, namely the Christ of the gospel. The Christ of the gospel (as center of Scripture) does not simply result from the sum of all New Testament passages which concern Jesus Christ, but rather represents on the basis of the testimony of the Old and New Testaments the *one* Lord and messianic Son of God in whose mission, cross and resurrection the *one* God of the Scriptures acted sufficiently for the salvation of Jews and Gentiles (cf. e.g. Rom 1:1–5; 2 Cor 5:18–21).

If we follow Paul and the gospel preached by him, this "center of Scripture" results not only from Paul's letters or the New Testament's writings, but represents the center of Holy Scripture, consisting of Old and New Testaments. This Christ-center of Scripture as a whole is to be distinguished carefully from an exclusive "canon within in the canon!" What we have just asserted results from the historical fact that the Old and New Testaments belong in a Christian perspective indissolubly together.

## V

A New Testament which has been detached from the Old Testament and understood by itself as Holy Scripture is a modern phenomenon. Only in Marcion does this have its (unfortunate) analogy in the Christian history of the canon. By nature the Old and New Testaments belong together in the closest possible manner. Jesus and the Apostles gave the

Church a share in the Holy Scripture of Israel. The Christian congregations of the first and beginning part of the second centuries read and interpreted the Law, the Prophets, Psalms and Wisdom writings as their "Holy Scripture." The New Testament writings were added to those of the Old Testament only gradually. From a canon-history perspective the New Testament supplements the Old Testament, but nowhere displaces it in the Church.

When one inquires about the limits of the Christian Old Testament, one has to recognize that the Bible of Christianity does not allow itself to be limited to the so-called Masoretic canon of the Jews. This is not possible for two reasons. First, Christians received the "Holy Scriptures" at a time in the first century A.D. when the three-part Jewish canon was not yet permanently established, but was still open with respect to which books should be included into the so called "Writings." Second, the Greek translations of the Septuagint were considered in Jewish and Christian communities of the first century to be inspired witnesses of revelation, just as the Hebrew and Aramaic books of the "Tanach." Third, apocryphal writings are cited as Holy Scripture in e.g. Mc 10:19; 1 Cor 2:9; 2 Tim 2:18, and the Letter of Jude. From this perspective it is necessary to consider the so-called Apocrypha of the Septuagint a part of the Christian Old Testament. In terms of tradition and canon history, these later books of the Old Testament (above all the Wisdom writings) stand far closer to the foundational strata of the Gospels and apostolic Letters than we ordinarily think.

For a theological interpretation of Scripture based on Rom 10:17, these facts mean that such interpretation should be theological exegesis of Holy Scripture as a whole, that it may not all too quickly demote the Apocrypha of the Septuagint to just "intertestamental literature," and it must consider very precisely when, how and where the Old Testament is presupposed, received and quoted in the New. Since the New Testament reception of the Old Testament is methodologically the same—even down to particulars—as the early Jewish use of Holy Scripture, one should also be theologically very cautious regarding the scientifically popular verdict concerning Christological interpretation of the Old Testament in the New.

## VI

The hermeneutical problem and comprehensive range of tasks of biblical interpretation for the Church are already outlined in the New Testament.

Just as for their Jewish contemporaries, the Holy Scripture (of the Old Testament) was also considered by the New Testament authors to be inspired by the Spirit of God (2 Tim 3:16). The *theopneustia* of Scripture means that only an interpretation which is borne by the Holy Spirit can really determine and pass on the inspired testimony of Scripture. Without participating in the Spirit who fills Scripture, a theological understanding of the Bible was and is not guaranteed. We find this to be the case for Jesus (cf. Mt 11:2–6 + 11:25–27), Paul (cf. 1 Cor 2:6–16), and the Gospel of John (cf. Jn 5:39; 6:63,68). The so-called later writings of the New Testament actually attest that (cf. 2 Tim 3:14–17; 2 Pet 1:16–21).

The New Testament witnesses had scarcely determined—in adaptation of and in confrontation with contemporary Jewish interpretation of Scripture—that Holy Scripture is not to be interpreted from Moses to Moses but from Christ to Christ (i.e. *ek pisteōs eis pistin;* cf. Rom 1:17), when a new, specifically Christian hermeneutical situation developed. The congregations had to be enabled by their teachers so as to be capable of responding to every one who required of these Christians an account of their faith and the hope which moved them (cf. 1 Pet 3:15). At the same time, however, these congregations had to be protected from a disintegration and false interpretation of their own foundation of faith by heterodox Christian groups, which developed further in the second century into Gnostic schools and docetic spiritualists. The confrontations with these groups appear in the Johannine Letters, in the Pastoral Letters, and e.g. also in 2 Peter.

The "apology" of the Christian hope of faith mentioned in 1 Pet 3:15 was carried out with the help of training in and appreciation of the Church's teaching of faith (cf. on this e.g. Rom 6:17; 1 Cor 15:3–5; 1 Tim 6:20; 2 Tim 1:12,14). Against growing docetism the confession of the full and complete incarnation of Christ was established (cf. Jn 1:14–18; 6:52–58; 19:34; 1 Jn 4:2f.; 5:5ff.). Against gnostic distortion of Paul's Letters, the tradition of the Gospels and the Old Testament, which is decried in 2 Pet 1:16ff.; 3:16, only a general ecclesiastical theory of interpretation could still help. It reads according to (the Pastoral Letters and ) 2 Peter as follows: The testimonies of the Old Testament, which were effected by the Spirit and are given to the congregation, the words of Jesus and the Letters of the Apostles are to be interpreted in terms of the tradition of faith, which is alive in the congregations from the Apostles. Spiritually salvific interpretation of the Old and (developing) New Testaments is an interpretation within the framework of the teaching of faith which derives from the Apostles.

The Ancient Church pursued this hermeneutical principle further and gave ecclesiastical biblical interpretation the so-called "*regula fidei,*" or the "*kanōn tēs pisteōs,*" as a theological standard. The "rule of faith" desires to be a summary of the essential content of faith to which the Scripture (consiting of Old and New Testaments) testifies. For this reason it can be decided on the basis of the "canon of faith" how the Holy Scriptures are to be interpreted. The person who has a share in the faith (of the Church), which is summarized in the "rule of faith," also has a share in the Spirit, and is therefore qualified for interpretation of the Bible in its fullness of the Spirit; the person who rejects the "*kanōn tēs pisteōs*" is not suited for theological interpretation of the Holy Scripture.

With these biblical and ancient Church parameters for theological interpretation of Scripture we come to a point which is decisive, but also dangerous, for the undertaking of the journal. It is decisive because all the churches to which we belong have adopted the above-named parameters and also affirm them in principle. A theological interpretation of Scripture which withdraws itself from dogmatic accountability is useless for the Church and unacceptable. A theologically comprehensive interpretation of the Bible consisting of Old and New Testaments is however not the exclusive prerogative of exegetical specialists, but lies rather in the joint responsibility of exegetes, Church historians, dogmaticians, teachers of practical theology, missiologists, and Christian witnesses of faith. EX AUDITU can therefore only succeed as a cooperative project which extends beyond individual theological disciplines.

The problem lies in the fact that our churches have, in the course of their history, split concerning the more precise identification and weighing of the above-named hermeneutical parameters, even to the extent of breaking church fellowship. The more we concentrate in this situation on the interpretation of the *biblical* traditions which we all have in common, the more helpful this will be for our still divided churches. None of them wishes to withdraw itself from responsibility to the testimony of Holy Scripture; all of them confess Jesus as Reconciler and Lord; all of them are currently faced with great missionary challenges. These challenges compel a drawing together of Christians and a joint reflection and contemplation of the biblical legacy. When we come together for such contemplation and reflection in the sense of EX AUDITU, then our work will, to the extent that it is possible, be theologically and ecclesiologically valuable.

# The Primacy of Consent and the Uses of Suspicion

Ben F. Meyer

This essay proposes a set of propositions on subject and subjectivity in interpretation: on the hermeneutical centrality of subjectivity, on the conditions of authentic subjectivity, and on authentic subjectivity as the condition of or key to objective interpretation.

We begin (part one) with the passing of the age of innocence, when issues of subjectivity were overlooked or underrated or suppressed or merely presupposed. There follows (part two) an account of the kind of subjectivity that is calculated to measure up fully to the task of interpretation. Here the accent falls on the role of critical realism in establishing a deeply and solidly based hermeneutics. Finally (part three), we discuss biblical interpretation, distinguishing conditions of possibility and conditions of excellence. Orientation to consent is the appropriate stance for interpretation in the strict sense, but "suspicion" is allotted a twofold role: first, in "analysis," whether antecedent to or consequent on interpretation; second, in critique, brought to bear not only on the text but on the interpreter himself.

## I

> . . . the more human studies turn away from abstract universals and attend to concrete human beings, the more evident it becomes that the scientific age of innocence has come to an end; human authenticity can no longer be taken for granted.
>
> Bernard Lonergan.[1]

The age of innocence was objectivist, a time when problems and solutions were discussed exclusively in terms of "objective data" or, at best, of "objective data and objective arguments." A late-blooming work markedly emblematic of this objectivism was Oswald Spengler's *Decline of the West*, according to which the life and death of Western, as of every, civilization is as predetermined as the evolution and life-span of a butterfly.[2] In this view, nothing that we, the bearers of Western civilization, think or decide or do make any difference.

The passing of the age of innocence has been signaled by the emergent theme of the subject, whose thinking, deciding, and doing make all the difference. The subject, celebrated in a cloud of unknowing by the Romantic movement, was diversely thematized in the works of Schopenhauer and Nietzsche, of Kierkegaard and Newman, and the theme moved toward maturity in our century with Heidegger, Jaspers, Marcel, and Maritain. Perhaps the most fundamental forward step on the philosophic and hermeneutical front has been the grasp of objectivity, not as the absence of subjectivity, but as the fruit of authentic subjectivity.[3]

Though the age of innocence has passed, there is hardly a day in which we do not hear

[1]Bernard Lonergan, "The Ongoing Genesis of Methods," in *A Third Collection. Papers by Bernard J. F. Lonergan*, ed. F. E. Crowe (New York/Mahwah: Paulist, 1985) 146–165, p. 147.

[2]Oswald Spengler, *The Decline of the West. Vol. 1: Form and Actuality. Vol. 2: Perspectives of World History*, trans. Charles Francis Atkinson (London: George Allen & Unwin, 1926–28). See the review by R. G. Collingwood, *Antiquity* 1 (1927) 311–325.

[3]Rudolf Bultmann, "The Problem of Hermeneutics," in *Essays Philosophical and Theological*, trans. J. C. G. Greig (London: SCM, 1958) 234–261, p. 239. Adding the crucial modifier "authentic" to "subjectivity," Bernard Lonergan, *Method in Theology* (London: Darton, Longman & Todd, 1972) 162–165.

the voice of yesterday. Not long ago the philosopher, Sidney Hook, responded in a mellow mood to a question about his atheism:

> I may, when I die, wake up in the presence of the Almighty, and if He were to ask me why I did not profess my belief in Him, I would reply, "Lord, you did not give me enough evidence."[4]

Overlooked in this nicely turned sentence is the possibility that what has been lacking is not evidence but the subjective conditions that would allow the speaker to grasp the evidence as "enough."

> In the ideal detective story the reader is given all the clues yet fails to spot the criminal. He may advert to each clue as it arises. He needs no further clues to solve the mystery. Yet he can remain in the dark for the simple reason that reaching the solution is not the mere apprehension of any clue, nor the mere memory of all, but a quite distinct activity of organizing intelligence that places the full set of clues in a unique explanatory perspective.[5]

In a word, it is not evidence that is lacking, but the intelligent act of placing the evidence in proper constellation. When this is done, the hitherto missing insight follows as the night the day.

We cannot say that if a tourist is unable to construe a sign written in a language unknown to him, there must be something wrong with the sign, nor that a nonliterary person's incapacity to construe a poem, despite having some hold on its every individual word and on many of its combinations of words, is a sure sign that the poem is a failure. Most poets would greet the formulas of mathematicized physics with even blanker incomprehension. What is regularly missing among the subjective conditions of our understanding of languages, of texts, of artifacts, of calculations, is mastery of "the code." The code is the key. In the concrete, however, the referent of the "code" metaphor can turn out to be less a magic password than a daunting demand for long-term personal development. One might have to scale a many-storied mountain before reaching the point at which Stravinsky and Shostakovich, or Rilke and Valéry, or Einstein and Heisenberg, or Russell and Whitehead begin to become luminously intelligible.

Habitually, we all know this. Selectively, we forget it again and again, for few of us have entirely let go of our pre-hermeneutical objectivist heritage. Recently, I reread a particularly fine article designed to introduce to English readers the work of Rudolf Pesch on the eucharistic words and on the way in which they can be seen to correlate with Jesus' public proclamation of the reign of God. The writer, Robert Daly of Boston College, concluded his exposition, however, in a spirit of extreme caution, offering a short but formidable list of items relevant to Pesch's argument and unfortunately unknowable: "(1) There is no presently known way of being sure about the genuinity . . . of the long text of Lk 22:19–20. (2) That the Last Supper was a Passover meal cannot be proven by historical-critical means. . . . " (3) That the early Christian eucharist was a unified meal celebration remains unproven. (4) Pesch's "genre-critical analysis that Mark is a historical account and not a liturgical text does not contain enough probative force to convince a sceptical mind."[6]

These negative observations, to be sure, are qualified to the extent that Pesch's argument, according to Daly, is "demolished" only if one takes it in "all-or-nothing" terms, the implication being that such terms are unreasonable. One might add to this that the four items in question are knowable in principle, and the fact that they are all disputed is no guarantee

[4]See Nathan Glick, "Sidney Hook, Embattled Philosopher," *Encounter* 75 (June, 1985) 28–32, p. 30, note 6.
[5]Bernard Lonergan, *Insight: A Study of Human Understanding* (New York: Longmans, 1958) ix.
[6]Robert J. Daly, "The Eucharist and Redemption: The Last Supper and Jesus' Understanding of His Death," *Biblical Theology Bulletin* 11 (1981) 21–27, p. 26.

of their unknowability. We have deep intractable disagreements on crucial issues in every sphere of human studies without exception. This does not make the truth about all these issues flatly inaccessible. Furthermore, Daly's own indications that the four unknowns may not be absolutely unknowable should be noted. Respecting the long text in Luke, there is "no presently known way" of establishing its genuinity. That the Last Supper was a Passover meal cannot be proven "by historical-critical means." That early Christian eucharist was a unified meal celebration remains unproven, not necessarily unprovable. Pesch's arguments for his genre-critical conclusions would not convince "a sceptical mind." Though the qualifications are slight or muted, they do take some of the edge off the claim that the right solutions to all four questions are unknowable.

Still, the last point, on what would or would not "convince a sceptical mind," is suggestive. It intimates the writer's conception of what is requisite to knowledge, namely, proof that will sway a sceptic. This has the look of epistemological insurance. What will sway a sceptic should easily be valid for the rest of us.

At this juncture, however, I would offer two observations. The first is that the implied requisite to knowledge is Cartesian overkill. The second is that this overkill is requisite to (and perhaps compensation for) prolongation of the age of innocence. That is, there is a strategy at work here: one makes the test of knowledge excessively rigorous to safeguard the assumption that any proposal passing the test will be generally accepted. To spell the assumption out: the generality of interested parties are reasonable men and women intent on understanding, equipped to understand accurately, and ready to judge in strict accord with evidence.

It is sobering, however, to reflect that even if Rudolf Pesch were to prove all four designated points beyond cavil, there would still be many exegetes of many lands and tongues and cultural communities and confessional allegiances to construe the data otherwise, to contest his arguments, and to reject his conclusions. For, no scholarly community, not even the community of natural scientists, to say nothing of social scientists, of historians, of literary critics and exegetes, is led simply by the careful marshalling and rigorous weighing of evidence.

When we say "sufficient evidence," we do not mean evidence sufficient to win the assent of everyone without exception; we do not mean evidence sufficient to win the assent of a two-thirds majority. We mean evidence sufficient to win the assent of a person of good judgment, i.e., of one able and willing to make his way to the truth. To concede the universality of such good judgment was the hallmark of the age of innocence. We have since come to realize that this generosity was ill-advised, misleading, and mistaken. Good judgment is neither universal nor commonplace. We have come to realize, in fact, that the heart of the hermeneutical problem is precisely here, in the categorical need to identify and bring to realization those factors in ourselves that facilitate insight and promote good judgment.

Moreover, when we are dealing with hermeneutics in relation to the Bible, the interpretation of which has generated distinct, separate, sometimes bitterly contentious religio-cultural communities, it is folly to suppose that the issue of what allows one, or positively leads one, to grasp evidence as sufficient (together with all the issues of meaning and value that this settles or at least impinges upon and colors) is squarely met by objectivist considerations of "data" and "argument." It is folly, in other words, to suppose that there is no need to take account of subjectivity, ranging from the habitually perverse to the habitually attentive, intelligent, reasonable, and responsible.[7]

[7]On the transcendental precepts (be attentive, be intelligent, be reasonable, be responsible), which accord with the four levels of human intentionality (experience = data, understanding, judgment, decision), see *Method in Theology* 53–55, 231f.

The root of our deepest divisions is not lack of evidence. It is the fact of opposed horizons and, above all, of irreducibly opposed horizons, as a moment's reflection on public controversies will suggest and as sustained reflection will confirm. Irreducibly opposed horizons are a massive human reality labyrinthine in its consequences, leading some sincerely to champion as true and good what others with equal sincerity repudiate as false and evil. In view of this baffling, if common, state of affairs, what is to be done? Since the question comes down finally to "what are we to do about ourselves?" it raises the foundational issue of human authenticity.

## II

The most illuminating conclusion to emerge from intentionality analysis in our time is that in virtue of the structures of intentionality the human person is variously self-transcendent and finds his fulfillment in the achievement of self-transcendence of many kinds. As knowledge is intentional self-transcendence, so love is affective self-transcendence, and the peak of self-transcendence is the primacy in one's life of the love of God. Love at its best moves the lover out of the relativizing and distorting reference to self into the freedom to dispose of his life generously. The tendency of the love of God is toward the most radical and thoroughgoing self-transcendence. At the same time, this tendency spontaneously enhances moral, affective, and cognitive self-transcendence. More than any other human impulse, the love of God energizes the wavering but instinctive human dissatisfaction with all that is shabby, shallow, hollow, and destructive. It nurtures the inconstant but deep-seated longing for human authenticity. Finally, religion, though allied with success, is peculiarly powerful amid failure, and so heals as well as fulfills.

As the ineradicable longing for human authenticity and fulfillment is still subject to overlays of illusion and distortion, so this drive to the most radical and thoroughgoing form of self-transcendence is liable to alloys and perversions, flawed forms that nevertheless presuppose and so attest the values they distort. Hence, though religion offers fertile ground for the exacerbation of opposed perspectives, convictions, and commitments, it also and more fundamentally offers great resources for the cultivation of acts and dispositions—self-suspicion and repentance, hope and love—that, if allowed free rein, would sweep away misconstrual and *ressentiment* and expose overblown oppositions as illusory, or minor, or in any case resolvable.

Moral self-transcendence subtly but thoroughly transforms ordinary men and women, making them good. The highest and best form of friendship is uncommon, according to Aristotle, because it supposes good men and good men are rare. But moral excellence not only makes the highest form of friendship possible; it also maintains the social fabric. Its contribution to human sensibility, manners, and taste is personally and socially indispensable. When the free flow of moral self-transcendence is reduced to a trickle, the culture turns into a slum.

The moral conversion that human knowledge and the love of God invite and demand is an effective commitment to values when values and satisfactions conflict. A moral stance of this kind assuredly does not do away with opposed horizons and human conflicts. But, like the self-transcendence that is the love of God, it is bifrontal, dissipating spurious oppositions as well as establishing oppositions crucial to the cause of society.

The intellectual dimension of subjectivity, though unlikely to come to full fruition in philosophic truth without the magnetic pull of religious and moral vitality, nevertheless has its own character and integrity. Its field of operation is the dialectic of sense and intelligence. Sense grounds a childish realism, intelligence an adult realism. Most lives are a symbiosis of the two, for the thousand learning adaptations that we make in childhood often prove to have lifelong staying power.

Russell Baker, the American autobiographer and humorist, offers an illustration and explanation. "O Romeo, Romeo! Wherefore art thou Romeo?" means, of course, "why are you Romeo rather than Silvio or Georgio?" But most educated adults, says Baker, will say it means "Romeo, where are you?" This simplicity is without excuse but not without explanation:

> The explanation of the error has to do with the lifelong persistence of misunderstandings which are born in early childhood. Juliet's opening words in the balcony scene are one of the first Shakespearean lines encountered in childhood. To an uninformed mind, incapable of grasping subtleties about the irrelevance of names, "Wherefore art thou Romeo?" can only sound like a call for Romeo to tell where he's hiding. . . . This tendency of the mind to reject the fruits of its education and lapse back into childhood's happy ignorance may explain the difficulty of rooting out nasty irrational prejudices.[8]

Thus, the child undermines the man. The "childish realism" alluded to above is a shorthand reference to a universal human experience. The primacy of sense life, beginning in infancy, defines the child's sense of the real. This is reflected in his spontaneous recourse to sense-resources for distinguishing his dreams from his waking hours, for keeping the stories he hears in a magic limbo at once held together with and held apart from the everyday world, and for seeing through the jokes, fibs, and subterfuges of his playmates. For the child the real is the live, moving, varied world that is seen, heard, touched, tasted, smelled.

This realism has enough staying power to defeat the efforts of most adults who undertake to ponder the real philosophically. So, Samuel Johnson, when Boswell remarked that Berkeley's idealism, though untrue, could not be refuted, cried, "striking his foot with mighty force against a large stone, till he rebounded from it, 'I refute it *thus.*' "[9] Since the real is what he can see and touch, the child is a realist, and the grown man may reaffirm, like Johnson, the realism of childhood or, like Berkeley, move out of it by appeal to the dependence of primary on secondary qualities and of secondary qualities on perception. In either case perception is king—just as in childhood.

A fundamental alternative to the perceptualism of naive realists, empiricists, and idealists alike comes to light from reflection on human wonder; for, wonder, supervening on perception, reveals itself in and through the questions that make wonder thematic. By contrast with perception, there is no limit on the kinds of objects that questioning may envisage. Whatever limit be posited, one may transcend it by questioning it, asking whether it exists, or what it is, and whether anything lies beyond it and, if so, what. The reach of wonder and, correlatively, the reach of the questioning that thematizes it cannot be restricted at all. Questioning is open *ad infinitum.* Questions intend, not nothing, but everything; not nothing, but being; not some modes and spheres of being, but all its modes and spheres. In questioning there is accordingly the possibility of a certain self-transcendence, and whenever a question is satisfactorily (i.e., truly) answered, this possibility is actualized. Without the questioner, to be sure, there is no question; but the truth of a truly answered question stands on its own.[10] Questions intend the real and true answers attain it.

This puts us on the track of fully human knowledge. As the realism of childhood identi-

[8]Russell Baker, "Why Art Thou Romeo?" *International Herald Tribune,* May 18, 1984.

[9]James Boswell, *The Life of Samuel Johnson* (London: Macmillan, 1922) 162.

[10]Bernard Lonergan, "The Subject," in *A Second Collection. Papers by Bernard J. F. Lonergan,* eds. W. F. J. Ryan and B. J. Tyrrell (London: Darton, Longman & Todd, 1974) 69–86, p. 70, on how, ontologically, truth resides only in the subject, but intentionally is independent of the subject.

fies the real with the objects of perception, so a fully human realism identifies the real with the object of true judgment. As one enters the world of the child through the senses, one enters the fully human world through wonder and questioning and question-answering and answer-checking, a process that begins in childhood, that first takes the habitual form of belief and, as time goes on, increasingly takes the form of independently weighing and selectively approving particular answers. Little by little, belief is confirmed or corrected, evidence gains in importance, and there come into view the lineaments of a world known to be real.

We are adverting here to a duality in our knowledge: elementary knowing, which is prior to questions, and fully human knowing, which follows on questions, includes the quest of answers, and culminates in the ascertainment that such-and-such answers are exact. The classic error in the theory of knowledge has been to make elementary knowing the paradigm of fully human knowing, as if, for example, fully human knowing were a high-class kind of seeing.[11] This misleading analogy generates mistaken inferences, e.g., that the object of understanding is clarified by the clearer case of the object of ocular vision. Just as a colored lighted object is a concrete determinant sufficient of itself to actuate sight (supposing that the eye is able to function), so the to-be-understood may be conceived as a concrete determinant sufficient of itself to actuate understanding. But if this were so, it would be difficult to explain why anyone should fail to arrive at a given understanding, or why persons asking themselves the same question do not, in fact, always come up with the same answer. Hence, the juxtaposition of seeing and of knowing turns out to offer clarification not by comparison but by contrast. The to-be-seen is simply there; the to-be-understood, on the other hand, only emerges as it is defined by a question. Further, the to-be-seen is simply seen, whereas the to-be-understood is pondered, clarified by illustration and experiment, readjusted to the question and revised. Finally, when the to-be-seen is seen, sight is fully actuated; but when the to-be-understood is understood, something is still missing in fully human knowing, namely, an answer to the further question, "is this particular understanding correct?"

"Critical realism" is a descriptive and analytic theory of knowledge designed to differentiate and correlate elementary and fully human knowing. The preceding paragraphs offer illustrations of the theory's descriptive function: upon examination one discovers that the traits of fully human knowing are not to be found in elementary knowing. Sense-knowledge yields neither "reality" nor "appearance," only "data."[12] The salient trait of wonder, on the other hand, as well as of the questions that specify it, is the boundless openness whereby the wonderer/questioner enters into relation not just to data but to reality and, in principle, to the whole of reality. Intending is an immediate relating of the intender to whatever he intends. There is nothing to keep him from intending the real. He could not keep himself from such intending.

The differentiation between elementary and fully human knowing implies no gap between the two, for it is data that give rise to wonder; wonder is objectified in questions; questions

[11]See *Insight*, 252f. on the distinction between elementary knowing and fully human knowing; 422f. on how failure to make and maintain the distinction (a failure epitomized in the tag "knowing is like seeing") generates the component of aberration in the dialectical development of philosophy. As Lonergan elsewhere puts it, the notions of knowledge and reality that are formed in childhood (i.e., the reduction of knowing to analogy with seeing and of the real to what is there to be seen) "down through the centuries have provided the unshakable foundations of materialism, empiricism, positivism, sensism, phenomenalism, behaviorism, pragmatism . . . " *Method in Theology*, 213f.

[12]See Bernard Lonergan, "Cognitional Structure," in *Collection. Papers by Bernard Lonergan*, ed. F. E. Crowe (New York: Herder and Herder, 1967) 221–139, p. 235.

call forth answers; answers solicit reflection; reflection culminates in judgment that a given answer is certainly or probably true or false.

Nor is it possible to make the case that fully human knowing may intend or aspire to the real but not attain it, for that is self-reversing. If the case were made that true judgments do not occur, then at least one true judgment would have occurred. Furthermore, one cannot deny that true ascertainments of matters of fact are recurrent in our lives, for the denial is contradicted by the habitual experience of what is being denied and hence is flatly void of plausibility.[13]

Taking account of the fact of true judgments, the analytic moment in critical realism addresses the issue of the objectivity in virtue of which such judgments occur. Once again, a grasp of the duality of elementary knowing and fully human knowing is indispensable. "Object" in the context of elementary knowing is simply the term of extraverted consciousness: whatever is seen, heard, touched, tasted, smelled. The condition of the objectivity of such knowing is the proper functioning of the senses. But "object" in the context of fully human knowing is whatever is intended by questions and known when the questions are satisfactorily answered. The objectivity of this kind of knowing is accordingly complex. An experiential component lies in the givenness of data. An intelligent component lies in the demand expressed by a question and met by an answer. A rational component lies in the further demand that the answer be true, met by the assembling of evidence and the reflective grasp of it as sufficient.

We can improve this account in the light of Bernard Lonergan's technically adroit formulation of "sufficient evidence" as "the virtually unconditioned"—an understanding the conditions of whose truth are known and known to be fulfilled.[14] Given this definition, the second and third components of objectivity may be more elegantly conceptualized as follows. Normative objectivity arises when the exigences of intelligence (namely, for insight in response to a question) and of reasonableness (namely, for the logic relating the insight to the conditions of its truth) are met. Terminal or absolute objectivity results from combining normative with experiential objectivity (the givenness of data), just as, by analogy, a syllogism (if X, then Y; but X; therefore Y) concludes in function of combining the major and the minor propositions.[15]

As the classic epistemological error lies in a confused amalgamation that partly reduces object and objectivity in fully human knowing to object and objectivity in elementary knowing, so the epistemological excellence of critical realism lies in the analysis of objectivity made possible by a clear and consistent differentiation between the two.

What counts for authenticity, according to Nietzsche, is not truth but life. Above we have sketched a sequence of philosophic reflections in the contrary conviction that life without regard for truth is headed away from authenticity toward ruin. And precisely because truth and a stubborn insistence on truth belong foundationally to human authenticity, we have attempted to highlight an option—critical realism—that affirms our need for truth and vindicates our access to it. No doubt, the living-out of truth—for example, in the unself-regarding generosity of friendsip, loyalty, love—shines with a clarity and immediacy that no human knowing can match. But to exclude objective knowing from the world of value is to ensure its ultimate collapse. Authenticity is intrinsically integral. It is a dynamic whole that, never perfect, never ceases to summon and assemble its diverse but functionally harmonious elements: intellectual, aesthetic, moral, and religious, individual, personal, and intersubjective, social, cultural, economic, and political.

[13]See *Insight*, 281–283 on the character and undeniability of true ascertainments of concrete matters of fact.
[14]*Insight*, 280f., 343–345; *Method in Theology*, 102.
[15]*Insight*, 280f. and "*Insight* Revisited," in *A Second Collection*, 263–278, p. 275.

Valid interpretation and human authenticity belong to and contribute to each other. Without valid interpretation, human authenticity is socially and culturally diminished. Without human authenticity, interpretation trails off into the capricious, thwarted by absorption in pretentious or unpretentious trivia (*fascinatio nugacitatis*). This includes, on the part of literary scholars who for whatever reason find themselves with nothing very compelling, or even very definite, to do, a misplaced hankering to break out into creativity and inventiveness. There follow declarations of independence from the tyrannies of philology and history, from the merely intended sense of the text, and finally from the text itself. But faddism is notoriously ineffective occupational therapy.

An honorable task for those who put a high premium on the text to be interpreted, interpretation is the three-step process of working out an understanding of the text, reflecting on and judging how accurate that understanding is, and presenting what one judges to be an accurate understanding of the text.[16] Understood in this sense, interpretation is not always necessary, for not every text poses problems of understanding. (If it did, then every interpretation would itself need an interpretation, and so on *ad infinitum*.)

Even where interpretation is appropriate, hermeneutics need not be. If the object of interpreation is to understand the text, the object of hermeneutics is to understand the understanding of texts. When interpretation is luminous, hermeneutics is superfluous. But just as interpretation becomes necessary when the text to be understood is in some way opaque, so hermeneutics becomes necessary when fundamentally diverse interpretations of the same text compete, and especially when the competition threatens to become chaotic. Then the situation calls for a reflective step backward in an effort to discover what has gone awry in interpretation.

We are concerned with the kind of interpretation that will measure up to classic religious texts that decidedly do call for interpretation. In Western civilization no interpretative effort has ever been mounted that would compare qualitatively or quantitatively with the tradition of biblical interpretation. For well over a century this tradition has been cultivated in the philological and historical mode, and for the greater part of this period German Protestant interpreters have taken the leading role. Two schools of theological interpretation (especially of the New Testament) have been successively predominant in Germany: first, liberal theology, which died out in the wake of the first world war; then, kerygma theology, which lost its ascendancy only in the last decade or two.

A conspicuous virtue of both schools was their philological and historical rigor. Both nevertheless exhibited basic shortcomings, as their interpretations of central New Testament themes make clear. For liberal theology the eschatological theme of the *basilieia tou theou* was moralized in thoroughgoing fashion, becoming an inner kingdom of repentance (*ein innerliches Reich der Sinnesänderung*, Ritschl). Against the liberals, kerygma theologians reaffirmed the centrality of the gospel, but they could not see their way clear to affirm its constitutent elements—the expiatory death of Jesus and his resurrection from the dead—at face value and in their intended sense.

The phrase "intended sense" evokes a theme of the highest relevance at this point, namely, the interpretative ideal. The test of kerygma theology was the "mythological" text, which on the one hand was central to Christianity and on the other was incompatible with scientific modernity. The solution was to transpose the mythical content of the text into existential terms. This procedure was, no doubt, liable to the objection that it made the text intelligible only by eliminating its intended sense. But kerygma theologians could respond that, if the procedure elimnated a superficially intended sense, it did so only to recover thereby the most

[16]*Method in Theology*, 155.

deeply and authentically intended sense of the text.[17]

This response hinged on a prior thesis having a philosophic and a literary aspect. On the philosophic side, the thesis described knowledge as a symbolic projection from an experiential matrix. Whatever the product of this projection—perhaps a maze of symbol or myth—the act of projecting was a charged self-expression. Among the direct consequences of this view were a hypothesis on myth and a corresponding interpretative strategy. The hypothesis defined myth as an objectified expression of self-understanding; thus, the thrust of all myth was anthropological. The interpretative strategy was to decipher the myth not, so to speak, on its own terms but rather by reference to the existentially grounded, self-revealing and self-defining act that produced it. Interpretation thus became an effort to locate in one's own experience the originating drive producing one's ideas and images, symbols and myths, and other objectifications. In this way Hans Jonas could find the unity behind the diversity of gnostic objectifications, and Rudolf Bultmann could work out a program of saving New Testament eschatology by finding its existential wellsprings.

The drawbacks of the "prior thesis," however, have been coming more and more relentlessly to light. On the philosophic side the gratuitous Neo-Kantian immanentism of its account of knowledge has been exposed by critical-realist critique,[18] and on the literary side the systematizing account of myth as objectified self-understanding has faded in the light of an empirically better grounded analysis of myth.[19]

The successive interpretative failures of pace-setting exegesis over the past hundred years or more—first, of liberal theology, then of kerygma theology—together with the exegetically chaotic scene to which these failures have manifestly contributed, attest the deep present need of hermeneutical renewal, if the kind of interpretation most appropriate to the text, theological interpretation, is to flourish again. In the meantime, kerygma theology's failed "prior thesis" on knowledge and the nature of myth strongly suggests that the interpretative ideal is back to where it had been and ought to be: it is the modest, if sometimes arduous, task of clarifying without changing the intended sense of the text.[20]

## III

Our question is: what does it take to perform this task well, when the text to be clarified is biblical? Thus far we have answered in the most general terms, broaching the theme of human authenticity and, under the heading of its intellectual component, asserting the full philosophic right to speak of validity, truth, and reality and to insist on their hermeneutical relevance. Having laid this groundwork, we hope now to get down to particulars on the subjectivity of the interpreter with a view to the objectivity of his interpretation.

No matter how well stocked his resources, the interpreter is truly equipped for his task

[17]James M. Robinson, "Hermeneutic Since Barth," in *The New Hermeneutic*, eds. James M. Robinson and John C. Cobb, Jr. (New York: Harper & Row, 1964) 1–77, p. 34: " . . . demythologizing does 'eliminate' the inadequate mythical conceptualization for the sake of stating more adequately the myth's meaning, and, if the objectifying conceptualization has been spun out into speculative *theologoumena* without existential meaning, such meaningless arabesques are to be 'eliminated.' "

[18]Frederick Lawrence, "Method and Theology as Hermeneutical," in *Creativity and Method, Essays in Honor of Bernard Lonergan*, ed. Matthew L. Lamb (Milwaukee: Marquette University Press, 1981) 79–104, see pp. 86–89, 96–100.

[19]Walter Burkert, *Structure and History in Greek Mythology and Ritual* (Berkeley: University of California Press, 1979) 1–34, 143–158.

[20]"Intended sense" throughout this paper refers to the author's intention only insofar as it is intrinsic to the text, i.e., expressed or encoded or objectified in the text. (The "intended sense" would fall under the strictures evoked by the catch-phrase "intentional fallacy" only if it could be shown—and, obviously, it cannot—that the sense intended by the author is not expressed or encoded or objectified in the text.)

only if he is "attuned" to it. Normally, this means being attuned to the texts to be interpreted. In view of the devastating alienations of our time, this being in tune cannot be presupposed as standard equipment among interpreters. Graduate schools do not pledge to confer or cultivate it and may never so much as mention it.

We can clarify this not really surprising state of affairs by drawing two distinctions: first, between conditions of possibility (that without which interpretation cannot take place) and conditions of excellence (that without which excellent interpretation cannot take place); second, between kinds or aspects of excellence. For the moment we wish to consider a particular aspect of excellence—not the philological nor historical but the religious and theological aspect—of interpretative excellence. In this specific but spacious context, being attuned to the text is part of being attuned to the world and its maker. In his remarkable phenomenology of festivals and festivity, Josef Pieper made being in tune with the world the condition of "celebration."[21] It is equally the condition of excellence in religious and theological interpretation, inasmuch as the texts to be interpreted, from Genesis to the Apocalypse, are themselves a movable feast, a peerless ongoing celebration that climaxes in witness to the act of God in Christ, reconciling the world to himself.

Nietzsche's idiosyncratic witness is pertinent once again. "The trick is not to arrange a festival, but to find people who can enjoy it"[22] and "to have joy in anything, one must approve everything."[23] Nietzsche felt, as few have, the absence of that comprehensive and permanent festivity that he knew to be somehow deeply right. The classical Greeks in their own way[24] and the Church Fathers in theirs attest its presence. "Our whole lives are a feast day" (Clement of Alexandria)[25] "We have unending holiday" (John Chrysostom)[26] "Festivity is everlasting in the house of God" (Augustine)[27] and "ours . . . is an eternal festival" (Jerome)[28] All these men placed the cross at the heart of Christian life, which removes the suspicion of empty optimism from their statements. More, it divulges the secret of their joy. "Cross" is not just pain, but pain redeemed, and theirs is a "joy that can endure despite the sorrow of failure, humiliation, privation, pain, desertion."[29] Nietzsche knew this splendid paradox only by the hem of its garment. He shrank from and entirely misconstrued it, never dreaming that it was in the pattern of the Isaian Servant and of the Christian kerygma that people were to be found in every era ready for festival. "Festivity" presents itself as a credible candidate for the status of specifically Christian authenticity. As such, it belongs high on the list of the conditions of excellent theological interpretation.

Contrary orientations subvert interpretation. Without having to consider manifest, almost gross, examples of estrangement from the biblical text (the deep ambivalence of Hegel and Schleiermacher, of Friederich Delitzsch and Adolf von Harnack vis-à-vis the Old Testament, the alienation of Bruno Bauer or Robert Eisler or Arthur Drews from the New), it is enough to adduce evidence of limited or selective estrangement. New Testament scholars, for example, have often tended to lose their poise and touch in the face of specifically apocalyptic themes. From Otto Pfleiderer to the present, efforts to grasp the Pauline theme of the com-

[21]Josef Pieper, *In Tune With the World. A Theory of Festivity*, trans. Richard and Clara Winston (New York: Harcourt, Brace & World, 1965).

[22]Cited by Pieper, *In Tune*, 10.

[23]Cited by Pieper, *In Tune*, 20.

[24]Pieper, *In Tune*, 38, cites Pythagoras on life as a festival, and Plato's *Laws* on every day a festival.

[25]Clement of Alexandria, *Miscellanies*, 7, 35, 5.

[26]Chrysostom, "De sancta Pentecoste," Migne, *Patrologia Graeca* 50, 454.

[27]Augustine, "Enarrationes in Psalmos," 41, 9; Migne, *Patrologia Latina* 36, 470.

[28]Jerome, *Epistola ad Algasiam* 121, cap. 10; Migne, *Patrologia Latina* 22, 1031. The patristic texts are cited by Pieper, *In Tune*, 38.

[29]Lonergan, "Theology and Man's Future," *Second Collection*, 135–148, p. 145.

ing resurrection of the dead yield many examples. That Paul harbored apocalyptic conceptions such as the salvation of the quick and the dead at the parousia was too well attested to be denied (e.g., 1 Thess 4:13–17; 1 Cor 15:22–28, 51–57). But exegetes well-disposed toward Paul and ill-disposed toward apocalypticism have repeatedly managed to save him from his lesser self and its immersion in apocalyptic remnants from Judaism such as the parousia and judgment themes.[30] Though Paul strangely clung to conventional images like the descent of a parousiac redeemer, his real thought would be better represented by the image of mystical ascent to the heavenly world.[31] It took some time for him to drop his inherently contradictory idea of resurrection, but he finally did so.[32] Whereas he had once thought of the saved as a tiny remnant, he eventually abandoned the fanatic and intolerant dualism behind this thinking, in favor of reconciliation to "experience."[33] Missionary accommodation led him to a "complete revision" of his apocalyptic eschatology, though he held on to themes like judgment even after they had "ceased to possess any real significance."[34] This whole line of thought, well represented over a period of more than a hundred years, was dependent on a demonstrably false reading of 2 Cor 5:1–10, but, far more important, was sustained by the interpreters' affect-laden recoil from apocalypticism.

This special and limited example is matched on other fronts. We have long grown familiar with the generic rationalism that finds prophecies and miracles unthinkable and impossible on *a priori* grounds, without regard either to the issue in its contemporary cognitional-theoretical dimension or to the particulars of individual cases.[35] In my opinion, this undiscriminating ideological stance has had a deeply negative impact on the exegetical and historical appropriation of the New Testament. Nevertheless, I would not wish to make the issue of the interpreter's "good will" or "orientation to consent" hinge on resolution of the more than ordinarily complex questions of prophecy and miracle.

Good will is an antecedent disposition of openness to the horizon, message, and tone of the text. The impersonal curiosity of the physicist is not enough for the interpreter. He does not confront mute nature; he enters into a dialogue, questioning and being questioned. He knows in advance only that without attention and sympathy he may not "hear" the text. The orientation to consent is a condition of such hearing, as Hans-Georg Gadamer, in concert with many others from John Henry Newman to the present, has insisted.[36] Openness to consent is ideally the openness of "basic horizon," the horizon of the thoroughly authentic man.

As the hermeneutics of consent reflects a prior acknowledgement that the human intentionality objectified in the text is in principle open to the whole of reality, so the hermeneutics of suspicion finds its proper object, not in the self-transcendence of the human spirit, but in the recurrent schemes and patterns of nature.[37] "Consent" goes with interpretation, "suspicion" with analysis. Interpretation deals with the text as text (*parole*, particular utterance); analysis deals with the text as language (*langue*, resources of speech). Insofar as the

[30]Otto Pfleiderer, *Paulinism*, trans. E. Peters, 2 vols. (London: Williams and Norgate, 1877) vol. 1, 261-276.

[31]Ernst Teichmann, *Die paulinische Vorstellungen von Auferstehung und Gericht* (Freiburg-Leipzig: Mohr, 1896) 72–74.

[32]R. H. Charles, *A Critical History of the Doctrine of the Future Life in Israel, in Judaism, and in Christianity* (London: Black, 1899) 394f.

[33]C. H. Dodd, "The Mind of Paul: II" (1934) in C. H. Dodd, *New Testament Studies* (Manchester: Manchester University Press, 1953, repr. 1967) 83–128, pp. 121, 126, 108.

[34]Wilfred L. Knox, *St Paul and the Church of the Gentiles* (Cambridge: Cambridge University Press, 1939) 128, 141.

[35]See B. F. Meyer, *The Aims of Jesus* (London: SCM, 1979) 99–102.

[36]Hans-Georg Gadamer, *Truth and Method*, trans. G. Barden and J. Cumming (New York: Seabury, 1975) 245–274.

[37]John C. Robertson, Jr., "Hermeneutics of Suspicion vs. Hermeneutics of Goodwill," *Studies in Religion/Sciences Religieuses* 8 (1979) 365–379.

text is a communication (*parole*), interpretation is prior by nature to analysis. But, if suspicion has no role whatever in interpretation taken strictly as the effort to grasp and mediate what the author has both intended to encode and managed to encode in the text, still suspicion has its place in literary study.

First, it is a stance appropriate to analysis, if not in all its modes, in many of them: those that are in some sense anterior to interpretation (text-critical, form-critical analysis, etc.) and those that bypass or follow upon interpretation (structuralist, psychological, historical, socio-economic, and many other kinds of analysis). Second, suspicion belongs to critique; that is, it belongs to the effort to say, not what the text means (that is the task of interpretation), but how adequately and authentically it means what it means. Critique in this sense includes the thematization of the interpreter's personal encounter with the text.

In bringing these general observations to bear on the concrete effort to read biblical texts well, the main matter is to maximize in oneself what Peter Stuhlmacher has called "the principle of hearing."[38] This, I would say, is first of all an orientation to consent antecedently sensitized by whatever measure of intellectual, moral, affective, aesthetic, religious, and specifically Christian authenticity that one can attain. Second, it is an acquired set of special competences belonging to historical and literary scholarship. In other words, to become attuned to the biblical text is to bring to realization the kind of subjectivity that, measuring up to the text, makes objectivity possible—an enormous challenge.

Suspicion, on the other hand, which is so much easier to hone to a fine edge, is a distinctly secondary matter. In the era since Benedict Spinoza and Richard Simon, suspicion has brought much to light. Inasmuch as it includes the hardy scepticism that is part and parcel of the historian's equipment, it has helped retrieve the common sense of changing societies over the thousand or more years that were the biblical period. Suspicion, moreover, meets the need to spot the traits of propaganda literature, be it from the court of Solomon or from Christian missionary centers in the diaspora of the Greeks.

But the reader must be alert to the distortions of bias not only in the text but in himself. It is the achievement of the masters of suspicion to have placed an array of surgical instruments at his disposal: the analyses of *ressentiment*, of screening devices and defence mechanisms and rationalizing legitimations; and these he may turn on the text to discern its biases and on himself to deconstruct those prejudgments that would block or deflect or otherwise spoil his responding appropriately to the text. This properly locates suspicion in analysis ancillary to interpretation and in the critique that follows upon it.

As Freudian suspicion generated psychoanalysis and Marxian suspicion the critique of ideology, so the suspicions of Reimarus generated the quest of the historical Jesus and those of Strauss and Baur, the inquiries into the nature of the gospel literature and into the drama of early Christian development. Still, all these adepts of suspicion—Freud and Marx, Reimarus, Strauss, and Baur—were reductionists whose work has had to be selectively salvaged by correction from outside their own suspicions. By contrast, the greatness of the great biblical interpreters of the past generation—to mention two, Gerhard von Rad and Joachim Jeremias—lay in the acuteness that informed their capacity to listen and to hear. It was greatness *ex auditu*.

[38]Peter Stuhlmacher, *Historical Criticism and Theological Interpretation of Scripture*, trans. Roy A. Harrisville (Philadelphia: Fortress, 1977) 85–87.

# Sources of Social Credit in First-Century Palestine: Immanence and Authority in the Jesus Movement

Richard K. Fenn

## Immanence

Some evidence for a first-century crisis in social credit is in the documents of the New Testament, which leave a picture of a world obsessed with authority. The documents themselves seem to be an extensive critique of a wide range of claims to social credit.

Some of these claims were based on visionary experiences: ascents of the soul to spiritual heavens, participation in angelic liturgies, or the reception of messages from God or Christ to be delivered as oracles to those who had ears to hear or to large crowds. Prophecy—authoritative speech—during the period of the 1st century presented conflicting messages and created a demand for a principle of interpretation that could neutralize competing claims to authority. The Jesus movement itself attacked claims based on the ability to follow laws for purity, on the interpretation of texts, on participation in the Temple cult or on lineage and descent. Here again, prophecy, clerical or lay, orthodox or heterodox, provided a bewildering set of messages that claimed authority even while exercising it. Every report of visionary experience or of messages received was also a command, and utterances therefore had an extraordinary illocutionary force.

In one sense, that world seems familiar, even modern. Sociologists studying new religious movements note that claims to authority are often based on esoteric knowledge or spiritual experience; every new priesthood creates a laity whose knowledge, in comparison, is tainted, partial, or profane. The hunger for status and social credit creates the demand for contexts in which one can receive special knowledge and can learn to speak with exceptional authority; on the other hand, every such context requires a certain self-abasement, adherence to rules for purity or abstinence of various sorts; every movement therefore withholds for a time the very powers that it promises to those who are eventually found faithful. In attacking the liturgies of conventional temples and by participating in esoteric rites, devotees of contemporary movements seek to enter into a gate from which they have previously been barred: the rather narrow gate on the way to authority itself. There are modern maharajahs, gurus, leaders of the People's Temples, and great Masters who, like Isaac in his Testament, "taught his household both that their earthly service resembled their occupation in the heavens, and that after a little time they would be engaged in holy angelic service," (Francis and Meeks 1975:183). Whether the purity required of modern devotees is dietary, or whether it requires abstinence from forms of contact with a race or a culture that are considered sources of pollution, new religious movements have promised their faithful that they will be honoured rather than deprived of their most sought-after and cherished goal; "great is their honour in the presence of the Lord" is a phrase that comes from an ancient text that promised great things to those who qualified to participate in the angelic liturgy, but its promise is peculiarly modern (Francis and Meeks 1975:178). The task is to be found worthy, to avoid being disqualified, i.e. to run the race and lay hold of the prize at last. To many sociologists looking at either the modern world or the first century, the prize, quite simply, is social credit: the right to speak with authority rather than to be subjected to endless probation, testing, and the threat of failure and disqualification. To be discredited, when all is said and done, is still the sting of death.

Nonetheless, the passionate, even desperate search for authority in the modern world may not help us to appreciate how serious and intense was the quest for such authority during the period in which the documents of the Christian faith were first edited and collected. Of course, in both the modern and the ancient world there was a demand for judgment: for an exercise of authority that would be final and incontrovertible. It may well be, for instance, that the Jesus movement sought to create a representative court to judge the cause of the people; in the apocalyptic literature that court might also include representatives of the gentiles as well as the tribes of Israel (cf. Charlesworth 1985). Whether or not the early church saw itself as the first gathering of such a tribunal, it was more than the locus of disputes over authority. At stake was something more than the claims of individuals to the sort of inspiration or religious experience that could be turned into the currency of social authority. There was a demand for a collective judgment that transcends individual claims: a judgment on communities of faith, on collectivities and peoples as well as on persons. It is crucial to know the powers and to foretell the eventual victory of some over others.

Now, it is true that a similar demand for judgment is widespread in the twentieth century. It is not individuals alone who seek vindication and credit, but ways of life, communities based on one lineage or another, peoples organized politically as well as spiritually, and nations themselves that are engaged in what appears to be a contest of near cosmic significance. Worlds are at stake; perhaps this world in particular. There are some, indeed, who appear to welcome a final confrontation between the forces of good and evil; Armageddon talk is widespread and dangerous. Nonetheless, I suggest that the first generations of Christians were far more serious about authority than modern contestants.

There are several reasons, I will argue, why the stakes in the struggle for authority in the first century were higher than in our own civilization: incommensurably higher, I should add. The first reason concerns the notion of immanence, a concept I will later develop in more detail. Here it may be enough simply to say that immanence connotes the fusion of a distant source of life and power with one's own immediate experience. Perhaps the best example is the way in which authority was expressed and created through ritual in ancient Israel:

> "The promulgation of the covenant code (Ex. 20–23), for example, is preceded by a narrative of the Sinai theophany, which is shot through with liturgical features such as the assembly of the people on a particular day of the year, the ritual cleansing of garments and the injunction of sexual abstinence, the prohibition of touching sacred precincts, the trumpet blast, and the column of fire and smoke" (Ex. 19:1–25) (Gaffney 1984:119).

This description, by Edward Gaffney, supports the conclusion of Berman and others that authority in ancient Israel was realized in various rites; that is to put it mildly. In such rites, the self, the body, and one's entire social world appear to be constituted by authority itself; one can only respond in purity of both body and mind. This is 'immanence,' and it achieves doctrinal expression in the notion of two substances, inseparable and yet twofold, inhabiting the same person. The perfect realization of such immanence, of course, is in a person whose will is both human and divine; it is in this sense, I would argue, that one can begin to understand such metaphors for authority as Son of Man, Son of God, etc. Despite their differences, these metaphors indicate the immanence of the divine in the human. Contrast such a viewpoint with contemporary perceptions of the sacred. No matter with what apparent reverence Americans may approach the documents and sites of the origin of the American Republic, for instance, not even the writers of the Constitution itself, however 'inspired,' represent such immanence.

There is a second reason for distinguishing the experience of authority in the first century from contemporary experience. Contemplate the presence of a statue of the Roman emperor in the Temple at Jerusalem in the light of the concept of immanence. Graven images are forbidden precisely because what they represent may inhere in the substance of the representation; the statue would bring to bear a potency that would entirely pollute, if not destroy, the sanctity of the Temple itself. Under these conditions, I am suggesting, magical thinking first projects powers of omniscience and omnipotence into persons who represent power and authority; second, magical thinking considers such powers to inhere in persons and their representations; a third step, by the same logic, represents defensive magic: a search for power no less omniscient and omnipotent than the one that inspires fear, hatred, and loathing. That is, Israel requires for itself a power commensurate with that of the Babylonian or Roman emperor.

The assumptions underlying this description derive from psychoanalysis and social anthropology; they cannot be developed here. Fortunately, recent work has elaborated them in detail (cf. O'Keefe 1983). Note, however, how the logic of defensive magic underlies the effort of Israel to achieve through the efficacy of ritual an authority commensurate with its enemies. The trumpet blast and the column of fire and smoke are no doubt intended not only to awe the adherents of the cult but to terrify and disperse the legions, however largely unseen, of the enemy (cf. Huntingdon and Metcalf 1979). It is not surprising, therefore, but entirely logical that Yahweh should have been for His people a source of power in history commensurate with that of the kings and emperors of Israel's enemies. Gaffney misses this point when he writes:

> ". . . many concepts currently thought of as religious in character, such as the unit of God and the centrality of the great commandments of love of God and neighbor, grace and the election of the covenant people, derive from the secular sphere of law, or more specifically from ancient Near Eastern Treaties" (1984:124).

It was a law that was understood and received under the auspices of the magical worldview.

The derivation of the notion of a covenant of grace and election, with its attendant blessings and curses, from ancient Near Eastern models is not simply an example of cultural diffusion. Sociologists have long noted that parties in conflict tend to adopt each other's characteristics and that movements of protest and reform often adopt a mirror-image of the very structures that they are opposing; rebellion and freedom-movements, if they are successful, often impose a new order that is in some sense a reflection of the authority that they have opposed. The Protestant movement against the priestly office, for instance, develops a bureaucracy structure of offices no less abstract and impersonal in its authority than the priesthood (cf. Martin 1981). A scholar who is comparing the texts of Hittite and Assyrian treaties with the covenant-theme in Israelite law might agree that "the monotheistic core of Mosaic religion originated at least in part as a result of reflection on the political relationship between ancient Near Eastern city-states" (Gaffney 1981:127). I am simply suggesting that the power of the imperial overlord over the "client vassal" city-states was so authoritative and compelling, attractive as well as fearsome, that Israel may well have wished to emulate the very power from which it sought to defend itself. The total, exclusive, and wholehearted allegiance of vassal to emperor finds its mirror-image in the great commandment of love for Yahweh (cf. Gaffney 1981:128). Apparently even diplomatic correspondence in the Near East urged that the vassal should "love the emperor like yourself" (Lohfink, The Great Commandment, 1968:93, quoted in Gaffeny 1981:128). Immanence, in other words, becomes a state of heart and mind, body and soul, that expresses the only proper relationship of the vassal to the lord, the faithful to Yahweh. Only a God who commands the same total and exclusive allegiance could provide a match for the emperor of Rome; the same power and authority, furthermore, would invest the followers of the Christian Lord with sufficient grace to withstand an emperor who inspired fear and profound respect bordering, at the extreme, on adoration. That would provide a form of bedrock social credit that could never be moved or destroyed.

It may be extremely difficult for modern citizens to understand the need for a divine king whose authority and power is indeed more than a match for the principalities and powers of this world. Our own principalities and powers, like the emperor in the fable, are often exposed to public view in a way that robs them of their powers of enchantment. In the second place, modern nation-states are likely to rest their claims on more abstract and rational foundations than do emperors who claim more divine sources of authorization. Legitimacy in the modern world depends at least as much on effectiveness as on adherence to tradition; charisma inheres in the office more than in the person of the politician. All of these are commonplace sociological observations about the development of legal-rational authority in a largely disenchanted universe. Even where sociologists are likely to discern religious symbols in political speech, the use of these symbols is liable to critical interpretation; the blast of the trumpet and the cloud of fire and smoke do not easily emanate from the careful wording even of Presidential speeches. The rites of Presidential inauguration hardly promote a new covenant of devoted obedience to a new lord; on the contrary, they serve notice that the existence and continuity of the regime depend on an abstract structure of constitutional law that is itself open to revision and reinterpretation. The process of forming authority has become open, continuous, and liable to more critical inquiry than ever greeted a trumpet blast. Under these conditions, despite the intrusions of the state on the prerogatives of a bureaucratized church, the authority of the state has fewer magical effects and requires less magical antidotes than the overwhelming presence of the imperial center in its incarnations on its several peripheries.

The distance between the world of the twentieth and the first centuries makes it difficult for sociology to use its usual categories in interpreting passages on authority. Sociologists, following Weber, are likely to distinguish between authority that is charismatic and that which inheres in an office or a tradition; it is a distinction lost on the first century. Sociology is likely to distinguish the person from the office in a way that is entirely inappropriate to New Testament usage. In speaking of the "rulers of the Gentiles" (Mark 10:42 ff.), for instance, Jesus uses a word that applies in the New Testament to specific individuals in various capacities, like Moses or Nicodemus, but also to categories of officials, like magistrates (Wink 1984:155–156). In other words, the modern distinction between person and office seems to be of little use in interpreting this term: an observation that apparently is even more applicable to *archē* than to *archon* (Wink 1984:155). Furthermore, the New Testament uses the notion of *archē* to apply not only to human but to spiritual powers, good and evil alike; the term can be used as well of Satan as of Jesus (Wink 1984:156). *The point is simply that the boundaries between the human and the social, the earthly and the spiritual, the good and the destructive are not clearly established; no wonder that individuals and officers were assumed to be the carriers of magical potencies and that contact with them could be profoundly beneficial or evil in its consequences.* In a world of immanence, these potencies were not easily confined, and one had to defend oneself against them as best one could. For many, only an extraordinarily powerful *archon*, Jesus, could in the long run provide adequate credit-protection against the rulers of this age.

In the dialectic between religion and magic, therefore, individuals invest the authorities with the imagined potency of omnipotence or omniscience, for good or ill. In reaction to a world peopled by such fearful powers, the individual required a defensive magic: an alternative potency with which to combat and safeguard oneself against the powers that be. It is remarkable, therefore, that the alternative posed by Jesus in this passage is not that of the insurgent *archon* but that of the servant. There may well be an attempt in the Jesus movement to break the dialectic between religion and magic: a move toward secularization.

There is ample evidence that in most tribal societies, especially those confronted by competitive communities or by an external and exceptionally powerful state, the alternative source of power is sought in what has been called the "big man" (cf. Wilson 1973). The "big man" is a charismatic leader who may enjoy particular prowess in fighting, skills in craft, hunting and fishing, or in medicine. The "big man" may have specific oratorical abilities that make him a political leader or engage in extraordinary oracular speech. Indeed, in many societies political opposition requires the individual to compete in oratory with established rulers: an arena in which differences in power are partially neutralized, as in debates between the incumbent and the rival candidate for Presidential office in the United States. Powerful, charismatic speech is indeed one major source of social credit in the struggle for succession to positions of authority.

In some societies, where tribal organization prevails and groups are scattered in various parts of a territory and engaged in segmented agricultural activities, conflict over the succession to the kingship, however bloody, in fact unifies the tribes; it is the kingship as an institution that prevails despite the sectarian struggles for power (Gluckman 1956;1967:44–47). A different system prevails where there is a "high degree of local concentration," as in towns or cities, and/or "a high degree of economic interdependence" among parts of a territory; there, succession among political leaders is more likely to be less violent, and choices of an heir to the throne are made from a single line rather than from competing lines of authority (Gluckman *ibid.*:47). It would appear that in Palestine of the first century prior to the destruction of the Temple, neither system was fully developed. There were enough centers of "local concentration" in Hellenized towns and cities and enough economic infrastructure to permit a more rational type of competition for authority and a more linear form of succession to develop. On the other hand, there were enough segmented and dispersed communities to make rebellions necessary, as it were, to solidify the nation in conflict over the succession to high priestly office and over what remained of central authority. Under these conditions, if Gluckman is right, political conflict would not be merely rebellious and leave intact the system of authority while changing the incumbents in high office; it would verge on the revolutionary, in which the system of authority itself is at stake (Gluckman 1961;1967:54 ff.). That is why, I would argue, that the saying by Jesus about the type of authority prevalent among gentiles was a signal not for one more rebellion, in which the system would remain unchanged, but for a fundamental change in the system itself. In that way, the dialectic between magic and religion, between powerful centralized authority and popular leaders would be neutralized once and for all. Credit, as a basis for authority, would be disenchanted. There is no mystery about service.

There was another dialectic during this period, equally loaded with magical thinking: the dialectic between the sources of purity and the sources of impurity. It was, after all, the rulers of the gentiles who were the target of Jesus' criticism. This clearly does not exempt the leaders of Israel from criticism; on the contrary, as I have suggested, the entire system itself was the object of revolution rather than of another cyclical rebellion. Jesus may have referred to *Gentile* leaders as though to sources of pollution. It is the dynamic interplay or dialectic between the opposite poles of purity and pollution to which I now turn the discussion.

## Dialectic Between Purity and Pollution

There was a dialectic in Palestinian social life of the first century that is quite central to our analysis: the interplay of the sacred and the impure. To put it another way, Jews of that period would have been exposed to a wide range of rules, many of them inconsistent with each other, on what is profane. By "profane" I mean that which is neither sacred, i.e. dedicated to priests (like tithes) or to the Temple's rites (like offerings), or impure (in contact with one of the many sources of impurity, e.g. corpses). The profane was the in-between world in which one might or might not be in contact with objects that were contaminated or which could belong to the cult in some way. I am arguing that it was the interplay between these two poles of social life, the one sacred and the other equally taboo for the opposite reason, that created a world in which one never knew quite what one should do. Credit was costly and required sacrifices, while it was too easy to be discredited by one's associations and contacts.

An "anomic" world, as sociologists often term it, is not foreign to an individual living in modern societies. Quite the contrary, it would appear superficially to be a very "modern" experience to be living in a society whose rules are vague, ambiguous, and often inconsistent or quite contradictory. The reasons for the anomic quality of social life in the first century, however, are quite different from those which underlie the confusion about what one should do in modern societies. There are relatively few extant taboos in contemporary American society: relatively few objects that clearly belong to the church for its worship, and relatively few which cannot be touched without risking impurity. Granted that there is a widespread fear of contamination from chemical or radiological sources of pollution; granted also that the courts are the scene of frequent litigation between the churches and other parties over the prerogatives of religious organizations. The parallels are superficial, however, since the scope and intensity of rules governing sacred and impure objects are greatly reduced in a complex society such as the United States. Of the total body of regulation, both formal and customary, to which an American must pay at least some attention in everyday life, those relating to the church, its clergy and its worship, are relatively few; the penalties for trespassing on the church's prerogatives, furthermore, are greatly diminished and are subject to relatively minor civil and criminal penalties rather than to the extreme practice, for instance, of shunning which literally excludes the offender from the company of the faithful. That company, furthermore, is no longer coterminous with civil society, and even if an individual were shunned, that person would have ample opportunities for association elsewhere. In the Palestine of the first century, however, the impure were those with whom one should have as few dealings as possible or, in extreme cases, none at all: dealings including the purchase of grains and ordinary social contact. Prohibitions regarding the sacred and the impure therefore had a wide scope and profound implications for the system and for the individual.

In a complex society such as the United States, however, prohibitions regarding impurity are rather specific in scope and low in moral or spiritual intensity. Of course, particular regions polluted by the effluent of chemical factories are likely to feel very much like residents of a small community in the first century: i.e. that their world has been spoiled. Pervasive toxic material can indeed damage a locale, disturb whole communities, and literally ruin the lives of many individuals and families. Most cases of pollution, however, or other forms of impurity affect specific products: contaminated batches of cheese or wine, for instance, or capsules intentionally poisoned with arsenic, as in the case of Tylenol. As these examples suggest, however, the impurities are specific, the remedies legal or technical, and restoration involves legal damages rather than rites of purification. More akin to the Palestinian case, however, might be the instances in which members of conservative religious groups have objected to certain types of television programming during hours normally reserved for "family viewing;" there is an attempt to keep the family free from such influences. A similar logic underlies the effort to keep small neighborhood stores like the 7-Eleven from selling erotic literature that might come to the attention of young people. The Rev. Jerry Falwell, whose organization (the Liberty Foundation) has been instrumental in protesting the sale of pornographic materials in such convenience stores, argues that "There will always be pornographic magazines available. It would just be better if (people) have to go to Sleazetown to buy them" (*Wall Street Journal* 4.14.86:31, in a colum signed by K. Blumenthal). The logic is the same as that which underlies attempts to declare an entire area of social life free from contamination by potent forces: i.e. the attempt to concentrate the forces of impurity, in this case, in a single area (Sleazetown). The same logic locates sources of impurity in an evil empire and seeks to purify the body politic of external influences. Even now, authorities need to acquire credit by discrediting their competitors and by threatening the demand with guilt-by-association.

The point, however, is that in a complex society the norms for maintaining purity become specific, i.e. in reference to particular products, to be consumed by the eye or the body. The intensity of the norms may vary according to which part of the population is surveyed; the majority of respondents to surveys conducted by various chain-stores were of no particular persuasion on the subject of pornographic magazines, but there were some shifts in awareness from one year to the next that prompted the owners to withdraw some of the magazines from the racks. The objections may be more intense, I would suggest, in small convenience stores that serve local communities than in stores less frequented by children or families, where anonymity and social distance may be greater. The point remains, however, that pluralism in the United States is associated with the relatively low intensity and scope of norms for purity, whereas in Palestine differences in viewpoint concerned a plethora of norms for purity that covered a wide array of objects, individuals and situations, and these differences mobilized a relatively high degree of moral intensity. Even those with other priorities would be required to take the norms into account, whereas in a complex society issues regarding purity are specifically related to a relatively few objects and situations over which differences of viewpoint are sustained, legitimate, and of relatively little immediate significance to most individuals in the transactions of everyday life. Secularization makes it relatively difficult for the authorities to discredit their competitors by accusations of impurity through improper association, since these associations are of such limited scope and intensity.

It would be unfortunate to underestimate the profusion of instructions regarding the sacred and the impure in Judaism of the period. Some groups attempted, in fact, to limit the profusion by focussing laws governing purity on practices and sacred objects directly associated with the Temple cult and its priesthood (Oppenheimer 1977:29–50). Other groups generalized these instructions so that they would apply virtually at any time and place: a generalizing that greatly increased the scope and intensity of prohibitions in social life (cf. Theissen Oppenheimer 1977:56). It was the purpose of the Pharisees, in fact, to soften the impact and limit the scope of these norms by distinguishing between what could be expected ideally and in theory from what might obtain in practice (Oppenheimer 1977:56): a liberalizing tendency offset by the demands for purity and perfection found in other sects and contexts in Palestinian society. Indeed, an obsession or preoccupation with purity was not limited to Judaism; contagion and purity were the sources of anxiety in the ancient Near East and in Hellenistic communities as well as in Judaism (Oppenheimer *loc. cit.*). The point is simply that structural characteristics of traditional societies tended to create such preoccupations, and it is worthwhile understanding that the corresponding uncertainty about proper norms fostered a type of anomie with which Western, contemporary societies are largely unfamiliar. The sources of credit have been largely clarified as well as disenchanted: a far cry from the mysterious *archontes* of the first century.

The "structural characteristics" I have in mind are contained in the notion of a dialectic: an interplay between the sacred and the impure aspects of social life. That interplay makes the sacred more successful, since the threat of contact with impurity intensifies the demand for rites of purification. On the other hand, the same interplay undermines the positive effects of the sacred. By "positive effects" I mean the creation of a sphere of social life, a set of objects and of people, which are profane, touchable, and without mystery or potential harmful effect. For instance, the effect of giving the first fruits of a flock or of a harvest of tithes to the priests is to render the remainder fit for human consumption. Otherwise, if one does not give the gods their due, so to speak, one may be consuming what belongs to them. The problem of purity, then, is an extension of the problem of authority: the task of the first century was to find the limits of the pervasive reach of an immanent authority. Tithing was a defensive strategy against such authority: a limited sacrifice, as it were, to protect the remainder. In a world, furthermore, where nature is perceived as animated with divine spirits and social life is a part of the creation, it follows that produce of any sort is potentially filled with manna: an unseen and yet potent divine presence. The *archontes* may be anywhere. The notion of "royalties" contains the residues of such a belief system and represents an analogy; one paid royalties to a monarchy whose rights extended to the produce of the land to which royalty had direct or indirect title. The presence of royalty extended only so far as its entitlements, and the enjoyment of the fruits of one's labor therefore depended on one's paying tribute to the unseen but nonetheless potentially present and potent owner of the fields. Although it was a radical notion for Locke to argue that the laborer also had property rights by virtue of having invested his or her person in the property in which one labored, the logic was still the same: A logic that depends on the infusion of nature with personal or spiritual properties. The distance of Locke's logic from contemporary assumptions about property, in which property is a commodity to be bought and sold and ownership is an abstraction, suggests how great a leap of the imagination is required of those who would enter into the anxious preoccupations over purity and authority in the first century. Credit in the twentieth century defines one's relation to a market, is often "revolving," and subject to quite transient and impersonal market forces.

One other word of caution: an anomic situation makes the social landscape itself exceedingly hard to describe even when one is a contemporary; from the distance of twenty centuries it is all the more tempting, therefore, to reduce the complexity by thinking of the 'am ha-aretz as a sect of the relatively impure or ignorant rather than as an amorphous element in a population subject to multiple and confusing instructions about various entitlements and prohibitions. That is why these cautionary remarks of Charlesworth are particularly appropriate:

> "It should now be clear that a sectarian approach to Early Judaism is anachronistic. That approach represents the time when scholars could talk about a normative Judaism; and it tends to warp a portrayal of the varieties of responses to Torah in Early Judaism" (1958:21).

There is something to be gained from focussing on the dialectic between the sacred and the sources of impurity in Palestinian Judaism; it helps to bring into sharper relief various sources of the struggle for social credit that center on the Temple, its cult, and its priesthood. Charlesworth notes, for instance, that

> "To acknowledge the centripetal force of the Temple is not to confess that the Temple was the norm for a monolithic Judaism" (1985:57).

On the contrary, as Charlesworth consistently has argued, there is no evidence for a normative, let alone a monolithic Judaism; it is difficult even to distinguish *between* Palestinian and extra-Palestinian Judaism or to weigh the relative importance of rabbinic or other strands *within* Palestinian Judaism (1985:47–57). The dialectic between the sources of purity in the sacred and sources of impurity would therefore create a wide variety of solutions, not all of which would center on the Temple, and it would allow varying degrees of freedom from the laws governing tithes and other offerings. On the contrary, the same dialectic could also generate competing centers of purity, as in the Qumran community itself: centers opposed to the Jerusalem cult precisely because it could not deliver the purity that it promised. Here is Charlesworth again:

> "Jews could and apparently did frequent the Temple in a spirit of disgust for the desecration of the sacred spot. The cult not only proved to be a unifying force in Judasim, it also tended to spawn differences, as the struggles for control, as well as the corruption, within the priesthood, produced opposition" (1985:57).

Charlesworth goes on to speak of the "rival priestly groups who struggled for control of the cults" (*ibid*.:57), but it would be unfortunate to understand these rivalries solely in terms of the *modern* struggle for social credit. They are not simply illustrations of such familiar entities as classes or status groups contending for shares of the market in public opinion or of the public treasury (cf. Theissen 1977). The underlying tension between the sacred and the sources of pollution made the struggle far more intense and serious even than contemporary politics in the Vatican or in the higher echelons of ecumenical office. The stakes were higher not only because fragments of political power were available; the struggle was quite literally between the two polar extremes of purity and impurity. Arrayed between these two poles were the various actors, drawn like the proverbial filings to the opposite ends of a magnet, in a variety of configurations.

The analogy with the magnetized filings is not intended to convey an impression of a helter-skelter distribution of polarized fragments in Palestinian Judaism; I agree with Charlesworth that "pre-revolt (pre-66) Palestinian Judasim was neither a chaos nor in anarchistic disarray" (1985:56). There is an order here, but it is fluid and dynamic within the constraints imposed by the dialectic itself. The extremes were in place, and even those who temporized with the demand for purity were no less subject to the pull of the dialectic than those who sought purity in the cult or within the community of the faithful. For instance, there were priests even among those who were "so abhorrent and unclean to the pious in Early Judaism: before 70 there were 'am ha-aretz priests" (Charlesworth 1985:57–58). There was no escaping the dialectic even for those who had the most to gain from exemption.

It is important to see this dialectic not as a sociological abstraction but as a process engaging the time, energy, attention, and perhaps sacrifices of individuals and groups that are caught up within its tension. At the risk of some repetition, here is Charlesworth's thesis concerning one pole of the dialectic: the cult centered at Jerusalem:

> "Jews throughout Judea and Galilee tended to acknowledge the central religious significance of Jerusalem (cf. Sir:36:13, the Eighteen Benedictions 14) and the cultic importance of the Temple, 'the Holy Dwelling of the Most High' (Ps. 46:5)" (1985:57).

Think for a moment of what is packed into this brief quotation. First, a transcendent God is acknowledged, who is the center of the universe, the Lord of History, the active agent in this history of His people, and a presence on earth through the cult at Jerusalem. Second, this high God is immanent in other ways; as I will argue later, the Temple and its several groups of priests had emissaries that kept a large area of social life under surveillance. One could not escape even by going "abroad" to cities such as Antioch. Conversely, as I have noted in connection with the rules for purity, many situations in everyday social life were defined, coded, and interpreted in terms of the central cult's prohibitions and permissions: even among those who were antagonized by its priests and sought to develop competing sources of priestly authority (Charlesworth *ibid.*:57). A High God who is a living presence that permeates social life and actively approaches His people to rescue and save or to punish: this is the theology that accompanies such a structure.

Now consider the opposite pole of the dialectic; Palestine was literally flooded with influences from the Roman, Greek, and ancient Near Eastern cultures. When Charlesworth speaks of these intrusions, he uses the metaphorical notion that Jewish culture had been "impregnated after the exile repeatedly by influences from Babylon, Egypt, Persia, Syria, Greece, Parthia, and Rome" (1985:61). As the metaphor suggests, Jews may not have been uniformly unwilling to be so influenced; after all, as Charlesworth goes on to note, there were large numbers of Jews who were "religious only for convenience, social respectability, or because of the perennial need for an efficacious 'god' " (1985:61–62). Under these conditions, the term cosmopolitan seems an appropriate one for Charlesworth to use for the culture within which Christianity gestated (Charlesworth 1985:61). On the other hand, the influences were not uniformly seen as neutral or benign; on the contrary, many Jews found their nation enslaved "to foreign idolatrous nations" (*ibid.*:64): an enslavement that made Israel's impregnation more like rape: a violation of the sanctity of its cultural borders and an unwanted forceful entry into its social life.

The *archontes,* as sources of impurity, in other words, were unavoidable, overwhelming, and may well have aroused the same violent passions as rape itself. Even those ambivalent or opposed to the Temple for its coercive or corrupt exercise of cultic authority would have been opposed to the "cosmopolitan" alternatives. *It was as if the world itself were a source of pollution; one could not escape by going abroad.* Contrast such a situation in which foreign religious imports are matters of consumer choice, optional and part of the leisure sphere of personal growth and enrichment; a world essentially private and subject only to occasional surveillance by the authorities of church and state, despite current anxieties over foreign cults. One can understand the appeal of a religious movement release from the obligations of purity and from the pervasive scrutiny of the rulers of the age. Secularity was freedom and redemption.

I dwell on the notion of impregnation for a crucial sociological reason which now may be more apparent. An individual who reads the texts of the first century may easily misunderstand cosmopolitanism or enslavement; he or she might consider cosmopolitanism to be an openness to a wide array of cultural choices or enslavement might interpret as subjection to a force that remains external to one's own culture. To a Jew or Christian of the period, however, such influences were never merely voluntary or involuntary, symbolic or external; they posed the threat of polluting the innermost sanctuary, the culture, the community, and the self. *Contact spelled contagion: an alteration in the metabolism and physiology, so to speak, of the body politic.* The critical sociological point is made by Swanson in his discussion of "immanence," and is worth quoting here at some length:

> "The notion of immanence resembles certain other ideas but is importantly different from them. Thus immanence refers to a real transfer of spiritual substances—of the powers of a spirit—and not merely to the influencing of one spirit by another . . ." (1967:4).

That is why I have emphasized the inescapability of cultural influences as well as of influences from the cultic center of Jerusalem; contact with either involves an element of incorporation of the external into the life of the local community or the self: both seen as an organism, like a human body, open to outside substances and capable of making them indistinguishable from the internal processes of the body itself. Swanson goes on to say:

> "Nor should immanence be confused with intimacy . . . [The] relation between spirits is characterized by influence and intimacy. Immanence also involves both of these characteristics, but the form of their presence, if immanent, is that of the incorporation by a recipient spirit of powers formerly part of another" (*ibid.*:4).

One thinks immediately, for instance, of the healings in which Jesus used spittle to transfer powers from himself to a sick person; like the bread and wine of the Last Supper, these elements became infused with his spirit and became capable of transmitting his spirit to another person in whom they became an aspect of the recipient's own person, i.e. incorporated. The capacity of a person's spirit to dwell in excretions or other discharges of the body has been, as I have noted, an important belief underlying early Judaism's preoccupation with purity.

The focus on bodily discharges, however, may distract our attention from the underlying pantheistic belief-system. Pantheism may seem a strange term to apply to a Judasim that had sought to distinguish between a transcendental God and divine activity in nature or history. Nonetheless, as Swanson (*ibid.*:6) points out, there were strong elements of pantheism apparent in early practices such as the casting of lots or consulting oracles; there is ample evidence, of course, that oracular utterances were prevalent in the first century, and certainly the disciplines sought to divine God's will through the casting of lots in choosing a successor to complete their number. As Charlesworth (1985:65–67) reminds us, the "cosmic theology of early Judaism" included events and emissaries that conveyed the force of the divine presence to people caught up in tragic events or in answer to their dreams, prayers, and aspirations. That present was even more concrete and concentrated in . . . "holy men, called 'Son of God,' who could speak to God directly and influence Him" (1985:67). Even Wisdom, the Word, and perhaps the voice of God, could be seen and heard, as it were, live and in person, on the social stage. The locations of immanence were many and potentially, if not actually, everywhere. The sources of social credit were so abundant that they could not easily be ignored or, on the other hand, easily judged. There was a glut of authoritative forces on the market.

The belief in immanence is therefore an expression of the dialectic; it was part of the problem, as we might put it. On the one hand, a powerful and potentially pervasive authority, centered in Jerusalem but with laws and emissaries requiring compliance over a wide area and in virtually every aspect of social life, would make the belief in the immanence of transcendent power exceedingly plausible. That is, in fact, Swanson's (1960) thesis in a book earlier than the one just cited, *The Birth of the Gods.* On the other hand, the intrusion of "foreign" cultures was so pervasive and penetrating that domestic practices and beliefs already incorporated many cosmopolitan influences: a fact of social life that could intensify the belief in immanence and support a magical worldview. There was no escaping the dialectic, therefore, between the demands for purity and the sources of impurity; they inhabited the self in a struggle akin to the experience of an individual possessed, as it were, by contending spirits or demons.

## Polytheism

No doubt, during the first century Jesus' words on authority would have had a variety of meanings depending on the context in which they were either heard or remembered. Take, for example, a teaching found in a variety of somewhat later sources on participation in the heavenly liturgy of angels; the Testament of Isaac speaks of those who will stand

> "in the presence of the Lord and His angels because of their pure offerings and angelic service, because their earthly service resembles their occupation in the heavens . . . And now be humbling yourselves to God . . ." (Francis 1975:178).

The author is discussing this document as shedding some light on the heresy at Colossae, and he finds parallels in a number of other passages in documents that, according to Charlesworth (1985:32), are either too late or still too problematic in origin to be useful for explicating passages in the New Testament. No doubt, also, that there were many countercultural variations among both Jews and Gentiles, some of whom used the angels' heavenly worship of God as a model for earthly asceticism and humility, while others venerated the angels themselves (cf. Francis *op. cit.*:176 ff). The point I wish to make here is a limited one, viz. that there were many contexts in which Jesus' words may have been uttered, heard, reported, interpreted, and reinterpreted: enough to make a single interpretation from the distance of many centuries a highly quesionable undertaking.

Despite such an obvious caveat, it is worth emphasizing that religious diversity in the ancient Near East is as important for our understanding as "immanence" and purity; there is a widespread polytheism during the period that operated as a counter-culture to any centralizing cult whether in Rome or Jerusalem. It is especially difficult for a contemporary interpreter to enter such a worldview, despite the apparent pluralism of religious and other cultural objects of veneration in American society. There is a certain homogeneity to our shrines and holy places; even the recent addition of imports from the orient does not disturb the consistency of their pattern, regardless of the variations among Protestants, Jews, Catholics, and those with more esoteric devotional tendencies. To enter the ancient Near East, however, is not only to enter a world in which neither the universe nor society have yet been disenchanted; it is to enter a world with multiple sources of immanence, enchantment, and of social credit.

Some of these sources are regional; shrines vary from one place to another. Some are expressions of the self-understanding of a particular town or city, of worship in a particular community, such as the Essenes, or of status groups and their particular variants of belief and practice. It may well be that a major source of polytheism in Palestinian or Hellenic communities was the household itself. To discuss these variations would be more than enough for an entirely different essay. Here I am simply making a reasonable sociological generalization: that groups and communities whose organizations are relatively autonomous and compartmentalized, whether or not they are continguous with one another, tend to develop a belief in a multiplicity of spiritual beings, such as angels (Swanson). This set of beliefs is, in Swanson's terminology, quite simply polytheism.

We are now in a better position to assess the difficulties of interpreting a passage such as the one on authority through service from the distance of the twentieth century. The gradual dissemination and institutionalization of religious values in Western societies has at least made it necessary to legitimate authority on the basis of its value to the individual. That is one of the "contradictions" of Western society. Sociologists have essentially agreed with Durkheim's evaluation that a society whose authority depends on its alleged benefits to the individual is fundamentally flawed. The flaw underlies the expansion of the welfare state, the increase in service-oriented occupations and institutions, and the resulting decrease in margins of productivity and profitability; the same flaw accounts for persistent, often increasing, and not infrequently unrealistic demands for security and satisfaction on the part of a wide range of social groups and movements. The evident contradiction of an entire society oriented toward selfless service has engendered some chronic distrust of public institutions and of the "service" professions; note the increasing litigation that has made these professions less profitable and is undercutting voluntarism in American society. The lack of immanence in modern societies has deprived secular authority of its capacity to enchant; the suspension of popular disbelief in a service society means that authorities must acquire social credit through their performances.

Nonetheless, despite their multiple sources of popular inspiration and objects of devotion, modern societies have developed highly consistent patterns in the standards and values that legitimate authority and provide the basis for criticism and protest; even counter-cultural movements draw their sources of inspiration and legitimacy from the same public wells. And the counter-culture, as Bernice Martin reminds us, only becomes "daemonic" when it escapes the discipline and rationality imposed by the ethic of responsibility and institutionalized in the churches and the professions (1981:185 ff.). Indeed, it is a testimony to the flexibility as well as to the stability of a highly rationalized and secular social system that the service professions have been able to absorb so much of the impact of what Martin calls the "expressive" revolution of the 1960's. Indeed, partly because of the gentlemanly or bourgeois ethos of education, teachers have been willing to develop the expressive potential of higher education at the expense of the clearly lower status occupations that stress merely useful knowledge, results, and success (cf. Martin 1981:197 ff.). At the same time as social workers and educators became professionally concerned with "quality of life," moreover, they were still continuing to engage in their traditional functions of keeping the young and disadvantaged off the streets and out of trouble. The service ethic has its civic functions as well as its more visible advantages to clients in need of professionalized attention. *Under these conditions, whatever may have been radical about identifying authority with service in the first century has largely been lost in the twentieth.*

What may still be a "flaw" in modern societies, i.e. the antithesis between authority and the willful pursuit of the individual's welfare or satisfaction, was a dangerous fault that could release powerful shocks to the social systems of the first century. The reasons for the difference are encompassed in Weber's notion of the institutionalization and even routinization of charisma. If charisma is the source of inspiration and radical leadership, and if one attributes to prophets or, as we have seen, to emperors the magical powers associated with such charisma, authority will no doubt be accompanied by rites, solemn proclamations, and the promulgation of blessings and curses to the sound of trumpets accompanied by clouds of smoke and fire. Equally apocalyptic imagery may be invoked by prophets whose retinues cannot afford the panoply of power but who insist on the same authenticating symbols.

Where prophecy can be co-opted by authority, imperial or otherwise, one finds only the beginnings of the "institutionalization" of charisma: a rite, as I have already noted, in which vassals align themselves with an emperor or in which tribes covenant with one another in the name of their God, Yahweh.

But the beginnings of such institutionalization in rites can be carried further. As prophets and chiefs or emperors are succeeded, their roles and responsibilities are assigned to followers who gain their predecessors authority and may also succeed to their powers. Charisma is thus concentrated rather than diffused or dispersed. The process has been too well described elsewhere to need elaboration here (cf. O'Dea 1966). Let it simply be said that for a movement to survive, the charisma of its leaders will necessarily be institutionalized. Making charisma routine is *a constructive process,* although it is sometimes miscontrued, even by those writing "a sociological analysis" of the New Testament, as a fall from grace (cf. Tidball 1984:128–134).

The point is that, in the first century, polytheism prevented charisma from being fully institutionalized. While magical powers were still attributed to those who exercised and claimed power, kings, high priests, and Roman officials or surrogates faced prophets and messiahs in a chronic and, at times, acute confrontation over the sources and substance of social credit. Those sources, being divine, were to be divined in oracle, extraordinary signs, and other less reliable forms of revelation. The rites of authority had failed to institutionalize charisma itself. Social credit remained too elusive to claim and to keep for any length of time.

I have been describing a process which is dialectical because it involves two contrary forces, so to speak, which intensify their mutual opposition and thus avoid either a stalemate, a clear victory of one side over another, or a new synthesis capable of reconciling the former opposition. The forces of social authority, on the one hand, consisted of political elites in the empire and the Temple cult; on the other hand the forces of personal charisma were located in prophets and messianic figures who claimed a wide range of sources of inspiration. The rulers of this world had generated an equally numerous and opposing number of messiahs and prophets. There was an inflation in social credit, widespread counterfeiting, and frequent crashes.

Their contest for social credit did not occur in a vacuum, however; pictures of the anomic and chaotic structure of Palestinian society may have been largely overdrawn on the basis of industrialized society. There were a few stable sources of social credit, and one was the household. Tidball (1984:822 ff.) is undoubtedly correct that the household was a major aspect of the social landscape and consisted of immediate relatives, clients, slaves either in bondage or freed into the intimacy of friendship, and long-term friends whose status in the community depended on their allegiance to a specific household. These were relatively autonomous units, capable of maintaining some degree of privacy, and able to adopt the religious orientations of its head without immediate regard for the worship of other households. This compartmentalization, heterogenous, and more or less contiguous pattern of social organization is conducive, as I have argued, on the basis of Swanson's cross-cultural studies, to polytheism. Polytheism, however, is hardly a source of cultural cohesion capable of sublimating or resolving the opposition between conflicting types of charismatic authority. On the contrary, this multiplicity of spiritual adhesions based on the household simply perpetuated one traditional type of authority incapable of providing the basis for the cultural unification of the peoples in the eastern Mediterranean. Immanence, whether in reference to the spiritual substances conveyed by prophet or priest, magician or emperor, made the conflict over authority exceedingly serious; polytheism made it necessary for the contestants to lay seige to loyalties still encapsulated in the institution of the household. In that institution the authority of the servant originated and could properly be understood. I hypothesize that *the Jesus movement borrowed that authority, however, as a principle with which to subvert the rule of all other lords.*

## Bibliography

James Barr, *The Semantics of Biblical Language* (Oxford University Press, 1961). SCM Press, Ltd.:1983.

James H. Charlesworth, *The Old Testament Pseudepigrapha and the New Testament* (Cambridge: Cambridge University Press, 1985).

Fred O. Francis and Wayne A. Meeks, *Conflict at Colossae.* A problem in the Interpretation of Early Christianity Illustrated by Selected Modern Studies. (Society of Biblical Literature and Scholars Press, 1975).

Max Gluckman, *Custom and Conflict in Africa* (Basil Blackwell, 1956; New York: Barnes and Noble, 1967).

Edward McGlynn Gaffney, Jr. "Of Covenants Ancient and New: The Influence of Secular Law on Biblical Religion," *The Journal of Law and Religion,* Vol. 11, No. 1, 1984:117–143.

Richard Huntington and Peter Metcalf, *Celebrations of Death.* The Anthropology of Mortuary Ritual. (Cambridge: Cambridge University Press, 1979).

David Martin, *The Dilemma of Contemporary Religion.* (New York: St. Martin's Press, 1981).

Daniel J. O'Keffe, *Stolen Lightning.* (New York: Random House, Vintage Books, 1983).

Thomas F. O'Dea, *The Sociology of Religion.* (Englewood Cliffs, N.J.: Prentice-Hall, Inc. 1966).

Aharon Oppenheimer, *The 'Am Ha-aretz.* A Study in the Social History of the Jewish People in the Hellenistic-Roman Period. (Leiden: E. J. Brill, 1977).

Guy Swanson, *Religion and Regime.* A Sociological Account of the Reformation. (Ann Arbor: The University of Michigan Press, 1967).

Gerd Theissen, *The Birth of the Gods.* (Ann Arbor: University of Michigan Press, 1960).

Derek Tidball, *The Social Context of the New Testament: A Sociological Analysis.* (Grand Rapids, Michigan: 1984).

Bryan Wilson, *Magic and the Millennium.* (London: Heinemann Education Books, 1973).

Walter Wink, *Naming the Powers.* The Language of Power in the New Testament. The Powers: Vol. I, (Philadelphia: The Fortress Press, 1984).

# The Basis of Empire, A Study of the Succession Narrative

Sean E. McEvenue

The Succession Narrative may be read in 2 Sam 9–20; 1 Kings 1–2.[1] Our study will attempt to discover the meaning of text by searching out the focus of creative effort manifest in the telling.[2]

## Historical Interest

The literary quality of this story is so striking, that it may be wise to begin our study in a counter direction, by stressing its bias toward what we might call hard historical facts. First of all, in a general way the author, without quite achieving the anti-hero cynicism with which we are familiar from the dominant literary modes of the sixties, still wrote a story quite without heroes. There is a refusal of myth at the heart of this writing, as we shall see in detail below, which would tend to present king, soldier, wise man, prophet, and priest as weak human beings, or worse. This refusal leaves the author little to work with except historical facts.

Secondly, one must admire the skill with which the author provides each personage in the story with a distinctive and consistent character, and the narrative art with which these personages are introduced and interwoven in a complex plot development. However, we must also note that some personages are introduced, and given no character, and not interwoven with any narrative skill whatever. For example we are told that Mephibosheth, before David brought him to Jerusalem, was living with Machir, the son of Ammiel, in Lo-debar (9:4,5). Much later in the story, when David had fled to Mahanaim, we are told that Machir, the son of Ammiel, from Lo-debar came there to help him out (17:17). This personage appears nowhere else, and seems to generate no narrative meaning in the text. He appears to be mentioned in the text *only* because he participated in the events. The same is true of an otherwise unknown Shobi the son of Nahash, who appears in the same verse apparently

[1]Cf. Leonhard Rost, *Die Überlieferung von der Thronnachfolge Davids,* (BWANT III 6), Kohlhammer, Stuttgart, 1926; *(The Succession to the Throne of David,* Almond Press, Sheffield, 1982). A most accessible and complete literary study of this narrative, with a useful survey of prior scholarship, may be found in R.N. Whybray, *The Succession Narrative, A Study of II Sam 9–20 and 1 Kings 2 and 3,* SCM Press in Great Britain, and Alec R. Allenson Inc. Naperville, Illinois, 1968. He characterizes the work as a "propagandist narrative" (p. 54), intent at the same time on illustrating specific proverbial teaching (p. 95), written by a wisdom teacher who was influenced by Egyptian models of "political novels" (pp. 115–116). The present paper might be considered an attempt to fill a lacuna to which Whybray makes allusion: "The question why the author chose to recount the events which led to Solomon's accession to the throne rather than some other story still remains unanswered" (p. 50). What were the aims of the author? For further bibliography cf. James W. Flanagan, "Court History or Succession Document? A Study of 2 Samuel 9–20 and 1 Kings 1–2," *JBL* 91, 1972, pp. 172–181; and also Anthony Campbell, *Of Prophets and Kings, A Late Ninth-Century Document (1 Samuel 1–2 Kings 10),* (CBQ Monography Series 17), Washington, 1986, esp. pp. 82–84. Campbell's claim that 1 Kings 1 is part of a different prophetic document is hard to accept, as the image of Nathan in that chapter is radically diverse from the image of prophets elsewhere in his proposed "Prophetic Record."

[2]The objectives and the justification of the method employed in this study are presented in chs. 1–2 of my forthcoming book dealing with the authority of the Bible.

just because he too turned up in Mahanaim. More striking is the mention of Mica, the son of Mephibosheth (9:12). In a succession story, a great grandson of Saul either should not be mentioned, or else, if mentioned, his role as threat to the throne or as successfully neutralized should be narrated. But our author is so distracted by facts, away from story forms, that he names Mica in ch 9, and then never mentions him again. One can only conclude that he mentions Mica simply because he was there, and that he narrates nothing further simply because he knows nothing further about him. Similarly the mentions of Ittai the Gittite (15:19–22; 18:2,5,12), and of Barzillai the Gileadite (17:27–29; 19:31–40), appear to carry no narrative value beyond the value of facticity. Again, the details of Shimei's error in 1 Kings 2:39–40 are otherwise irrelevant, and therefore must be understood as historical facts. Finally, even the artful presentation of David's uncertainty in the disposition of Saul's wealth between Mephibosheth and Ziba (16:4; 29:29) must be historical, if only because such wealth was too visible to be lied about, at least for many generations afterwards.

This paper is concerned with the historicity of the text only to the point of establishing what kind of narrative this is. These few observations should be sufficient to show that this writing is historical, in the sense that it is truly rooted in historical facts and realities.

## Narrative Structures

The narrative proceeds by a series of vignettes, each of which is skillfully turned. Moreover the clever interweaving of separable stories about Mephibosheth, Ziba, Joab, Shimei, Nathan, and Bathsheba, through the larger story of David and his sons, serves to knit the incidents into a continuous development. But beyond this there is a further continuous story line, which the reader feels obscurely as a deeper unity, even if one cannot easily identify it. What is the underlying narrative about?

Leonhard Rost recognized a narrative line from Yahweh's election of Solomon in 12:24–25, through the elimination of competitors (Absalom and Adonijah) to the establishment of Solomon on the throne in 1 Kings 2:46. There is no reason to doubt that that narrative line exists in the text. However it is difficult to agree that it is the point of the text, or that it does justice to the concerns of the author. For example, if the story is about Solomon, how explain that Solomon himself plays a very brief role in the story line? And if it is about succession, how explain that the idea of succession is adverted to only at the very end? And how explain the wealth of material in the text which is very remotely, or not at all, connected with this story line? The story line itself is so obscurely present in the text that one major study denies its very existence.[3]

Moreover, one can point to a second underlying story line which is equally present in the text: namely, a story of sin and punishment, in five phases. This story begins with David the king attempting to do good things, (to take care of the descendants of Saul in 9:1, and to be loyal to the Ammonites in 10:1–2), and with Yahweh very firmly on David's side in 10:12–14,18. In a second phase, the focus is on sin. First, David sins: adultery leading to an odious murder. God promises punishment (chs 11–12). Then David's son Amnon also perpetrates a sexual crime, and another son, Absalom, also becomes guilty of an odious murder, while assuming the role of punisher of sexual folly. Absalom then proceeds to punish David, but finally ends up murdered himself (13–18). In a third phase of the

[3]Cf. James W. Flanagan, *op cit.* who argues that the material concerning succesion, i.e. the Bathsheba incident and 1 Kings 1–2, are a separate story, from a different source. For the purposes of this paper, it is not necessary to refute the source-critical arguments of Flanagan and others. Whatever the history of the weaving of this text, this paper addresses continuities in narrative, attitude, and style in this slice of the present biblical text, which produce a specific effect in readers of the Bible.

story, David has done penance (12), has accepted the curses heaped upon his exile by Shimei (16:11–12), and has accepted as from God's hands all that he suffered from Absalom (18:5,33). In a final phase of the story, David is restored to his kingdom (19–20); and his son by Bathsheba is established on the throne (1 Kings 1–2). That is a plausible reading of the text. It is a story line which is undeniably present in the text, even if its presence is just about as obscure as that of the succession story.

A third underlying story line can be pointed out. It might suggest further source analysis, and it may be closer to propaganda than story, but it is a unifying theme within the text. And it is clearly tributory to the main succession narrative. It is the story of David's vindication: how he is proven not guilty of the blood of Saul. David is a devious and sinful man, but he is not guilty of regicide. The political value of such a story to Solomon, or any later successor of David, is obvious.[4] This story line is carried with particular clarity in the vignettes about Shimei. Shimei curses David, precisely because he believes that David's defeat is a proof that Saul's blood is on his head. (16:8) It is important to note that David himself is presented as not being sure but that Shimei may be right (16:12). When the rebellion has been defeated, Shimei realizes he was wrong and begs forgiveness (19:18–20). David states that he too has recognized a proof of his innocence in this victory, and he is so overjoyed that he will not allow Abishai to kill Shimei (19:22). Finally, the death of Shimei forms a kind of climax in a series which reaches beyond Shimei: all those who endangered the consolidation of Solomon's succession to the throne are killed or exiled: Absalom, Adonijah, Abiathar, Joab, and finally Shimei. The first three are punished because they contested Yahweh's choice of David and then Solomon for the throne. Joab is punished because he had brought blood on the head of David and his family. Shimei is punished for imputing blood guilt to David and his house.

The reader must ask why these plots are so interwoven as to be almost hidden in the text. One could imagine three possible answers to this question. It could be because the author is struggling with too many historical details, and unable to bring out clearly the points he wants to make? Or it could be because the author is a wisdom writer, who chooses to write in an indirect riddling style, inviting the reader to figure out what lies beneath the surface? Or, finally, it could be because the author uses the story lines as an underlying framework, but does not focus on them because his or her main interest does not lie in story at all, but elsewhere?

It can hardly be the first, because there is not a single sentence in the text in which one can see the author struggling to establish any clear points. There are no generalizations. There are no summaries. There is no introduction, and the conclusion is only one half verse in length.

The second is more plausible, but it too has to be rejected, when one thinks concretely about the points actually in question. This brilliant writer simply cannot be imagined to have written so complex a document in order to invite readers to riddle out these three lessons. There is no riddle about the fact that Solomon was chosen by God. This must have seemed all too obvious to those Jews who lived during the splendor of his empire, or within memory of it. Or again, that David had sinned, been punished, and then restored to power, is a truth which is not so much subtly concealed in this story, but rather one

[4]The vindication of David seems also to have been one of the main concerns of the "Rise of David Story," which may be read roughtly in 1 Sam 15–2 Sam 8. For a history of research cf. the classical introductions to the Old Testament, and especially Brevard Childs, *Introduction to the Old Testament as Scripture,* Fortress Press, Philadelphia, 1979, pp. 266–271. Cf. further, David Gunn, *The Story of King David, Genre and Interpretation,* Sheffield, 1979, and S. McEvenue, "The Rise of David Story and the Search for a Story to Live by," in *Creativity and Method, Essays in Honour of Bernard Lonergan,* Milwaukee, 1980 pp. 185–195.

which is weakened and almost denied by the graceless ending to David's life which is portrayed in the final two chapters. Finally, that David is vindicated of blood guilt by his victory over Absolom, and by the crowning of Solomon, might justify a riddling treatment. However, this theme can explain only the last part of the narrative, leaving the whole of chs 9 to 15 unmotivated.

Now it is true that wisdom is much discussed in the text, and that, as we shall see below in some detail, much of the author's genius is involved in portraying communication by indirection. However it is also true that the author does not really admire indirection, as s/he consistently associates indirection with unsavoury accomplishments. For example, Jonadab is described as "wise" (13:3) when he shows Amnon how to go about raping his sister, an act which is later characterized as folly (13:12–13). Joab sends a "wise" woman of Tekoa in order to wheedle David's consent to the idea of restoring Absalom, an idea which proves to be a disastrous mistake. When David figures out the manipulation, s/he compares his "wisdom" to that of the angel of God who knows all things. In this context, even angelic wisdom turns out to be a dupe! Another "wise" woman (20:16) intervenes as a negotiator, and succeeds by betraying Sheba the son of Bichri. David calls Solomon "wise" (1 Kings 2:9) because he will be able to kill Shimei, circumventing David's oath. Similarly Solomon's "wisdom" will enable him to bring Joab to an evil end (1 Kings 2:6). Even the more elegant word "counsel," reserved for the great courtiers Hushai, Ahithophel, and Nathan, signifies nothing more elevated than astuteness, craft, or wilyness on the pen of this author (cf. 16:23; 17:7,11,14,15,21,23; 1 Kings 1:12.). The author has the wise woman of Tekoa flatter David by comparing his "wisdom" to that of the angel of God (14:17), but when the author himself, or herself, seriously praises the "counsel" of Ahithophel, she compares it, not to God's "counsel," but to God's "word" (16:23). In this case Ahithophel's "counsel" was correct, but Yahweh intervened to defeat this good counsel (17:14). This author describes astuteness and manipulative communication within history, but places God, and the story's unidentified narrator, outside it. Such an author can hardly be expected to relate to his/her own readers in this mode.

As a final argument, I would ask whether the reader's pleasure in reading this story is enhanced when these hidden story lines are pointed out. When we read the text, with the hypothesis that these plots govern the basic meaning, that they are the "whole point" as it were, do we not feel rather disappointed and bored? Do we not feel that we are missing something, or else that this clever author could easily have made these "points" more effectively?

We must conclude, therefore, that the third explanation is correct, namely that the author is interested in something other than these hidden story lines. The central meaning of the text is to be found elsewhere.

## The Central Focus

If the author of The Succession Narrative draws upon history, and uses interwoven story lines, where does he or she apply and display creative interest, original thought, passionate talent? What are these stories really about?

A first answer, and an important one, is that at their best they are about communication, deception, manipulation. This can be seen in a rapid survey of the major stories. Ch 9 is, in fact, a good example, but we will reserve it for later consideration. Ch 10 deals with war, and climaxes in definitive victory over Syria. However that part of the story is told as a a colourless chronicle. All the authorial creativity has been concentrated in relating the misinterpretation of David's intentions in sending mourners to the Ammonites, and in their humorous response. Ch 11 is a story of adultery and murder, and yet almost no time or effort is spent depicting those events. Even the emotional and moral aspects are reduced to a single verse (11:26). All the energy in the story is derived from contrasts in communication. On the one hand, the directness of David's communication to Bathsheba (11:4,27,24), and to Joab (11:6), and of the servants' communication to David (11:10), and of Uriah's to David (11:11) provide a uniform background. On the other hand, another series of communications form a very striking contrast against it: namely the manipulative deception of David's communication to Uriah (11:8,12), and the detailed portrayal of circumspection and indirection in Joab's communication to David (11:18–24,28). This element absorbs the whole interest and creative energy of the story. Similarly the sequel in ch 12 is not at all a straightforward story of prophecy and repentance. First, we see Nathan employing an indirect approach (12:1–4), remote from prophetic forms but similar to that of the wise woman of Tekoa in ch 14. Second, David's grief turns out to be not just grief, but rather a posture in prayer. Third, the author focuses the readers' attention on a communication problem experienced by David's servants (12:18–23). Finally, the end of the chapter wraps up the war with the Ammonites begun in ch 10, but the focus of interest is not on the victory, but rather on Joab's astuteness in having David secure the image of victor for himself.

Ch 13 presents the rape of Tamar, and it focuses on the technique of tricking her. Tamar's reaction centres only on appearances and reputation (13:12–13), and then on a technique of communicating her state to the family (13:19). The rest of the chapter deals with the concealment (13:20), the delayed deception by which Absalom takes revenge, and the way in which David finds out about it (13:20–36). Ch 14 deals with Absalom's return to Jerusalem, but the author has conceived it as a story about communication and persuasion in the royal court. Ch 15 presents David's defeat in Jerusalem, and ch 16 deals with his flight. The interest in the story is maintained by reflections on how Absalom created a good opinion of himself (15:1–6); how he deceived David (15:7–12); how David set up a communication system for himself (15:24–28) and a perverse wisdom for Absalom (15:32–37; 16:15–19); and finally how Absalom communicated his victory to the common people (16:20–23). Ch 17 deals with the contest in persuasion between "counsellors," and the messenger system set up by David. Ch 18 relates the death of Absalom, but even here the whole of vv 19–33 are dedicatd to the story of how the news of it was brought to David. Chs 19–20 present David's complete return to power in a manner consistent with the foregoing, though not remarkably focused on communication.

Finally 1 Kings 1–2 relate Solomon's accession to the throne, and David's final advice and death. Ch 1 is exclusively about communication: it is a kaleidoskopic study of creating appearances and manipulating information in order to create power. The point is not that Solomon became king, but precisely the manipulative process by which Solomon became king. Ch 2 then deals with craft in government.

It must be concluded that, to an astonishing degree, the central and almost exclusive interest of this author consists in his/her ability to depict the role of communication, deception, and manipulation in history.

A second answer to our question about the focus of our author's creative interest is intimately related to the first. The Succession Narrative is a clever study of David, provided by a narrator who has no access to David's inner thoughts, but who appears to be a member of the court (9:11 "Mephibosheth ate at *my* table, like one of the king's sons."), who witnesses David's actions and gestures and decisions from close up. The author has no privileged information about David's motives. S/he does know what individuals said to David in relative privacy, as in ch 19 where Joab urges David to cease grieving for Absalom; and also what such individuals might have reported of their private conversations, as in ch 14, for example, the conversation with the wise woman of Tekoa. But there is never a glimpse of David's own thinking. The genius of the presentation is that David is consistently shown as acting or speaking, on the basis of motives which are unknown, or ambiguous. There results a figure who fits very convincingly at the centre of a story of communication, deception, and manipulation.

Ambiguity arises at the very start, in ch 9. The reader's doubts will be slight at first, but they will grow even larger as David's duplicity is revealed, and as the author allows ambiguities to accumulate without ever giving counter-indications about David's motives. The story opens with David proffering a generous gesture toward a grandson of Saul. David says he intends to "show him the kindness of God" (9:1,3). However the reader is left unsure about David's motives. Mephibosheth is to live in Jerusalem and eat at the royal table. Is this an honour, or a form of imprisonment? The reader must note that Mephibosheth's helplessness is mentioned in 9:3, and then placed as a final comment on the story in 9:13. Moreover David now places Ziba in control of all the land of Saul, and tells him to bring in all the produce for Mephibosheth. What will Mephibosheth do with it, now that he is to eat at the king's table? David considers Ziba himself to be a servant only of Saul, not of Mephibosheth (9:9–10). Later in the story, Ziba will lie about Mephibosheth, and as a result David will give him all that had belonged to Mephibosheth (16:4). Later again, when Mephibosheth clears his name, and David does not know whom to believe, David will show no trace of "the wisdom of Solomon," but rather will hastily divide the land between Mephibosheth and Ziba as though it were a matter of small consequence (19:29). In this sequence we see David's initial magnanimity take on an ambiguous note, and then gradually be revealed as a political manipulation. And David's inability to decide which was the liar, Mephibosheth or Ziba, somehow leaves David in complicity with deception.

In ch 10 the author gives us only David's word for it that his purposes in regard to the Ammonites is only condolence. We see David letting Joab lead the battle until the king of Syria appears on the scene. Then David takes to the field (10:17). This is uncommented in the text. Later, in 12:27–30, David will again take to the field, this time for the moment of glory. In ch 18:2–4 there is a great discussion about whether David should risk his neck in battle, and the decision is he should not. Again the author gives no clue as to the real motives, and the reader is left just slightly unsure about David's military honours.

Of course the Uriah story presents David at his deceptive worst. Moreover, in ch 12, David's impressive grief over the loss of Bathsheba's first child, and his immediate recovery upon the child's death,leaves the reader wondering. Is this strong religion, or weak theatre? Here again the author chooses to leave the ambiguity intact.

David's relationship with Joab is ambiguous. Clearly they begin as allies in war and in crime in chs 10–12. Clearly they end up as enemies, and David explains that it is because of Joab's murder of Abner and Amasa (1 Kings 2:5). However, the reader knows something of Joab's contempt for David from his manner of instructing the messenger in 10:18–21, and the wise woman in 14:1–3, about how to manipulate David. And we know that Joab directly disobeyed David in murdering Absalom, and then hypocritically assumed the honest-statesman role, convincing David that he must resume his leadership and cease his indulgence in grief (19:1–8). Just five verses later we see David appointing Amasa to head the army! The author makes no comment about this implicit demotion of Joab. The reader is puzzled. Did David learn who had murdered Absalom? Or was this simply astute politics, promoting a former enemy? Later, in ch 20, Joab manages to kill Amasa, and simply reassumes his position at the head of the army. What did David think of this? Again the author leaves the reader without any clues, until the end, when David tells Solomon to kill Joab.

David's concern that Absalom not be killed, and subsequent grief, in chs 18–19, seem authentic. But then we immediately see David securing his power in Judah and in Israel by manipulation and violence (19:11–15;20–6). One cannot doubt, after reading the Shimei encounter in 16:5–14 that David firmly believed that his kingship was given him by Yahweh. However it is equally clear that David felt called upon to use every means, fair or foul, to protect Yahweh's choices! In this context, the grief over Absalom appears to be both genuine and also a political gesture.

In the final scenes, we see David blatantly manipulated by Nathan and Bathsheba to give the nod to Solomon. In his own words, his decision is based on his oath to Yahweh (1 Kings 1:11–31). And his dying advice to Solomon begins with an admirable exhortation to virtue (1 Kings 2:1–4)[5], but this is followed by a return to the scheming and vindictive politician, assuring rewards for his friends and revenge on his enemies (1 Kings 2:5–9).

The ambiguity about David is accompanied by other more minor ambiguities in the narrative. Some characters are relatively colourless: for example Absalom, Amnon, Zadok, and Abiathar. Others are stereotypes, such as Bathsheba, the dumb blond, or Joab, a prototype of contemporary images of the Pentagon. However Mephibosheth and Ziba remain enigmatical to the end of the story. And Nathan is remarkably ambiguous: he is given prophetic responsibility for Solomon in 12:25; and in 1 Kings 1 he is again called a prophet in vv 22–23, and he plays a decisive role in securing the throne for Solomon. Moreover he is allowed to use the formula "Thus says the Lord" in 12:11. However his style is that of a wise man in ch 12, and of an unscrupulous courtier in 1 Kings 1. The reader does not know what to make of him as a person, even if Yahweh has used him to His own purpose.

Such then is the genius, the charm, and creative contribution of this writer in narrating David's end and Solomon's accession to the throne. S/he writes of deception and ambiguity. Presented this way, it sounds like a situation comedy. But it is clearly far more serious than that. We see here a literary technique by which the author, and hence the reader, does not finally know the human reality which underlies this history. Or rather we know that the human reality was always ambiguous, and never decisive. However, there was a decisive reality underlying the events, namely a series of divine decisions. And this reality is largely taken for granted, though quietly mentioned, by the author. It demands faith on the part of the reader. It is the tension between these two elements of ambiguity and certainty which makes this, not only a clever, but also a powerful, text. It is to the divine reality that we must now turn.

## The Interventions of Yahweh

The belief system which forms a background to this story understands that God is very much in charge of outcomes. "Man proposes but God disposes" is very much the view of history represented here. For example, when Joab is set to go to battle against the Ammonite-Syrian coalition, he understnads that his battle is in defence of the "cities of our God; and may Yahweh do what is good in his eyes" (12:10). A New Testament translation of this wish is "Thy will be done." And this must not be taken for a meaningless phrase, for we see this to be a serious principle in a later story, which determines David's actions. In 15:25–26, David expresses readiness to be restored or to come to an end as God sees fit, and this pious affirmation is shown to be operative in ch 16. There, David fleeing the city, is cursed by

[5]These verses are sometimes ascribed to a Deuteronomistic editor.

Shimei for the murder of Saul's family. Abishai wants to kill Shimei, but David is very much afraid that Shimei is right, and that his present suffering is due to Yahweh's intervention. Killing Shimei would not, therefore, stop Yahweh. Rather it would remove all chances of satisfying God's wrath with some punishment short of death. David hopes for a reprieve in return for suffering this insult: "Possibly Yahweh will witness my guilt-suffering, and Yahweh may restore blessing after his (Shimei's) cursing today" (16:12). Thus, for David, all manipulation of persons and events by himself is powerless against divine decisions, and indeed might prove counter-productive.

In this line of thought, one might further reason that all manipulation of persons and events toward furthering divine decisions will be appropriate. Our author offers no such generalizations, but this one would explain and justify David's remarkable shift from passivity, in chs 14–18, to decisive and energetic activity towards restoring his position in Jerusalem, once he is sure that Yahweh wants him to continue as king, in chs 19–20. It would also explain the shift from David's hands-off policy regarding his sons throughout the story (particularly Amnon and Absalom), to his decisive action in securing the throne for Solomon, once Adonijah has threatened that divine decision. Moreover, it is clear that the wise woman of Tekoa held this doctrine (14:11,17).

In this story, Yahweh is not at all involved, and is almost never mentioned, in the world of intrigue, of communication, of manipulation. However, the author presents very specific moments of divine intervention, which it will be well to enumerate. First, if we are to trust Joab's and David's piety in leaving the outcome in Yahweh's hands, as we saw above, then we must conclude that Yahweh gave the victory over the Syrians and Ammonites in chs 10 and 12. Moreover we shall see below that Yahweh is said to have given David the victory over his foes, though this is a slightly different category.

Second, we are laconically told that Yahweh was displeased with David's adultery-murder (11:27), and then that Yahweh will punish the crime by causing armed strife in David's family, by humiliating David sexually, and by taking the life of the illegitimate child (12:10–14). These three threats are carried out in the ensuing story. In regard to the second and third of these, the text itself explicitly points out the divine intervention (12:15,22; 16:21–23). Similarly the punishments which Solomon gives to Abiathar, Joab, and Shimei, are attributed to Yahweh (1 Kings 2:27,32–33,42–46).

Third, it becomes evident that Yahweh has decided, in fact, that David should be returned to the throne in Jerusalem. We are told that David prayed Yahweh to confuse the counsel of Ahithophel (15:31); and later that Yahweh had decided "to defeat the good counsel of Ahithophel, so that Yahweh might bring evil upon Absalom" (17:14). Three times it is said that Yahweh has given David victory over his enemies (18:19,28,31). In 19:22 David says that "this day I know I am king over Israel." However, the author does not choose to indicate how David knows, or to confirm this with another specific statement.

Fourth, we are told that Yahweh loves Solomon at his birth (12:24–25), and that the throne was given to Solomon by Yahweh (1 Kings 2:15). Moreover we are assured that Yahweh will grant eternal peace to this dynasty (1 Kings 2:33).

In summary, Yahweh intervenes to give victory in war, to punish evil, and to choose the monarch.

## The Subliminal Teaching of this Narrative

The theological teaching of this text is not at all obvious. It contains a teaching about divine intervention, outlined in the previous section, but this is more a background than a positive affirmation of the text. If any biblical text can be said to be secular, this witty piece surely is it.

Within the context of the Deuteronomic history, one could align it with those texts which are opposed to the monarchy. An exilic Deuteronomist, who wrote Dt 17:14–20, and who edited 1 Sam 7–12 by the insertions of 7:3–4;8:6–20a;10:18–19; and especially 12:6–25, and who viewed the monarchy as a corrupt institution from the start, and destined to bring about the end of Israel, would certainly have enjoyed this story as exemplifying royal corruption.[6] Such a reading would rightly argue that the conclusion of a text usually indicates "the point" which is intended. In this case, 1 Kings 2 consists mainly of David's malicious advice, and Solomon's craftiness in following it. And the closing incident shows how Shimei is killed on the pretext of a trivial offence. The final closure consists of a single sentence, which reads: "And the kingdom was established in the hand of Solomon." The closure seems to signify that Solomon's imperial power is to be explained by the foregoing narrative, i.e. its origin lies in the political manipulation which brought Solomon to the throne, and in the devious violence which secured him there.

However, this paper would like to seize the original meaning of The Succession Story prior to specific subsequent moments of interpretation through larger contexts of the canon.[7] It would like to do so, partially because that meaning is still there, however much subsequent biblical and post-biblical tradition may have overlooked it; and partially because the canon, or the Deuteronomistic history, have seldom, if ever, been read as continuous units by the faithful in the churches or synagogues. Our faith has been formed on the basis of small segments of texts, and the voice of this faith must not be lost.

The fact is that, even if it is not articulated textually, there is a distinctive message in The Succession Story which leaves its mark on the reader. There is a Voice in the text, which is the creative aspiration of the original writer, and which is obscurely heard in every pericope. This writer remains ambiguous about David and Solomon as human persons. However s/he did not use any words such as "malicious," or "devious," or "violent." S/he does not condemn these kings as we have done in the last paragraph. We feel the author's pleasure in revealing ambiguity, but we do not detect any trace of indignation or anger. If the author lived during the time of Solomon, or shortly after, then he, or she, lived in a period of Israel's history where the kings provided political stability, personal security, financial wealth. The author's voice invites the reader to recognize the deception of appearances, and of political postures, and to embrace these human beings for what they were. At the same time, it invites the reader to identify and rely on the divine decisions which form reality and give shape to history.

In formulating this message, one is tempted to take modern proverbs such as "The Lord writes straight with crooked lines," or else to return to ancient authors such as Plato who taught his disciples to seek "truth" *(aletheia),* in preference to "opinion" *(doxa).* But the voice of this text, while counting on the straightness and truth of God, does not spend much time on it. It's focus is not there, but rather in the complexity of deception. There is an iconoclastic message in the text, which demands that we abandon awe before royalty, since

[6]For the source analysis and themes of the exilic Deuteronomist in Samuel and Kings, cf. Norbert Lohfink, *Rückblick im Zorn auf den Staat, Vorlesungen zu ausgewählten Schlüsseltexten der Bücher Samuel und Könige,* Frankfurt, 1984, pp. 44–110, esp.p.61.

[7]For critical discussions of the powerful hermeneutical principles proposed by Brevard Childs, written within the same basic philosophical presuppositions, cf. *JSOT* 16, 1980, the whole issue, and also *Horizons in Biblical Theology, An International Dialogue,* 1980, vol 2, section 2 pp. 113–211. My own critique is published in an article, "The Old Testament, Scripture or Theology" which was reprinted in the first issue of *Ex Auditu,* and further in a book review in *CBQ* 1980, pp. 535–537.

it presents David and Solomon as ambiguous at best; abandon admiration for the army, since Joab is presented as a ruthless schemer; abandon the cult of prophets, since it presents Nathan as a court politician; abandon respect for wisdom, since the wise are presented as manipulative and deceptive. It is so certain about well-being at the hand of God, that it takes pleasure in laying bare the uncertainty of human institutions through which God operates. It lays them bare, without hating them. It embraces life, reality, without myth, because that is where God does operate.

This is a unique literary genre. Where the edifying literature of the Deuteronomist explains prosperity (blessing) by civic virtues, or prophetic literature explains doom by human sins, or much of wisdom writing invites us to seek the causes of events in the hidden patterns of human nature, the sparks of divinity within creation, this writing delights in showing that human virtue and vice and the patterns of nature are only shifting appearances, froth on an ocean of reality. This is an approach which loves discussing ambiguous human process, precisely because it relies on divinely determined outcomes. This genre could be called adult, realistic, history. It is truly adult, because it is not cynical, or satirical. Rather it understands and embraces human ambiguity, rather than withdrawing in distaste. And it is truly realistic, in the sense that it finds God's work within human lives, rather than by covering these with myths or aesthetics.

There are biblical Proverbs, which are close to the thought of this text, and which will help to clarify its meaning. We may begin by first citing two helpful texts from the Succession Narrative itself: first, Joab's code that we should do our best, leaving the outcome in the hands of God:

> Be of good courage, and let us play the man for our people, and for the cities of our God; and may Yahweh do what seems good to him (10:12).

Second, David makes several rapid decisions, and expresses the same code, as he flees Jerusalem:

> Carry the ark of God back into the city. If I find favor in the eyes of Yahweh, he will bring me back and let me see both it and his habitation; but, if he says "I have no pleasure in you," behold here I am, let him do to me what seems good to him (15:25–26).

Some proverbs make humans responsible for the antecedents of events, but God alone responsible for the public event which occurs, even distinguishing preparatory thoughts from publicly uttered words. This view is close to that of our author, for whom the public acts are real, but the motives are shadowy, and ambiguous, hidden under devious words which fascinate but are finally irrelevant. We might consider the following three Proverbs:

> Commit your work to the Lord,
> And your plans will be established (16:3).
>
> A man's mind plans his way,
> But Yahweh directs his steps (16:9).
>
> The plans of the mind belong to man,
> But the answer of the tongue is from Yahweh (16:1).

In particular, it is the decisions of the king, and his actions, which are real, and created by God. David flees from Absalom precisely because he is not sure, as we saw above, about his own blood guilt, and whether Yahweh wanted him as king, or Absalom. Only when this question is answered by the death of Absalom does David take charge again. This belief in the divine right of the king has been supplanted in our time by rights based on majority vote, or the divine rights of the people. In our society, a leader must wait for a new mandate by the electorate before enunciating new policy. For us the divine will is expressed by democratic process; for David, as we saw, the divine will is expressed in success in war, in life and death, and in the ceremonies of enthronement. Consider the following Proverbs:

> It is the glory of God to conceal things,
> But the glory of kings is to search things out (25:1).
>
> My son, fear Yahweh and the king,
> And do not associate with those who change;
> For disaster from them will rise suddenly,
> And who knows the ruin that will come from both (24:21–22)?
>
> Inspired decisions are on the lips of a king;
> His mouth does not sin in judgement (16:10).

Even though what matters is what the King does or proclaims, still it remains true that it does not finally matter what the king thinks:

> Many seek the favour of a ruler,
> But from Yahweh a man gets justice (29:26).
>
> As the heavens for height, and the earth for depth,
> So the mind of Kings is unsearchable (25:3).

With such a view of reality, it is little wonder that our author studied the words and deeds of David so attentively, presenting them as they were, with subtle inuendo and implied questions, but ultimately little concern about the motives which lay behind them. It was not in creation, or in nature, but rather in politics that this author could experience the reality and love of God. The realm of his/her search was the ambiguity of human communication, but divine action was found in the stable realities of political power. The voice of this author, subliminal and therefore all-powerful in the mind of the reader, demands a similarly adult and realistic way of living religiously.

For many readers, this text may seem to teach nothing at all regarding the topic of this symposium, namely the implication of biblical texts for Church and state relationships. The easiest way to show implications, if it is an allowable one, may be to indicate the challenge this text directs to myself, with my own peculiar history. I was brought up as a member of a despised religious minority in the city of Toronto, during the 30's and 40's. During those years I learned to feel that government was simply corrupt and corrupting, foreign to true religion, and totally within the purview of what I believed to be an heretical religious establishment. In other words, my attitude to political authority was analogous to the position of the exilic Deuteronomist toward the king, as I mentioned earlier. Personally, I was unaware of the exilic Deuteronomist until recent years. Rather, my attitude seemed to be sufficiently justified by glib interpretations of Jesus' words: "Render to Caesar the things that are Caesar's, and to God the things that are God's." However, later in life, when I no longer felt powerless, or marginalized in society, or free from social responsibility, well then that angry escapist attitude was not enough! It did not constitute an adequate political theology, to say the least. And yet the subliminal message of this text is so inimical to all those early feelings that it has taken me fifty years of living with it, and of growing in other ways, before I could understand and accept its challenge.

## Conclusion

The author of this narrative chose to write about the succession because these were the major events he or she had lived through as an involved spectator, and mostly because he or she had searched for and discovered a traditional faith, not in the past, not in traditional myths or language codes, but in the experience of ambiguous human interaction. The reader who seeks "objective" historical data, or who admires literary skill, will find much to praise in this text. But the reading will be somewhat sour, unless one habitually lives as a radically responsible citizen.

# Christian Community and Governmental Power in the Gospel of Matthew

Ulrich Mauser

We are accustomed to think and to speak about the relationship of Church and State. In the context of this Symposium, dedicated to the theological interpretation of Scripture, the task was set that we should inquire of the New Testament in what way it might provide us in our time with some direction in our desire to live as members of the Christian Church and as responsible citizens of one State or another.

At the outset, however, it may be wise to put a note of caution. A "State" in the modern sense of the word does not exist in the time of Jesus and the nascent Christian community, neither does the "Church" if we understand by that term the summation of social, cultural, legal, and political realities shaping a community which has inherited close to 2000 years of Christian tradition. The modern State is dominated by a constitution which provides unity and order to all within its borders, regulates the balance of power among its citizens, and furnishes a communal identity in whose exercise it can relate like a person to other States around it. By the same token, the Church is, in the experience of most of us today, an identifiable body of people who are also expressing themselves through, and are governed by, a constitution with much the same powers as that possessed by the State, however significantly and characteristically it may vary in content and spirit from the constitution of a State.

When we turn to some observations on the relation of the Christian community to governmental powers in the Gospel of Matthew, we have to bear in mind that in the purview of the Matthean community neither Church nor State conform to our grid of realities.

We assume that the Gospel of Matthew was written within the last two decades of the first century AD in a Syrian city. It originated in a Jewish-Christian community in close and constant contact with a Jewish population shaped by the influence of the reform movement led by the Pharisaic rabbis under Johann ben Zakkai. But these Syrian Jewish Christians had already before, at the time preceding and during the horrendous Jewish-Roman war of 66–74 AD, suffered the shock of expulsion from the Jewish synagogues with resultant hardships and a threatened loss of identity. In the wake of the failure of their mission to their Jewish kin they had turned, perhaps for the first time, perhaps with painfully sharpened previous convictions, to a vigorous mission among the non-Jewish populace of their area.[1]

This Syrian Christian community found itself tossed upon the waters of hostile governmental powers against whose tides it had no protection on earth (Mt 8:23–27).[2] Both in its memory and in its present experience it had plenty of reason to be wary of government. Its memory was focussed on the person of Jesus whom the community worshipped as Israel's true king and as the Son of Israel's God, and into their memory extended the dark-

[1] For recent surveys on the historical setting of the Matthaen community, see U. Luz, *Das Evangelium nach Matthäus* (Mt 1–7), EKK 1/1, Zürich and Neukirchen: Benziger and Neukirchener Verlag, 1985, 61–82, and E. Schweizer, "Matthew's Church" in *The Interpretation of Matthew*, ET ed. by G. Stanton, Philadelphia and London: Fortress and SPCK, 1983, 129–155.

[2] To Mt 8:23–27, the essay by G. Bornkamm remains important, "The Stilling of the Storm in Matthew" in G. Bornkamm, G. Barth and H. J. Held, *Tradition and Interpretation in Matthew*, ET London: SCM, 1983², 52–57.

ness of governmental forces who combined to destroy him. The memory stored the deadly contact with the long and strong arm of Roman imperial administration in the figure of the governor Pontius Pilate and his soldiers, it had engraved on it the image of the Sanhedrin in Jerusalem, the high court which combined the highest legislative and administrative authority for Jews in cases civil and religious, and it contained the figures of some Jewish kings whose life story shrank in Christian memory to the one point of their hatred unto death of the Messiah and his predecessor.

But there was also the community's present, or very recent, experience with confrontations with local, and largely independent, governmental agencies. The hellenistic *polis* could govern its own affairs to a large extent by its own rules; and in its festivals, schools, and even in its numerous clubs civil and religious matters were so intertwined that their separation was virtually impossible. Within the *polis* there existed in many cases a strong Jewish community whose synagogues were permitted to take care of Jewish concerns, including legal proceedings, to such an extent that the synagogue produced a *polis* within the *polis*. Although the statements in Matthew's Gospel alluding to this experience are general, and indeed formulaic, owing to their dependency on long preformed Old Testament language about the persecution of the prophets and the righteous,[3] they enforce the conclusion that the Matthean community encountered significant harassment, and occasionally death, at the hands of both pagan and Jewish civil authorities.[4] Only here and there can the community find relief from the hostile alliance of governments around it, in the person of some representatives from the ranks of military and civil personnel, Jewish and Roman alike, who act as harbingers of possibilities for better relationships. But nowhere is there any evidence in the Gospel that the Christian community could rely for its safety and peace on any of the multiple governmental authorities around it, let alone offer its cooperation for fruitful partnership. The offer of its teaching and healing mission, from now on at least mostly to the non-Jewish world, is its only task and its only security. From here we can turn to some details.

## I. Governmental Powers as Enemies

In the genealogy at the beginning of the Gospel of Matthew (1:1–17), Jesus is introduced as the Messiah (1:16) from the royal line of David. From the beginning, Matthew wants his readers to understand that the story he is about to tell deals with the true king of Israel. The Evangelist favors the title "Christ" which occurs 16 times in the Gospel, notwithstanding the radical modifications which the messianic concept is to undergo in being determined by Jesus of Nazareth.

It is, therefore, clear from the start that the Gospel deals with the exercise of royal power and, hence, with the most concentrated manifestation of governmental authority. Together with his messenger, John the Baptist, and in words identical with his, Jesus begins his work with the announcement, "the kingdom of heaven is at hand" (3:2; 4:17), and at the Gospel's climax the risen Christ commissions his disciples for further work because "all authority in heaven and on earth has been given to me" (28:18). Whatever transformations of traditional concepts of power will be required, it is clear already through the composition that Matthew's Gospel is concerned with power, with the right and the ability to govern, and with the source of this authority.

[3] O. H. Steck, *Israel und das gewaltsame Geschick der Propheten,* WMANT 23, Neukirchen: Neukirchener Verlag, 1967.

[4] D. R. A. Hare, *The Theme of Jewish Persecution of Christians in the Gospel according to St. Matthew,* Cambridge: University Press, 1967.

However, there is immediate, constant, and—at least on the surface—effective resistance against the power which releases God's rule in the world. It is a resistance most determined on the part of those who occupy already positions of governmental authority. Matthew provides room in his narrative for two Jewish kings, Herod the "Great" (2:1–19) and his son the tetrarch by the same name (14:1–12). (The reference to Archelaus in 2:22 is without weight). Herod the "Great" has his place in Matthew's prologue (1:1–4:17, or 4:22) in which the nature of the Gospel's central person is presented, the inclusion of the pagan world into the people of God is anticipated, and the ensuing conflict between the royal power of God on earth and those who hold the actual powers of government is introduced. Along with a broad tradition in antiquity, the birth of a future ruler of great importance is met instantly with violent opposition by the present rulers, which places the newborn into mortal danger from which he can be delivered only be divine help.[5] The Herod of Mt 2:1–19 is painted entirely with the colors appropriate for the archetypical enemy of the newborn hero: he schemes destruction with cunning deceptiveness (2:8), and sets in motion a massacre of children (2:16) thereby manifesting what he truly is—the executioner of his own people whose deed is interpreted by the lament of Rachel, the mother of Israel, who mourns her dead offspring (2:18). In the body of the Gospel, the tetrarch Herod only follows the pattern, on the plain of observable history, which his archetypical father had set in the medium of evaluative saga. The tetrarch murders the Baptist (14:1–12) and with him the man through whom the impending advent of God's way of governing was first announced.

The episodes of the two Jewish kings selected by the Evangelist provide an insight into Matthew's evaluation of governmental power. The two Herods are seen exclusively as enemies of the coming kingdom of heaven. Their "history" is thematic in the Gospel only in so far as it exhibits their death-dealing opposition to an order of things on earth which is the fruit of God's exercise of power. It is obvious that this picture can only be achieved by a radical concentration on one point, and the elimination of all factors which belong to historical reality but do not serve to sharpen the single vision.

The account of the Baptist's execution at the midpoint of the Gospel is, of course, told as anticipation of Jesus' execution brought about in cooperation between the ultimate governmental authority of Judaism, the Synedrion, and the representative of the power of Rome, Pontius Pilate. The highest Jewish court (26:59), represented in Matthew mostly through the high-priests and the elders (26:3, 14, 47; 27:1, 3, 12), has decided to kill Jesus (25:4), conducts a trial against him in whose course he is convicted of blasphemy and found guilty of a capital offense (26:57–66). Since only the Roman power could carry out the execution, the case was presented to Pilate who, in spite of his better judgment (27:24) and a solemn warning from his wife (27:19), ordered the crucifixion on grounds of rebellion against Rome as a messianic revolutionary (27:37). The subtleties and nuances of Matthew's passion story cannot here be discussed. Suffice it to say that the dark picture of governmental authority, begun in the portrait of the two Herods, is in the passion story confirmed. No doubt can linger any longer in the mind of the Christian reader of Matthew: governments which are confronted with the claim of God's rule on earth manifest themselves as bastions of opposition, no matter what ethnic or religious claim to power they possess.

In Mt 20:25–27 we find a saying of Jesus in which the disciples' obligation to be servants is contrasted to the habit of pagan rulers to exercise ruthless authority over their subjects. The teaching states in its first part: "you know that the rulers of the Gentiles lord it over them, and their great men exercise authority over them" (20:25). The way of contrasting pagan ways of living as a foil over against which the attitude and action expected of disci-

[5]Cf. the useful table of parallels in U. Luz, *Das Evangelium nach Matthäus,* 84.

ples stands out more clearly, is similar to sentences in the Sermon on the Mount: "If you salute only your brethren, what more are you doing than others? Do not even the Gentiles do the same?" (5:47), and "in praying do not heap up empty phrases as the Gentiles do . . . do not be like them" (6:7f.). In the saying on the Gentile rulers it is taken for granted that pagan government construes the power placed in its hands as licence to oppress those who have no power. The cool rationalism of this sentence is remarkable. There is no hint at an idea of the divine right of kings, or at the exercise of governmental power in the service of God. It is simply assumed that outside the knowledge of the God of Israel power is understood to be the means by which the will of the ruler is enforced without regard to the needs and aspirations of the subjects. The saying assumes also that in Israel, specifically now when Israel's law is newly interpreted by Jesus with unparalleled authority, power must be understood very differently. But while the consequences are drawn with regard to the disciples' servanthood, no conclusions are offered what this might mean for Jewish kings and for Jewish forms of government.

In 20:25 the power-brokerage of Gentile governments is alone in view. The picture is enlarged, and the verdict on the nature of human dominion in the world is radicalized, in the third temptation of Jesus (following Matthew's order of the temptations, 4:1–11).

> The devil took him to a very high mountain, and showed him all the kingdoms of the world and the glory of them. And he said to him, "All these I will give to you, if you will fall to your knees and worship me." Then Jesus said to him, "Begone, Satan! for it is written, 'you shall worship the Lord your God and him only shall you serve.'" (4:8–10)

The temptation stories are difficult to interpret, primarily because their vocabulary draws from important stock-words of Old Testament and early Jewish tradition in which tradition these words received extremely rich connotations defying uniform meanings. It seems clear, however, that in Matthew's third scene of the temptation the devil acts as the owner of the world. He is able to present the panorama of all the kingdoms in the world and their glory, and it is within his power to endow dominion over them if his claim is recognized to be the source of world-supremacy.[6] The notion of Satan as the Lord of the world appears to have developed on the basis of Old Testament reinterpretations of foreign gods as angels of nations. Apocalyptic thought made the angels of the nations an army of demons and put at its head a satanic commander of the entire demonic force. The third temptation adopts this apocalyptic picture. No longer is pagan government contrasted to authority in Israel, as in 20:25, but the rule over the world as such is now enveloped in the shadow of satanic power. The insinuation of the devil to Jesus is a temptation precisely because he is the one who is designated to rule heaven and earth (28:18). Satan understands correctly that the one he faces is sent to inaugurate God's way of ruling ("kingdom of heaven"), and he understands that this form of power is diametrically opposed to his own. Jesus' command "begone, Satan!" is the affirmation of the decision to be the true king of Israel exclusively in the power of God who alone is to be worshipped and whose way of having power demands total allegiance. It is to be shown in the narrative of the gospel through the account of Jesus' words and deeds, which begins after the temptation, what power of God it is which conquers heaven and earth (28:18) in whose anticipation the present rule over the world, as far as the eye can see, is branded as a rule of the devil.

[6]The Lukan version of the temptation story explicitly states Satan's ownership of the kingdoms of the world by adding the sentence, "it has been delivered to me, and I give it to whom I will" (4:6), but there is hardly any question that Matthew's scene presupposes the same apocalyptic idea.

## II. The No to Revolution

The gospel of Matthew was written in the aftermath of the great Jewish-Roman war of 66–74 AD. The tremors of this earthquake which shook Jewish life down to its foundation are still felt in Matthew's pages.

The war of liberation against Rome was fomented and led by a variety of Jewish groups who together advocated military force in the effort to break the yoke of Rome. Josephus lumps them all together in the term "robbers," and no attempt is made here to differentiate between them. These groups of revolutionary activists were united in some presuppositions. Their revolt against Rome was to them a supremely religious task. It was undertaken not only as a holy war but in the conviction that the end-time had arrived, and that God's promises of old about Israel's eventual triumph over all world powers were to be actively pursued. If anywhere in Judaism, eschatology was to be realized there and then, and the sole worship of Israel's God was to be concretely established in the actual organization of the state. The first and inevitable step in pursuit of this aim had to be the total elimination of every form of domination by a pagan power, and hence the war against Rome became an article of faith.

Matthew 24, Jesus' speech about the end of the present evil world, is based on Mark 13, although Matthew has made far-reaching editorial changes. In this speech, already in its form in Mark and even more so in Matthew's stress on the ethical consequences, the Christian community is warned against becoming victimized by eschatological intoxication. War and its accompanying sufferings are not to be seen as means to force into being the kingdom of God, but as the disasters brought about by messianic and prophetic pretenders.

The warnings against eschatological pretenders in Mt 24 are dominated by some leading ideas which show a remarkable similarity to the description of the Jewish war parties in Josephus (see the list below). The greatest danger in Mt 24 is the arising of pseudo-messiases and pseudo-prophets, mentioned repeatedly with heavy emphasis either separately or linked together (24:5, 11, 24). These pretenders must on no account be followed: four times the solemn warning not to be deceived is issued against them (24:4, 5, 11, 24). The pseudo-christs and pseudo-prophets will perform "great signs and wonders" (24:24) as in the time of Israel's first liberation from Egypt, and the warning against them includes the prohibition against following a summons to the wilderness (24:25) because it is in the wilderness that the new liberation will begin in analogy to the wilderness beginnings under Moses.

The same pattern of association is observable in Josephus' description of the Jewish revolutionaries during the war with Rome. A whole sequence of messianic pretenders incites the people to war: Simon in Peraea who with his troops burns the royal palace in Jericho (Bell 2, 57), the shepherd Athrongaeus who charges his followers to kill Romans, royalists, and disloyal Jews alike (Bell 2, 60–62), the zealot leader Menahem who, after capturing Masada returns to Jerusalem "as a king" (Bell 2, 434), Simon bar Giora who demands recognition as a king (Bell 4, 510). At the same time, self-styled prophets also lead in the cause of war: there is an unnamed pseudo-prophet the obedience to whom costs a great number of Jewish civilians their lives (Bell 6, 286), there is Theudas, mentioned also in Acts 5:36, who calls himself a prophet (Ant 20 97), and there is an Egyptian Jew claiming the same distinction (Ant 20, 169; in Bell 2, 261 called a pseudo-prophet). The accusation is frequent in Josephus that all these claimants to messianic and/or prophetic office were deceivers (Ant 20, 98; Bell 6, 287 and 2, 259). These imposters mislead the people by promising to re-enact the liberation of Israel by performing new miracles in the wilderness. The clearest analogies to Mt 24:24f. are Josephus' reports of false prophets who lead people into the wilderness to demonstrate these "signs of liberation" (Bell 2, 259) and the account of deceivers who allured the masses to move into the desert where they would be shown "signs and wonders in accordance with God's providence" (Ant 20, 167f.).

Other details in Mt 24 show the same pattern reflecting the still vivid memory of the tumults of the great war. The connection between the warning about heeding the claim of pseudo-messiases and the immediately following statement "you will hear of wars and rumors of war" (24:4f) is, on this background, self-explanatory: it is precisely the message of those false Christs to take up arms to establish now the kingdom of God. The betrayal and hatred of one another, in 24:10, reflects an inner-Christian danger, but it echoes also a general situation of Jewish society immediately before and during the war in which constant infighting among rival groups belonged almost to the order of the day; an example among many may be found in Simon bar Giora's battle against the zealots (Bell 4, 514). The same Simon seems to have been proverbial for the hatred of his own kin (Bell 7, 266). Matthew states that in this chaos lawlessness will be multiplied (24:12), Josephus chooses the same word (otherwise very rare in his writings) to characterize the revolutionary actions of a group of Idumeans and zealots (Bell 7, 268).[7]

If these observations lead into the right direction, it must be said that the Matthean community saw the messiahship of Jesus in complete antithesis to those Jewish groups which encouraged the war of liberation for the establishment of a Jewish government meant to bring about conformity to the sole rule of God over his people. Definite similarities between the Christian and revolutionary groups notwithstanding (expectation of the immediate coming of God's kingdom, messianic and prophetic convictions, the zeal for the primacy of the first commandment), the Matthean congregations are warned against that kind of revolutionary activism which exterminates its perceived enemies by military and political force.

The Gospel of Matthew contains a whole series of references to oppression, and even persecution, of Christians. In the last of the beatitudes, those who are reviled and persecuted are called blessed (5:10–12), in their mission the disciples will be brought up before local courts to stand before Roman and Jewish authorities of government (10:17–18), and parables speak of the arrest, ill-treatment, and even killing of the servants of God (22:6; 23:29–29). These passages must refer to experiences of harassment and punishment by organs of government, both Jewish and pagan, in the vicinity of the Syrian home of Matthew. Since it has been demonstrated that up to the years immediately preceding the outbreak of the Jewish war we have no evidence of any organized persecution of Christians in Palestine or Syria,[8] it becomes a natural assumption to connect the experience of oppression on the part of the Christian communities with the chaotic disorder brought about by the eschatological fever which whipped Judaism into war. It is certain that groups of Jews, Jewish Christians included, who resisted the war propaganda were liable to be met with intense hatred that did not hesitate to use local courts to discipline, and bring to death, all who dared to disagree with what was fancied to be a divine call to arms. We propose, therefore, to understand the persecution passages in Matthew as having been shaped, in part, by the influence of Christian resistance to the revolutionary movement which sought to defeat Rome on the field of battle.

[7]Martin Hengel has collected an impressive list of parallels between the situation described in Mark 13 and the tumultuous condition of both Judaism and the Roman Empire in the years immediately before the outbreak of the Jewish-Roman war, see his book *Studies in the Gospel of Mark,* ET Philadelphia: Fortress, 1985, 14–28. For Matthew, the chaos of the years preceding and during the war is still vivid memory.

[8]D. R. A. Hare, *Persecution,* 19–79.

## III. The Right of Government

One asks oneself, after all that has passed before us, what is left of governmental order and justice in Matthew's Gospel? Is the Evangelist advocating a total withdrawal of the Christian community from any existing form of government, be it in the form of a totally nonpolitical individualism, or in the form of a retreat to a small sect which lives in isolation from the doomed world around it obedient only to its own ideals?

One thing is quite certain. An interpretation of Matthew in a strictly individualistic sense is impossible. The Sermon on the Mount is addressed to a community with the intention to declare this explication of Israel's law binding and fulfillable for its members in their conduct to one another, and indeed to those outside the community's bounds: it is communal law. Matthew's congregations are subject to an authority to bind and to loose, i.e. the authority to declare what is legal and to impose sanctions attaching to this declaration, which derives from a special mandate to Peter (16:19) and which is incorporated in the community's power to bind or to loose (18:18). Chapter 18 contains rudimentary rules for the order of the community including provisions for disciplinary action; they are a far-cry from a "Book of Order" but they nevertheless rule out the possibility of a consistently individualistic interpretation of the Gospel.

It belongs to this aspect of the matter to observe that Matthew's reinterpretation of Israel's law, not only in the Sermon on the Mount, retains elements of Jewish legislation in spite of the concentration of all law in the love commandment. The Sabbath is observed in Matthew's community (24:20), and even the most critical indictment of the behavior of Jewish law experts does not cancel out the obligation to listen to them (23:3). The pericope 17:24–27, on the question of the Jewish temple tax, appears symptomatic for the attitude in Matthew's congregation to Jewish law. On the one hand, Peter states in this passage without any hesitation that Jesus himself pays the temple tax. On the other hand, Jesus' dialogue with Peter maintains that there is essentially freedom from this obligation, only in order not to offend is the payment of the tax continued. Jesus' words to Peter employ the nucleus of a parable: the sons of a king do not pay tax but the servants of the king do. The point is very radical: Jesus and his disciples are free sons of god, while the Jewish community outside this new "society" remains in bondage to the law. But the freedom of the sons is not exercised in the refusal to pay the tax, rather it is used to conform to a piece of Jewish legislation that does not cancel out the dedication to the kingdom of heaven.

Even with regard to the power of Rome, the Gospel leads into the same direction. Matthew retains the story of the healing by Jesus of a centurion's servant (8:5–13). Not only is this narrative retained in spite of Matthew's insistence that Jesus' and his disciples' mission was to be conducted among Jews alone (10:5) to manifest God's steadfastness in his call of Israel until the final refusal of this fidelity not only by Jewish leadership but by the population at large (27:25). Beyond that, the story presents the officer of a pagan military force as a model of faith whose response to Jesus puts to shame those who as members of Israel ought to live in this type of trust (8:10). All dogmatism of election is broken in this narrative; the representative of a pagan authority over Jews is declared righteous, and the fact of his being an officer of a foreign government cannot invalidate this judgment. The same is true to an even higher degree of the centurion under the cross together with his soldiers (27:54). Regardless of the exact meaning of the centurion's words, the very detachment of troops charged with the execution of real or suspected revolutionaries is conducted into the light of the Christian confession.

Interestingly, it is another passage in Matthew on taxes which, similarly to 17:24–27 regarding Jewish tax legislation, provides a paradigm for the relation to the Roman administration. In 22:15–22 Jesus is confronted with controversy concerning payment or nonpayment of tax to Rome. The question is political dynamite because the refusal to pay Roman taxes was one of the cardinal tenets of the Jewish eschatological revolutionaries. Jesus' answer, "render to Caesar the things that are Caesar's and to God the things that are God's" (22:21) does not invite the casuistic attempt to define neatly what might rightfully be God's and what might rightfully belong to Caesar. The spirit of the whole Gospel forbids this question because it is axiomatic in it that the supremacy of God's rule on earth suffers no infringement. However, the story seems to be entirely clear in saying what is Caesar's: it is the money which bears his image, was produced in his mints, and supports the commerce in his realm. The one who has come to restore the world to the sole supremacy of its one true God does so as one who is so poor that he has less sheltering property in the world than its foxes and birds (8:20), and who has warned against putting any trust in possessions (6:19–21, 24). He and those who follow him can, for that reason, give back to a government what this government has produced to begin with; their mission does not depend on it, nor is it denied by it.

### Leading Ideas in Matthew 24 and in Josephus' Description of the Jewish Revolutionaries

| *Matthew* | | *Josephus* | |
|---|---|---|---|
| *I. Pseudochrists* | | | |
| v.5 | Many will come and say I am the Christ | Bell.2, 57 | Simon makes himself king and consorts with robbers (Ant.17, 273f) |
| | | Bell.2, 60ff. | Athrongaeus assumes kingship and assembles a band to kill Romans, Royalists, and Jewish sympathizers |
| v.24 | There will arise false Christs together with false prophets | Bell.2, 434 | Menahem captures Masada and returns to Jerusalem as revolutionary leader like a king |
| | | Bell.4, 510 | Simon bar Giora commands allegiance as to a king |
| *II. Pseudoprophets* | | | |
| v.11 | Many false prophets | Bell.6, 286 | Jewish refugees in Jerusalem killed because a false prophet deceived them |
| v.24 | False Christs and false prophets | Ant.20, 97 | Theudas called himself prophet |
| | | Ant20, 169 | An Egyptian calls himself prophet (in Bell.2, 261, false prophet) |
| *III. The deceivers* | | | |
| v.4 | Warning against some who will deceive | Ant.20, 98 | Theudas deceived many |
| | | Bell.6, 287 | A certain false prophet is called the deceiver |
| v.5 | False Christs decieve | Bell.2, 259 | Deceivers and imposters pretend inspiration to incite revolution |
| v.11 | Pseudoprophets deceive | | |
| v.24 | Pseudochrists and pseudo-prophets will arise . . . to deceive | | |

*IV. The new exodus*

| | | | |
|---|---|---|---|
| v.24 | Pseudochrists and pseudo-prophets will perform great signs and wonders | Bell.2, 259 | Deceivers lead into desert expecting God's signs of freedom |
| v.26 | the cry is heard, "he is in the wilderness" | Ant.20, 167 | Imposters lead into the wilderness to show wonders and signs |

# Romans 13.1–7—A Charter for Political Quietism?

James D. G. Dunn

Rom 13.1–7 is a classic test case for any Christian hermeneutic which wants to root discipleship firmly in scripture. For it is one of very few NT passages which give any guidance on a Christian attitude towards the state or secular authorities.[1] Moreover, it appears to provide a clear statement of principle, which is not tied to any particular situation or hedged around with qualifications.[2] 'Let every person be subject to the governing authorities. For there is no authority except from God . . . He who resists the authorities resists what God has appointed . . . For rulers are not a terror to good conduct, but to bad . . . He is God's servant . . .' and so on. As a statement of general principle it has for centuries provided biblical validation for a theology of the state—as the secular arm of the one divinely ordered commonwealth (Corpus Christianum), or as an essential expression of the order of creation or of natural law in the overall scheme of things.[3] At the same time, modern interpreters cannot forget that the same passage provided justification for use of state power to suppress Baptists and other radical groups at the time of the Reformation,[4] or that German Christians could appeal to it as the ground for their support of the Third Reich. And in our own time the substantial movement of Liberation Theology in its challenge against state oppression of the poor and the politically weak poses equally uncomfortable questions to our passage with regard to its hermeneutical relevance and import. So in any consideration of Rom 13.1–7 the issue cannot be avoided: whether such a passage can still function as a guideline for Christian social ethics, and if so how? Or are attempts to abstract a universally valid theology from such a passage doomed to failure because they have demanded too much of the hermeneutical task or have failed to make sufficient allowance for the particularity and context specificity of a passage like Rom 13.1–7?

An important aspect of such a debate is the question of the degree to which historical exegesis can contribute to the debate. Can we determine the historical reference of the text?—and if so, so what? Does a limited historical reference impose a similar limitation on all subsequent interpretations? If the exhortation of Rom 13.1–7 was written with a view to particular historical circumstances of the time, which soon changed anyway, can it be given a different or wider reference, and if so, on what grounds and by what criteria? Is there an assumed framework of thought, some christological or eschatological reservation, and if so, should that continue to condition the significance of the text, or should we simply read the text in the light of our own theological framework and presuppositions? In short,

[1]The most obvious others are Mark 12.13–17; 1 Pet 2.13–17; 1 Tim 2.2 and Tit 3.1 (cf also Rev. 13).

[2]The passage appears to be so unrooted within the context of the letter that some have argued that it is a later insertion. So most recently, J. C. O'Neill, *Paul's Letter to the Romans* (Harmonfsworth: Penguin, 1975) 207–9; W. Schmithals, *Der Römerbrief als historisches Problem* (Gütersloh: Gütersloher, 1975) 191–7. E. Käsemann, *Romans* (London: SCM, 1980) calls it 'an independent block' and allows the phrase 'an alien body' (352). See also n. 24 below. But see n. 28 below.

[3]For the history of the understanding and use of Rom 13.1–7 in the history of Christianity see U. Wilckens, *Römer* (EKK VI/3; Zürich: Benziger/Neukirchen: Neukirchener, 1982) 43–66.

[4]There is something of an echo of this in Käsemann's repeated thesis that Paul writes here as elsewhere to combat 'enthusiasm'—'Principles of the Interpretation of Romans 13', *New Testament Questions of Today* (London: SCM, 1969) e.g. 206; also *Romans* 351, 359. Cf. P. Althaus, *Römer* (NTD 6; Göttingen: Vandenhoeck, 1932/1966) 130; Wilckens, 'Römer 13:1–7', *Rechtfertigung als Freiheit* (Neukirchen: Neukirchener, 1974) 229–30.

how does such a biblical text continue to function as scripture for Christians in the late 20th century? How should it be heard today?

To help set up the discussion with reference to Rom 13.1–7 my task, as a NT specialist, is clearly to offer such a historical exegesis of the text—to set it in context and to see how specific or general it was in its original reference. If the original reference has *any* relevance in determining subsequent significance we need to inquire carefully into that original reference. I will attempt therefore, first, to set Rom 13.1–7 as firmly as possible into the historical context of the time and situation to which it was written, and second, into the context of the argument of Romans. Only then will we be able to turn to the passage itself to see what further light we can gain from an examination of its principal themes.[5] I am well aware that this is only one part of the hermeneutical task, but I am quite sure it is an essential part, to be neglected at our peril.

## I The Historical Context

Since Paul's letter to the Romans was written to the capital city of the Empire it would be surprising if this did not influence the letter writer. And on this topic in particular (the only time Paul addresses the issue of his readers' relation to the secular authorities) we can hardly avoid the assumption that Paul had in mind at least to some extent the political realities within which the Christian congregations in Rome had to operate. If we are to understand Rom 13.1–7 therefore we must certainly inquire into the political circumstances of the first Christian groups in Rome. Fortunately we have more literary data for conditions in Rome than for any other large city of this time, and a good deal of epigraphical material besides. So, despite the silence of the Christian tradition about the initial appearance of Christianity in Rome,[6] we can glean a surprisingly full picture of its historical circumstances.

Crucial in the whole discussion is the relation of the first Christians to the Jewish community in Rome. Here we must start from the probability that Christianity first emerged *within* the Jewish synagogues. This is what we might have expected in the case of a movement which began as a sect of Judaism and whose first missionaries were all Jews. And this *a priori* plausibility is confirmed by such evidence as we have. In particular we may note the following:

(1) The earliest reported link between Christianity and Rome is the presence of Jews from Rome among the Jerusalem crowd who witnessed the effect of the Pentecost outpouring of the Spirit (Acts 2.5,10). No matter how accurate or otherwise that report may be, it is wholly plausible that the first Christians to appear in Rome were Jewish merchants and other travellers taking their faith to Rome directly or indirectly from Palestine. We know that the Jewish community in Rome in the first century may well have been as large as 40,000 or 50,000.[7] We know that there were frequent contacts between Rome and Palestine: for example, the warm relationship between Herod Agrippa and the imperial family, particularly Caligula and Claudius; the movement of business people like Priscilla and Aquila; the implication of Acts 28.21 that the Roman Jews looked to maintain a correspondence link with the mother country; the movement of temple tax and pilgrim traffic (implied in the Pentecost narrative); and the later testimony of regular visits of leading rabbis.[8] We

[5]I follow here the same structure as V. P. Furnish employs in his *The Moral Teaching of Paul* (Nashville: Abingdon, 1979) 117–39.

[6]For Christian beginnings at Rome a recent summary treatment is provided by R. E. Brown & J. P. Meier, *Antioch and Rome* (London: Chapman, 1983) 97–103.

[7]Brown, *Rome* 94.

[8]Brown, *Rome* 96.

know also that, particularly since Pompey's conquest of the East, the movement of oriental religions to Rome the capital city was a feature quite often remarked upon by Roman writers. As Juvenal was to note: 'the Syrian Orontes has long since poured into the Tiber, bringing with it its language and customs . . .' (3.62–3).[9] Paul, who as a Jewish Christian missionary first appears in Acts as emissary of Antioch on Orontes, was not the only one who saw it as his goal to preach his message in Rome (Rom 1.15; 15.23–4).[10]

(2) The pattern of early Christian evangelism was very probably rooted in the synagogue. This is how Christianity began in the third largest city of the Empire (Antioch) and, according to Acts, it was also Paul's strategy to begin his preaching in the synagogue where possible. We have no good reason to doubt this portrayal, despite the misgivings of some.[11] So long as the new movement saw itself as a form of Judaism, and that is a fair generalisation for the period up to AD 70, the synagogue was the natural community centre and forum for intra-Jewish preaching and discussion.

(3) The famous report of Suetonius, that Claudius 'expelled Jews from Rome because of their constant disturbances at the instigation of Chrestus' (*Claudius* 25.4), also provides important confirmation. It is generally agreed that 'Chrestus' means Christ, and that the reference is to disturbances between Jews regarding Jesus, that is, to disagreements between Jews who had accepted the Christian claims.[12] This almost certainly indicates a significant presence of Christian beliefs within the Jewish synagogues already within about ten years of the first proclamation of Jesus' resurrection.

(4) Priscilla and Aquila are first introduced to us as Jews who had to leave Rome because of Claudius' expulsion order (Acts 18.2). Since their conversion is not reported in Acts 18, as it surely would have been if Paul had converted them, we must assume they were already Christians before they left Rome—that is, Jewish Christians in Rome, believers in Jesus Christ but functioning within the Jewish community.

(5) We might simply add the evidence of Paul's letter to Rome itself. For though it is clearly writen with Gentiles particularly in view (1.6,13–15; 11.13,17–21), it also presupposes a thorough knowledge of the OT and a considerable concern with Jewish self-identity. This could conceivably be a matter of Paul's self-indulgence, writing to satisfy his own concerns, regardless of whether his readership was able to make much sense of what he said.[13] But this is very unlikely: the situation of the Roman Christians already outlined above would almost certainly mean that questions of Jewish self-identity were questions for many Jewish Christians in Rome as well as for Paul; and the preservation of the letter by Roman Christianity implies that it was valued for its relevance in Rome.[14] It should also be noted that knowledge of the OT within the ancient world was confined almost wholly to Jewish and Jewish-derived communities: the LXX is not known in Greco-Roman literary cir-

[5]I follow here the same structure as V. P. Furnish employs in his *The Moral Teaching of Paul* (Nashville: Abingdon, 1979) 117–39.

[6]For Christian beginnings at Rome a recent summary treatment is provided by R. E. Brown & J. P. Meier, *Antioch and Rome* (London: Chapman, 1983) 97–103.

[7]Brown, *Rome* 94.

[8]Brown, *Rome* 96.

[9]See further F. Cumont, *Oriental Religions in Roman Paganism* (New York: Dover, 1956) chap. 2.

[10]'It was a matter of pride and, indeed, of missionary strategy for every religious movement to establish a foothold in Rome'—E. Bammel, 'Romans 13', *Jesus and the Politics of his Day*, ed. E. Bammel & C. F. D. Moule (Cambridge University, 1984) 368.

[11]E.g. G. Luedemann, *Paul, Apostle to the Gentiles: Studies in Chronology* (Philadelphia: Fortress, 1984) 159–61.

[12]See e.g. *GLAJJ* 2.116–7.

[13]So E. P. Sanders, *Paul, the Law and the Jewish People* (Philadelphia: Fortress, 1983) might argue.

[14]Who truly belongs to Israel was a real issue for more than one stream of thought within Judaism (e.g. 1 Enoch 1; PsSol 3, 13; 1QH 2.6–37).

cles. Consequently to be able to assume such a knowledge of the scriptures as Paul does in Romans he would have to assume that his readership by and large had enjoyed a substantial link with the synagogues in Rome.

(6) A final point to note is that only with Tacitus, writing of the period after Romans was written, can we detect an awareness that Christians had become a distinct entity (*Ann* 15.44.2–5). The implication is that prior to that time the movement had been neither strong enough nor distinct enough to be marked out from a larger group of which they had previously been counted part. That larger group would, of course, have been the Jews.

In short, it must be judged highly probable that the synagogues of Rome were the natural matrix for emerging Christianity in Rome, and that Paul either knew for a fact or could take it for granted that most of his Gentile listeners in Rome had been either proselytes or God-fearers.[15]

This being the case, we can proceed on the assumption that Roman attitudes to Jews at this period may well give us some indication of the sort of pressures the new Christian congregations were experiencing. The character of Judaism within Rome and Roman treatment of the Jewish synagogues can be expected to shed light on the context to which Paul wrote and on the emphases he makes. Here the central factor is *the ambiguous and vulnerable status of the Jews.*

(a) We know that many Romans, the intelligentsia in particular, were very suspicious of foreign cults, and Jews were no exception. For example, Cicero in 59 BCE, in his defence of Flaccus accused of stealing Jewish gold, speaks of the 'odium' of Jewish gold, of Judaism as this 'barbaric superstition,' inimacle to all that is Roman (*Pro Flacco* 28.66–69). Seneca tells how in his youth, in the time of Tiberius, interest in strange cults, as evidenced by abstinence from certain kinds of animal food, brought liability to prosecution. So he desisted from his own practice of abstinence (*Ep.Mor.* 108.22). Pliny the Elder designates the Jews as 'a race remarkable for their contempt for the divine powers' (*Nat.Hist* 13.46). And Tacitus, of course, is well known for the savagery of his anti-Semitism: 'The Jews regard as profane all that we hold sacred . . . (and) permit all that we abhor;' 'the other customs of the Jews are base and abominable, and owe their persistence to their depravity;' and more in the same vein (*Hist* 5.4ff.—here 5.41 and 5.5.1).

At the same time there is clear evidence that the Jewish community in Rome was quite influential. For example, a population of 40,000 to 50,000 made them a substantial minority ethnic group within Rome itself, and because of Jewish support for Julius Ceasar Jews were given special privileges denied to other religious groups 'to assemble and feast in accordance with the native customs and ordinances' (Josephus, *Ant* 14.214–6). Cicero in his speech on behalf of Flaccus says he will speak softly since the attendant crowd were liable to favour the Jews (*Flacc* 28.66–67). Horace speaks of the success of Jewish proselytization—'we, like the Jews, will compel you to make one of our throng' (*Serm* 1.4.142–3).[16] Judaism evidently proved attractive to not a few, including ladies of nobility like Fulvia and Poppaea, the wife of Nero (Josephus, *Ant* 18.82; 20.195). And early in the second century Juvenal complains about the way Judaism spread its influence by gradually winning over whole families—pork abstaining and sabbath-observing fathers who were surpassed by their sons going on

[15] A. T. Kraabel has persistently questioned the existence of 'God-fearers' within or on the fringes of diaspora Judaism—see particularly his 'The Disappearance of the "God-fearers"', *Numen* 28 (1981) 113–26. If his complaint is simply against 'God-fearer' being used as an established technical term in our period, his question has some substance (though even then the soon to be published Aphrodisias inscription undermines his case). But that there were many God-fearing Gentiles associated in some degree with diaspora synagogues is too well attested in Josephus to be dismissed (e.g. *JW* 7.45; *Ap* 2.123,280,282); and see also below.

[16] For comment see *GLAJJ* 1.323.

to embrace circumcision and the whole Jewish law (*Sat* 14.96–106). No doubt it was precisely this attractiveness to some which made the Jews all the more hated and feared by others.[17]

b) Roman hostility to its Jewish minority had in fact boiled over several times. Twice within Paul's own lifetime Jews had been expelled from Rome in large numbers. In AD 19 most of the Jewish population had been expelled by Tiberius, several thousand of them shipped to Sardinia (Tacitus, *Ann* 2.85.4), the reason being, according to Cassius Dio, that their proselytizing was too successful (Dio 57.18.5a; cf. Suetonius, *Tiberius* 36). And in AD 49, as we have already noted, Claudius, despite his long friendship with the Jewish royal family, followed suit. It is a highly plausible suggestion that this latter expulsion helps explain the degree of Gentile/Jewish tension which is evident in Paul's letter to the Romans. For if the Jewish Christians had been expelled along with their fellow Jews (as was the case with Priscilla and Aquila), the Christian congregations in Rome would have become exclusively Gentile. This alone would go some way to explaining why Paul felt it necessary to warn his Gentile readers against any feeling of superiority over their Jewish fellows (Rom 11.17–21). Moreover, Jews must have begun to return to Rome in significant numbers in the 50s (since their influence continued through the second half of the first century). So we may assume that Jewish Christians returned too. Their return after a period when leadership of the Christian congregations had rested solely in Gentile hands must have caused some friction in at least a few cases.[18] Part of the problem and sensitivity on the part of the Gentiles would presumably be the result of the doubtful legal status of their Jewish brethren: by accepting them back into their congregations, were they putting themselves and their congregations at greater risk from the authorities?

c) A third factor we should note is that in terms of organization the Jewish community in Rome appears to have been very weak. We know of many Jewish synagogues in Rome during this period, but each synagogue seems to have been regarded as an independent unit. Unlike the larger Jewish minority in Alexandria there seems to have been no single controlling organization which could act on behalf of the Jewish community as a whole, no ethnarch to represent his people before the authorities.[19] This would naturally leave them in a more exposed position politically, since without the special protection which Julius Caesar had accorded them, they would always be vulnerable to actions against sects and *collegia* even when these were directed against others.[20] It is very likely that the Christian house congregations were in the same plight, for if they had any official status it would be as types of Jewish synagogue or *collegium*. Moreover, the fact that Paul addresses his readers as 'all the beloved of God who are in Rome' (Rom 1.7) and never speaks of 'the church (in Rome),' as is his usual practice elsewhere (1 Cor 1.2; 2 Cor 1.1; Phil 4.15; Col 4.15; 1 Thess 1.1; 2 Thess 1.1; cf. Gal 1.2), strongly suggests that the Christian congregations shared something of the same fragmented existence. The Christians functioned as several 'churches' in Rome (cf. Rom 16.5), but were not seen as a single entity—and if not by Paul, still less by others. Without a strong and unified political status, and less than ten years since the Jews were last expelled from Rome, Paul's readership would certainly be wise to keep in mind the political realities within which they had to live.

[17]Cf. E. M. Smallwood, *The Jews under Roman Rule* (Leiden: Brill, 1981) 139, though she probably exaggerates Jewish exclusiveness on p.123. See also W. Wiefel, 'The Jewish Community in Ancient Rome and the Origins of Roman Christianity', *The Romans Debate*, ed. K. P. Donfried (Minneapolis: Augsburg, 1977) 101–5.

[18]So particularly Wiefel 111–3, who, however, exaggerates the extent to which the house church form exacerbated the tensions between Jewish and Gentile Christians (113).

[19]See Wiefel 105–8 with fuller details; Bammel, 'Romans 13' 368.

[20]On *collegia* see *OCD* 254–6.

d) The final piece of background information which can hardly be ignored is given us by Tacitus. In *Annals* 13 he reports that the year 58 was marked by persistent public complaints regarding indirect taxes. Nero's initial response was to propose the abolition of all indirect taxes. But the senators warned strenuously about the likely consequences—fall in revenue and demands to abolish direct taxes as well. Nero relented, but it was generally agreed that tax-collectors' acquisitiveness must be restrained. This report of Tacitus is sufficient to suggest the strong likelihood that in the years prior to 58 the collection of taxes was a sensitive matter within the public domain. Jews, by virture not least of their special privileges regarding the temple tax, would be all the more open to charges of tax evasion. And Christians, identified with Jews, would be equally vulnerable in situations where tax-collectors were levying additional duties, for example, on shipments and property. Should they refuse or complain and so leave themselves exposed to legal action, even if the tax-collector had demanded more than his right? Or should they pay up and say nothing to avoid drawing hostile attention to themselves?[21] It was, after all, only about seven years since the last banishment of the Jews and only another seven or eight years before Christians were being hounded as scapegoats for the fire of Rome. Christians might well be advised to 'keep a low profile' on such a politically sensitive matter as public taxation. It is not surprising then that Paul's exhortation on Christians' responsibility vis-a-vis the state should end with firm advice about the payment of taxes (Rom 13.6–7).[22]

All in all then, we can be fairly confident that Paul would be aware of the ambiguous and vulnerable status of the Christian congregations in Rome and that he framed his advice to them accordingly. What this might mean for the meaning of Rom 13.1–7 then and for its continuing significance is an issue to which we must return. But first we must attempt to locate 13.1–7 within its literary context, within the movement of thought in Romans itself.

## II The context in Romans

One of the chief difficulties in 'locating' 13.1–7 within Romans is that the logic of the letter has been so frequently misunderstood. The key here is to grasp the proper function of chapters 9–11. If Romans is understood as Paul's exposition of the gospel essentially in *individual* terms, then it is natural to see the climax of the letter in chap. 8, with chapters 9–11 as a kind of appendix. Chapters 12–15 can then be read as a sequence of ethical corollaries which do not follow thematically from what has gone before and which may have been somewhat randomly chosen—perhaps a standard paraenetical pattern which could have been attached to any theological exposition, or a summary of lessons learned by Paul elsewhere—Corinth, the place of writing, being the most obvious candidate.[23] In which case the literary context would provide little help in the exegesis of 13.1–7.[24]

This will not do, however. So to regard Romans is to neglect the fundamentally *corporate* dimension of Paul's argument in Romans. For what Paul was doing in Romans was, in effect, to redefine the people of God. The gospel proclaimed in this letter is not simply about the individual sinner being offered grace and salvation in a direct one-to-one relation with God. It is about the solidarity of sin—'*all* have sinned and fall short of the glory of God' (3.23). It is about membership of the eschatological people of God, embracing Gen-

[21]For the power of taxcollectors and the fear and hostility they inspired see Philo, *SpecLeg* 2.92–5; 3.159–63.

[22]See also J. Friedrich, W. Pöhlmann & P. Stuhlmacher, 'Zur historischen Situation und Intuervention von Röm 13.1–7', *ZTK* 73 (1976) 156–9; Furnish, *Moral Teaching* 133–5; Bammel, 'Romans 13' 369–75.

[23]Cf. Rom 12.3-8 with 1 Cor 12 and Rom 14 with 1 Cor 8,10.

[24]Bammel, for example, while in full agreement with the first section (see n.21 above), regards the passage as 'a foreign body when seen from the general viewpoint of Pauline theology' ('Romans 13' 381).

tiles as well as Jews—'Is he not the God of Gentiles also? Yes, of Gentiles also, since God is one' (3.29–30). It is about being the seed of Abraham, 'the father of many nations' (4.17). It is about incorporation into the new humanity of Christ over against the old humanity of Adam (5.15–6.11). As K. Stendahl argued persuasively 25 years ago, Paul's message of justification was not addressed to the conscience smitten sinner seeking peace with God but aimed to break down the barrier between Jew and Gentile, assuring both that God's acceptance is open to all, Gentile as well as Jew.[25]

In other words, one of Paul's chief purposes in Romans was to redraw the boundaries which marked out the people of God. For the great mass of his Jewish contemporaries the boundaries were clear: the people of God was defined ethnically as the descendants of Abraham, marked out by circumcision in particular; the people of God were those who lived within the law, under the law, performing works of the law as maintaining their membership of the covenant.[26] In his argument in Romans 2–4 and 9–11 in particular Paul sought to undermine that attitude, to break down the old boundaries and to draw ones that were more appropriate to Israel's monotheism and to the original convenant purpose and promise of Israel's God. So the argument of Rom 2.17–29 is precisely that being a Jew, having the law, bearing the mark of circumcision, makes no difference. There is no ground for boasting in the law, for relying on the works of the law as proof of belonging to the people of God's favour (2.23; 3.20,27–30). Faith in Christ is the new boundary, circumcision of the heart by the Spirit is the real mark of the true Jew, of eschatological membership of God's people (2.28–9; 3.21–6;4). The line of the covenant is by election, not by flesh, through God's call, not through works of the law (9.6–13). Righteousness is not something exclusive to Israel over against the Gentile, but is *God's*, to all who believe (10.3–13). Membership of God's olive tree is by faith, for Jew as well as Gentile, for Gentile as well as Jew (11.17–24).

This whole argument, of course, would have profound ethical and social consequences for his readers. For under the old definition of the people of God the ethical guidelines were clearly drawn. To be a member of the convenant people was to live within the boundary set by the law: 'the man who does these things shall live his life by them' (10.5). By following these guidelines and living within these boundaries the mutual relationships of the covenant members were also determined, as also their relationship with others outside the boundaries. But once the boudaries had been blurred or changed, the ethical characteristics of the people of God needed to be re-expressed. Where group identity was not longer determined by the law and the works of the law, the question of how the group may define itself in social intercourse was one which could not be ignored.

This was the task which Paul undertook from chapter 12 onwards—to expound the ethical and social expression of the new corporate identity of the eschatological people of God. The immediate resort to sacrificial terms in 12.1–2 ('hand over yourselves as living sacrifices . . .') should therefore occasion no surprise. For ritual is an important part of group identity. And Israel's sacrificial system was one of the main ritual expressions which marked out and maintained Israel's covenant distinctiveness as the people of God. But in Paul's redefinition of the people of God that identity and boundary marker no longer remained: indeed,

[25]K. Stendahl, 'The Apostle Paul and the Introspective Conscience of the West', *HTR* 56 (1963) 199–215; also *Paul Among Jews and Gentiles* (London: SCM, 1977): the 'doctrine of justification by faith was hammered out by Paul for the very specific and limited purpose of defending the rights of Gentile converts to be full and genuine heirs to the promises of God to Israel' (2).

[26]I have developed this observation in a series of essays; see particularly 'Works of the Law and the Curse of the Law (Galatians 3.10–14)', *NTS* 31 (1985) 523–42. As Galatians shows, this was not a new perspective imposed on Paul by the special situation of Roman Christianity (against Wiefel 115).

one of the most remarkable features of the new movement Paul represented was precisely its *lack* of a sacrificial system. In exhorting his readers in sacrificial terms Paul in effect acknowledges this—the boundary of cultic ritual is transposed from the cult to the life of every day and transformed into a nonritual expression. What was to mark out the redefined people of God was not a daily sin-offering or annual passover or anything quite like that, but the daily sensitivity to the will of God which comes from complete commitment.[27]

So too in 12.3–8, the corporate identity of the eschatological people of God is wholly transposed from the category of ethnic Israel to that of the body of Christ, and the mutual relations of this new entity are defined in appropriate terms—no longer in terms of fixed 'offices' (high priest, elder, scribe, etc.) but in terms of the mutual interdependence of charismatic ministry. And in the verses which follow (12.9–21) the range of relationships which Paul holds in view gradually broadens out as he seeks to bring to expression what the new corporate identity of the covenant people means for relationships within its boundaries and across its boundaries—'love one another with brotherly affection . . . bless those who persecute you . . .' (12.10,14).

It is wholly natural that in 13.1–7 therefore Paul should turn his attention to the question of how the redefined people of God relate to the state. For under the old definition there were clearly marked out guidelines. Ideally Judaism was a state religion, with the law allowed to govern the whole range of relationships, political as well as social and religious. But even when that ideal was impossible to realize, it was still possible for the Jewish people to live within the covenant by maintaining their distinctive ethnic identity—with special privileges allowing the continuation of ancestral customs, including the right to send the temple tax each year to Jerusalem, and in cases of large Jewish population, as in Alexandria, able to function for most purposes almost as a state within the state, with their own administrative and judicial powers.[28] One of the principal concerns of diaspora Judaism was to maintain the freedom to live their lives as wholly in terms of the Torah distinctives as possible—to live within their own boundaries as Jews even in an often hostile environment. And much of the political manoeuvering of Jewish communities in the diaspora, as attested by Philo and Josephus, was precisely directed to that end.[29]

But Paul's redefinition of the people of God no longer made that possible. A community which no longer identified itself in ethnic terms could therefore no longer claim the political privileges accorded to ethnic minorities. Paul must have been very conscious that by redrawing the boundaries of the people of God in nonethnic terms he was putting the political status of the new congregations at risk. Whatever he might claim about Gentiles being grafted into the olive tree of Israel, the political reality was that the new congregations were in process of shedding the identity of ethnic Israel, and the sociological reality was that the believers in Jesus as Christ were breaking down or ignoring the very boundaries which had given the Jews their distinctiveness and so also functioned for their protection.

It is no surprise either that in the following paragraphs[30] Paul goes on to remind his readers what the redrawn boundary of the Torah involves—love of one another. Membership of the convenant people is no longer to be understood in terms of 'covenantal nomism'; the law is fulfilled in loving one's neighbor (13.8–10). And after the pointed reminder of the

[27]E. Käsemann, 'Worship in Everyday Life: a note on Romans 12', *New Testament Questions of Today* (London: SCM, 1969) 188–95.

[28]See Smallwood, *Jews* 225–7.

[29]Smallwood, *Jews* 136–143.

[30]I need not go into the structural links between 13.1–7 and the surrounding context since this has already been adequately done by Friedrich *et.al.* 147–55 and Wilckens, 'Römer 13.1–7' 205–216; also *Römer* 30–31,37,38,39.

shortness of the eschatological perspective (13.11–14), it is wholly in character that he devotes the final long section of his paraenesis to one of the most sensitive problems caused by his redefinition of the people of God. For two of the clearest boundary markers of ethnic Israel were sabbath and food laws.[31] No wonder then that it was precisely these two issues which the Christian congregations at Rome, still sheltering under the cloak of Judaism, found most problematic. To name the Jewish Messiah as Lord but to abandon the Jewish characteristics of sabbath and food laws was to enter unknown territory. Those who wished to continue the practice of both would have been motivated, wittingly or unwittingly, by the need to maintain a clear-cut self-identity and one which would be well recognized by the other inhabitants of Rome.

In short, one of Paul's principal concerns in 12–15 was clearly to draw out the ethical and social consequences of his exposition of the gospel in its corporate character. A crucially important dimension of that would be the Christian congregations' political standing within the Roman state. Paul would be conscious that the Jews in Rome had a clearly defined status and privileges to match. He would probably be just as conscious that his redrawing the boundaries of Israel was liable to expose the Christian congregations to greater risk. Some treatment of their relationship with the authorities would be highly appropriate. And this is precisely what we find in 13.1–7.

## III Particular Issues in 13.1–7

We are now in a position to make sense of Rom 13.1–7 in its historical context. Fully to set the passage in its historical context would of course require a breadth of knowledge and depth of sympathetic appreciation for the concerns of Paul and his readers which is hardly possible to us. But at least we now have some awareness of the situation of his readers and some sense of the flow of Paul's thought in the letter, so that we can have some hope of hearing the text with the meaning and force which Paul intended his first readers to hear—so to hear the text, I take it, being the primary task of exegesis. As we proceed it will become increasingly apparent how well these verses fit into the historical context of the Christians in Rome outlined above (I) and provide a nautral and important element of Paul's overall purpose in writing this letter (II).

V.1—'Let every person be subject to the governing authorities. For there is no authority except from God, and the powers that be have been established by God.' In turning abruptly to the relation between the Christian congregations and the authorities in Rome,[32] Paul's first concern is obvious. Within the political structures of the Roman state the responsibilities and powers of government were clear. These responsibilities and powers were exercised by a few by right of birth, or connection, or wealth or ruthless self-advancement. For the rest, the great majority, there was no political power and no realistic hope of wielding it. For modern commentators accustomed to a centuries old tradition of developing democracy, the political realities of ancient society, including not least the Roman Empire, are hard to grasp. It would not even have occurred to Paul and his readers that they could exercise political power in a Roman city, far less that they by their efforts might change its structures.

[31]See n. 26 above.

[32]Against the view that the *exousiai* are the heavenly powers which stand behind this worldly authority—associated particularly with O. Cullmann, *The State in the New Testament* (London: SCM 1957); cf. C. D. Morrison, *The Powers That Be* (London: SCM, 1960) with further literature—see e.g. A. Strobel, 'Zum Verständnis von Röm 13', *ZNW* 47 (1956) 67–93; C. E. B. Cranfield, *Romans* (ICC; Edinburgh: T. & T. Clark, 1979) 656–9; Wilckens, *Römer* 32; W. Carr, *Angels and Principalities* (SNTSMS 42; Cambridge University, 1981) 115–8. It is now generally recognized that Paul would *not* call for subjection to *heavenly* powers.

All they could do was to live *within* the structures which existed, accomodate to them, as everyone had to, and seek to benefit from whatever rules or rights the governing authorities granted.[33] So Paul's opening words ('Let everyone be subject to the governing authorities') were no new or unheard of slogan. They were simply the obvious assumption for the great mass of the powerless in the daily business of living within the corporate state. They did not even constitute what might be called a policy statement. They were simply common sense wisdom, which other Christians were also to advocate (1 Pet 2.13; Tit 3.1). Since politics was the business of so few, the rest who wanted to be about their own business naturally took it for granted that they must operate within the constraints laid down by the ruling authorities. For any exposition of how the eschatological people of God should live within the political realities of the Roman state this was the obvious first thing to be said. The reason why Paul states it as an exhortation was presumably not so much because his readers might think otherwise, but rather because the recent history of Jews in Rome made them that much more vulnerable. Paul's reminder is in effect to say: since you cannot change the terms under which you live, and since your position is already hazardous, remember the political realities of the politically powerless and live accordingly.[34]

The rationale for this basic exhortation is also clear: political authority is from God. Here again Paul enunciates no new principle. On the contrary, it was one which was familiar in Jewish wisdom.[35] As in Prov 8.15–16—'By me kings reign, and rulers decree what is just; by me princes rule, and nobles govern the earth.' Wisd 6.3 likewise reminds those that rule over multitudes and boast of many nations that 'your dominion was given you from the Lord, and your sovereignty from the Most High' (similarly Sir. 10.4; 17.17; Arist 224; Josephus, *JW* 2.140). More to the point here, it was a principle to which other Jews, confronted with the overwhelming might of a conquering state, had quite often clung to in preceding centuries. Thus before Nebuchadnezzar and Cyrus (Jer 27.5–6; Isa 41.2–4); and Daniel repeats it frequently in the face of Syrian oppression—'the Most High rules the kingdom of men and gives it to whom he will' (Dan 2.21, 37–8; 4.17,25,31; 5.21). And 1 Enoch 46.5 echoing the vision of the Danielic Son of Man makes the same point (cf. 2 Bar 82.9). Such assertions must have been particularly meaningful for Jews living in the diaspora, as aliens living under a foreign power, and often as slaves and dispossessed. To be able to affirm that God is one, *their* God is one, and so also God of the Gentiles, meant in the logic of the times that *all* rule and authority must have come from that one God, *their* God. The comfort of such a belief was not that it made them any less vulnerable to the whims of such rulers—the Maccabean crisis had been proof enough of that. The comfort was rather that such rulers were by definition responsible before God, and so were under the constraint of God's final judgment. That particularly Jewish belief would, of course, have little impact on the rulers themselves, but at least it gave their oppressed Jewish subjects the assurance that rulers who flouted their responsibility before God would come under the judgment of God sooner or later—as Nebuchadnezzar had found to his cost in the Daniel story (4.13–17,23–5; 5.20–21). So too the whole point of Wisdom's asserting that kings receive their dominion from the Lord was to warn them that the Most High would inflict severe judgment on those who 'did not rule rightly, nor keep the law, nor walk according to the purpose of God' (6.4). Similarly in fiercer tone, 2 Bar 82.4–9. And in 4 Macc 12.11

[33]Cf. Käsemann, 'Romans 13' 205; also *Romans* 354,356.

[34]Cf. Furnish, *Moral Teaching* 127. Cranfield, *Romans* 660–2, reads too much into the use of the verb *hupotassesthai*, which is a quite natural word to use (see BAGD); the thought that the subjection is limited by the terms of the ruler's God-given authority is correct, but is the point of the clauses which follow.

[35]See particularly W. Schrage, *Die Christen und der Staat nach dem Neuen Testament* (Gütersloh: Gütersloher, 1971) 14–28; Friedrich *et.al.* 145–6. Rabbinic references in SB 3.303–4.

the tyrant is rebuked for abusing his responsibility given to him as king from God.

It is this line which Paul takes up in the second half of v.1. The point had a double importance. For one thing it gave a solid theological undergirding to the practical wisdom restated in the first half of the verse. But just as important in this instance, it constituted a reaffirmation of Jewish wisdom, a taking over of the practical faith by which ethnic Israel had lived under the rule of regional superpowers of the time. That is to say, in redrawing the boundaries of the people of God, Paul nevertheless retains the older boundaries between the people of God and the secular authorities. The perspective from which the people of God were to view the political powers-that-be remained the same even when the definition of the people of God itself was being altered. The continuity of the chosen of God under an authority which determined the structures of political existence, and which might do so in an oppressive way, remained through the discontinuity between ethnic Israel and eschatological Israel.

In the following four verses the logic of this basic restatement of Jewish wisdom is pressed home, in what might be termed a theology of the orderly state, of good government. The principle is simple and would have commanded wide assent: a society needs constraints in order to ensure 'the good'; and it is one of the chief roles of a ruler that he is responsible for administering such constraints, for commending the 'good' and punishing the 'bad' (vv.3–4).[36] In theological terms, the corollary of asserting that God gives dominion to kings and rulers is that he does so for the good of his creatures. In the matter of exercising political authority rulers are 'servants of God' (note again the echo of Wisd 6.4; cf. Jer 25.9). Their power is not their own; it comes from God. To resist them therefore in the exercise of their God-given responsibility is to resist God and so to incur his judgment and wrath (vv.2,5).[37] Hence he can even say that submission to political authority is a matter of 'conscience,' a word which had come into Jewish thought through its overlap with Hellenism (e.g. Wisd 17.11; Philo, *Det* 146; Josephus, *Ant* 16.103). Once again, therefore, Paul undergirds the principle of good citizenship with the firm theological reasoning which he drew from his own (Jewish) tradition.

It should be noted here too that this is not a specifically Christian line of reasoning. There is no implication here that Christ has overcome the 'authorities' or anything like that.[38] The argument does not depend on the assumption that a new state of affairs exists by virtue of Christ's ministry. These are rather the conditions under which the people of God have operated for centuries. Indeed, since the theology of good government applied also to the Jewish state during its years of independence (as, e.g., in 2 Sam 12.8) it can be said that this is the condition under which the people of God always exists. In other words, the argument is theological, not christological; it is expressed in terms of the normal circumstances of social order, not in terms of *Heilsgeschichte.* Nor is it particularly eschatological as indicating a state of affairs which is temporary and from which the people of God will soon be delivered.[39] It is simply a recognition that this is the way society operates, always has and always will, but given a crucially theological and moral dimension by repeating the Jewish affirmation that God has so ordered it for the good of humankind in society and with the corollary that both ruler and ruled are responsible to God in consequence.

[36]For the importance of 'the good' as a desirable moral category see e.g. LSJ *agathos* I.4, II.4; BAGD *agathos* 2. For the thought here cf. Philo, *Leg* 7.

[37]*Orgē* as usual means divine wrath (see e.g. *TDNT* 5.440–1).

[38]This remains true despite Cranfield's justified assumption that Paul would presuppose certain convictions which he shared with his Christian readers (*Romans* 653–5).

[39]Cf. Käsemann, 'Romans 13' 204–5; also *Romans* 352; Wilckens, *Römer* 40. Though note also M. Dibelius, 'Rom und die Christen im ersten Jahrhundert', *Botschaft und Geschichte* II (Tübingen: Mohr, 1956) 184–5; K. Aland, 'Das Verhältnis von Kirche und Staat in der Frühzeit', *ANRW* II.23.1 (1979) 186.

It is a striking fact that the discussion builds up to its climax (vv.6–7) on the subject of paying taxes. This is unlikely to be accidental, and vv.6–7 should not be regarded as an anticlimax or simply another argument.[40] For nowhere else does Paul include such instruction in any of his letters, so there must be some reason for his doing so here. And we have already seen that there was probably considerable unrest in Rome on the matter of paying taxes in the middle 50s, at the time when Paul wrote to Rome. The clear implication therefore is that Paul knew enough of the political circumstances in Rome to know how sensitive was the issue of paying taxes; and also that he framed his counsel at this point because he suspected (or already knew) that the Christian congregations needed to take particular care on this issue.[41] This is borne out by the fact that he seems deliberately to distinguish the two main types of tax—*phoros*, the direct tax, and *telos*, the indirect tax—reminding us that it was precisely because of the abuses of indirect taxation that Nero was soon to propose its abolition. Again the implication is clear: the abuses of the indirect taxation system were such that the Christian merchants and traders in Rome were in a particularly vulnerable situation. Failure of a number of Christians to pay even an inflated tax might draw the authrorities' attention to the little congregations and put them at risk. Paul's advice is not entirely clear as to whether he would have his readers pay excessive taxes without protest; but certainly his intention is clear that what the state could levy as a tax, indirect or direct, ought to be paid faithfully.

Here too Paul does not hesitate to undergird this policy of political prudence with firm theological assertion. The authorities in their function of levying taxes are 'servants (*leitourgoi*) of God' (v.6); taxes are the equivalent of the offerings and sacrifices brought to the altar; within the state as ordered by God tax officials are the equivalent of priests within the cult.[42] As in 12.1–2, the boundary which separated the cult (of Israel) from the daily business of living in a busy city has been broken down. Whether it is a case of sacralizing the state or rather of desacralizing the cult is left open. And here again in his final exhortation Paul echoes the traditional Jewish commendation of reverence for the king (Prov 24.21),[43] drawing on the inherited wisdom of his native faith to give guidance to the newly redefined people of God, but still living under alien and potentially repressive rulers.

## IV Conclusions

1. In response to our opening questions we can now give clear answers. (a) Rom 13.1–7 is *context specific*. Paul is here clearly writing for Christian groups in Rome at a difficult time of political transition: the Jewish community with whom the Christian groups were still largely identified had not long before been expelled; and there was mounting trouble over the taxation system which bore upon Christians as well as the other residents of Rome. Paul writes with these specific circumstances in view. (b) His exhortation is *related to the larger argument of Romans*. Paul is attempting in this letter to spell out the social and political reality of the newly redefined people of God. In taking seriously the corporate reality of the people of God's promise he takes seriously the reality also of their social setting within the political structures of the time.

[40]See particularly Furnish, *Moral Teaching* 126, 131–5.

[41]See n. 22 above. Wilckens, *Römer* 34 is more doubtful.

[42]It is not the use of *leitourgos* alone which is significant, since it can indeed by wholly secular in meaning (LSJ); it is the fuller phrase, 'ministers of God'.

[43]A distinction between 'fear' and 'honour' may be intended, in view of 1 Pet 2.17 (so most), but the suggestion that Paul would use 'fear' only in reference to God (as in 1 Pet 2.17) may take too little account of the stark political realities of the situation in Rome (cf. *m Abot* 3.2); cf. Wilckens, 'Römer 13.1–7' 222–3. And given the theology of good government 'fear' is a proper response to *God*-appointed authority (cf. Arist 194).

2. Within this double context (Rome and Romans) Paul opts for *a counsel of political realism*. What this means can be summed up most straightforwardly in a series of negatives. For one thing Paul does not idealize the situation he is addressing. He does not pretend the authorities of whom he speaks are models of the good ruler. His advice does not particularly arise out of his own experience of Roman protection and the *pax Romana*. He and his Jewish readers in Rome knew well enough the arbitrary power of Rome. The tradition of Jewish wisdom on which he draws had already been well tested by the fires of persecution. Paul would have no illusions that a quiet subservience would be sufficient to guarantee peace. But his advice is not conditional on Roman benevolence. It is simply a restatement of the long established Jewish recognition of the reality and character of political power.

Paul's political realism also meant that he gave no thought to the Zealot option which was currently gaining strength within Palestine itself. Nor is there any indication that his readers were in any danger of being seduced by that option: however realistic it might appear to be in Palestine, it could hardly be entertained, even on theological grounds, within Rome itself. But neither did he advocate a policy of withdrawal from the corruption of the metropolis, as though the desert or the Qumran alternative could provide a model for Christians in general or Roman Christians in particular. That too was a non-starter. Political realism for Paul meant living *within* the political system even if that meant living to a large extent in the terms laid down by that system.

We should also recall once more that this position is neither christologically nor eschatologically inspired as such. As the carry over of Jewish wisdom, it is creation theology if it is anything. Paul's political realism grew out of the recognition that ruler and ruled is the nature of human society. To be sure, 13.1–7 is set within an explicitly Christian context: as the immediately following paragraphs indicate, the model for 'the good' is love of neighbor (13.8–10; cf. Mark 10.42–45; 12.29–31), and there is an eschatological perspective to cheer those who are suffering (13.11–14). But Paul's political realism is based simply on the recognition that power to levy taxes, to judge, to punish is part of the social fabric of this age.

3. What then is there of lasting value in exhortations given to such a specific historical context? And does the passage provide any guidance for those in different political situations where, for example, the state oppresses Christianity as such? Does Paul say anything to the debate about the need for civil disobedience or even violent revolution in some situations? Two observations seem appropriate.

(a) The passage here does give a basis for a theology of political power. The fact and inevitability of political power is affirmed and validated—for *every* person. The state on the corporate scale is the equivalent of the body on the individual scale—it is the means of corporate existence in this world. As there is no basis for a spirit/body dualism in Paul, so there is no basis for a social dualism, whereby political power and political activity is regarded as evil or antithetic to religion. On the contrary, Paul seems to go out of his way to eliminate any such division. State officials not simply *can* be, but properly speaking *are* 'servants of God.' For Paul who lived his whole life as one of priestly ministry (Rom 15.16), there was no clear division between sacred and secular. Christians could be involved in the political structures of the time and wield political power without ceasing to be Christians and indeed as part of their Christian service.

(b) Beyond that we cannot go with confidence. Paul does not envisage the possibility of a Christian political party or a Christian state. At that point I suspect a different set of theological principles would come into play; for he would certainly be fearful lest any other political or national entity made the same mistake as his fellow countrymen had—that of identifying God's purpose of salvation with one particular nation's material well-being and political dominance. Nor does one speak to the issue of whether civil disobedience or non-violent resistance can be Christian. Here we must recall that his advocacy of political quietism was in the context of the political powerlessness of most members of the ancient state. In contrast our modern democratic traditions make it possible for individuals to exercise some political power and to pass judgment on whether rulers are operating for the good of their citizens.[44] At the same time there has been a decrease in the typical ruler's sense of responsibility towards God or the gods, and so a drastic reduction of the constraint on a ruler's freedom to abuse the ruled which belief in a final judgment provided. Where there is no longer any effective self-constraint on the oppressor provided by a theology of political power, it is wholly legitimate that such a theology should come to expression in the defence of civil rights and democratic principles on behalf of the oppressed. At the same time it would have to be said that where a government was *not* serving God for the good of its citizens, any appeal to this passage as a way of maintaining their subservience would be a complete distortion and an abuse both of Paul's purpose and of its continuing scriptural significance.

[44]Cf. Wilckens, 'Römer 13.1–7' 241–5.

# The Trial of Politics and Religion*
# John 18:28–19:16

Thomas W. Gillespie

A cartoon in *The New Yorker* depicts two clergymen in serious conversation. One is obviously a wisened veteran, the other clearly a novice. The senior member of the duo is saying to his young colleague, "If you wish to be successful in the ministry, Higgenbotham, you must studiously avoid two subjects—*politics and religion*."

Whoever composed the Fourth Gospel in its canonical form avoided neither of these topics. In the story of the trial of Jesus, Pilate and the chief priests are bonded in a manner which contradicts the modern maxim that politics and religion do not "mix." The narrator knows that apart from that mixture this story could not be told.

The trial episode unfolds in seven discrete scenes in which Pilate moves back and forth between the courtyard and the hall of the praetorium. The dramatic effect, as C. H. Dodd notes, is "two stages . . . a front stage and a back."[1] In two, and only two, of these seven scenes, Pilate and Jesus engage in face-to-face dialogue.

That these two scenes belong together formally is confirmed by Raymond Brown's astute observation that the entire episode is cast in a seven-point chiasmus.[2] Thus Scene One, (18:28–32), in which the religious establishment accuses Jesus of a capital offense, has its counterpart in Scene Seven (19:12–16), in which their demand for the death penalty is met. Scene Two (18:33–38a), narrating the first dialogue, corresponds to Scene Six (19:9–11), relating the second. Scene Three (18:38b–40) and Scene Five (19:4–8) correspond on the basis of Pilate's pronouncement of the innocence of Jesus in each. Scene Four (19:1–3), in which the ironic investiture of Jesus is portrayed, serves as the hinge.

The relationship between Scenes Two and Six is not merely formal, however, but material as well. The topic in Scene Two is the sovereignty, the kingship, which Jesus implicitly claims for himself. In Scene Six the conversation focuses on the power, the authority, which Pilate explicitly claims for himself. The crucial issue is how this sovereignty and this authority are, if at all, related.

Consider first the explicit claim of Pilate. Scene Six (19:9–11) opens with Pilate back inside the praetorium interrogating Jesus about his alleged divine sonship. "Where are you from?" he demands to know. Exasperated by the silence of Jesus in response to his question, Pilate threatens him with the boast that he has the *exousia* to crucify or to release him. The Greek term can mean "authority" or "power," and the Revised Standard Version opts for the latter translation. The former, however, is preferable.

John Schuetz defines "authority" as "the legitimate use of effective power."[3] Thus "authority" includes the notion of "power" that is both "effective" and "legitimate." Without

*Sermon preached during the Morning Service, August 17, 1986.

[1]C. H. Dodd, *Historical Tradition in the Fourth Gospel* (Cambridge: Cambridge University Press, 1963), p. 96.

[2]Raymond E. Brown, *The Gospel According to John (XIII-XXI)* (New York: Doubleday & Company, Inc., 1970), pp. 858f.

[3]John Howard Schutz, *Paul and the Anatomy of Apostolic Authority* (Cambridge: Cambridge University Press, 1975), pp. 1–21.

"power," "authority" is banal. "Power" without legitimacy, however, is only "force." Pilate's boast of "authority" is thus not empty. He legitimately exercises the judicial power of life and death within his Roman jurisdiction.

Like the story of the two Englishmen who were arguing the relative authority of the bishop and the magistrate. "The bishop has the greater authority," said one, "because the bishop can say 'Ye be damned,' while the magistrate can merely say, 'Ye be hanged.' " "Aye," responded the second, "but the difference is that when the magistrate says, 'Ye be hanged,' ye are hanged." Pilate enjoyed that kind of authority.

The rejoinder of Jesus to this boast both confirms and defuses it: "You would have no authority over me unless it had been given you from above." Paul Duke comments aptly: "What power Pilate has is his only by higher authority. Even Pilate could not fail to fathom this *double entendre*: Jesus speaks less of the Caesar above Pilate than the God above both Caesar and Pilate."[4] The reader of the Fourth Gospel cannot miss this double meaning either.

In the earlier episode attesting the conversation between Jesus and Nicodemus, Jesus spoke of the "birth" which comes "from above." The reader is well aware that the phrase "from above" (*anothen*) has a theological reference. Thus the question is how Pilate's authority is derived from *this* "above."

Bultmann interprets this saying of Jesus along the lines of Paul's brief treatment of the authority of governments in Romans 13.[5] The phrase "from above" for Bultmann thus refers to the ultimate source of the political authority which Pilate exercises as a representative of the Roman state. The reference of Jesus to this Source, accordingly, calls Pilate's attention "expressly to his responsibility before God. . . . "

Ernst Haenchen chides Bultmann for speaking naively of the state here, calling attention to the fact that for the Evangelist there was no abstract entity called "the state" but only the *Imperium Romanum*.[6] Granting Bultmann's anachronistic use of language, it remains difficult to see how the substitution of the *Imperium Romanum* for the abstract entity called "the state" blunts Bultmann's point. For the *Imperium Romanum*, as Raymond Brown puts it, is "the Roman incarnation of worldly power,"[7] which is precisely what a "state" is.

Perhaps that is why Haenchen offers no alternative to Bultmann's interpretation. Father Brown, however, does. He argues that here "the Johannine Jesus is not lecturing Pilate on the God-given rights of the prefect's office, nor, *a fortiori*, on the relations of Church and State."[8] The saying must be understood rather in the light of the previously attested claim of Jesus that no one can take his life from him, for he alone has authority to lay it down (10:18). Now that Jesus has voluntarily entered "the hour" appointed by his Father (12:27) when he will lay down his life, "the Father has permitted men to have power over Jesus's life." His conclusion is this: "Although Pilate does not realize it, the reason he has the power he boasts of is not simply because he has legionaries at his disposal. The power is his because God has assigned him a role in 'the hour.' "[9]

Notice, however, that the one assigned this role in "the hour" and thus empowered for it is not merely an anonymous "him." It is specifically Pilate—the Roman procurator or prefect, whichever is historically the accurate title of his office. The point is that Pilate would not be assigned this role if he did not occupy this office.

[4]Paul D. Duke, *Irony in the Fourth Gospel* (Atlanta: John Knox Press, 1985), pp. 133f.

[5]Rudolf Bultmann, *Das Evangelium des Johannes* (Göttingen: Vandenhoeck & Ruprecht, 1959), pp. 511-513.

[6]Ernst Haenchen, *John 2: A Commentary on the Gospel of John Chapters 7–21* (Philadelphia: Fortress Press, 1984), pp. 182f.

[7]Brown, *op. cit.*, p.863.

[8]*Ibid.*, p. 892.

[9]*Ibid.*, p. 893.

Is it then legitimate to separate the role from the office as neatly as Professor Brown seeks to do? It would be if Pilate were granted mere "power" over Jesus in this his "hour." What is actually given to Pilate is "authority," the "legitimate use of effective power." What legitimates the "power" given to Pilate is the office assigned to him by Caesar. And it is the "authority" of this office which is "from above" in the double sense intended.

The respective interpretations of Bultmann and Brown are not antithetical, therefore, but complementary. The reference of this enigmatic saying is to the judicial authority which Pilate exercises as both a political and a providential figure in the unfolding drama of "the hour" of Jesus. Pilate's authority in either sense is "from above," and to that Source he is both responsible and accountable. Nothing less than this is required by the cryptic remark of Jesus which concludes this exchange: "Therefore he who betrayed me to you has the greater sin."

What would be the basis of pronouncing Pilate's final decision in this case "sin" if his office is ruled out of consideration? The irony which characterizes this scene depends upon Pilate's malfeasance. For already his political authority has been hopelessly surrendered to the crowd outside. Pilate may pronounce the final verdict, but it is the crowd that is making the judicial decision. As Paul Duke puts it: "No matter what Pilate claims about a power to release, he is now destined to play a part in killing Jesus; and for all his blustering about his importance in this affair, the little governor will not even rate the larger share of guilt."[10] That he has any guilt at all, however, is predicated upon his exercising an official authority which has its ultimate source not in Caesar but in God.

Consider second the implicit claim of Jesus. Scene Two (18:33–38a) also presents Pilate inside the praetorium interrogating the accused. "Are you the King of the Jews?" he demands. Jesus responds ironically: "Do you say this of your own accord, or did others say it to you about me?" In other words, "Is your question an acclamation (of belief) or an accusation (of unbelief)?"

With this question Jesus turns the trial away from himself toward Pilate. For Pilate the issue cannot be what others think of Jesus but what *he* thinks. In this context, Pilate's retort, "Am I a Jew?," hints at the deeper question, "Are you *my* king?"[11]

Jesus responds to this by saying, "My kingship is not of this world; if my kingship were of this world, my subjects would fight, that I might not be handed over to the Jews; but my kingship is not from the world." Note well that this too is a claim to authority. Pilate takes it as a harmless claim precisely because it is a claim to authority which confesses its inability to exercise effective power. Jesus' admission that he lacks "subjects" willing or able to fight for him against his accusers relieves the Roman of his anxieties. Once the concession of powerlessness is made, Pilate concludes that this claim to sovereignty represents no political threat. Now he can toy with the prisoner.

"So you are a king?" is a question which asks what kind of sovereignty this might be which lacks power. "You say that I am a king," Jesus answers. "For this I was born, and for this I have come into the world, to bear witness to the truth. Every one who is of the truth hears my voice." This final remark invites Pilate to enter the door that has been opened to him and to engage the issue of the identity of Jesus. But Pilate declines the invitation. He is content to conclude the exchange by simply asking the profound question, "What is truth?"

Would that the text could convey to us the tone of that question. Then we would know whether Pilate is speaking out of scorn or cynicism or incomprehension or possibly even

[10]Duke, *op. cit.*, p. 134.
[11]*Ibid.*, p. 130.

an honest hunger to know the answer. Cynicism has received the most votes in the history of interpretation. Francis Bacon summed up the majority opinion when he wrote, " 'What is truth?' said jesting Pilate, and would not stay for an answer."

Whatever the intention of the question, however, it is clear that Pilate made no connection between truth and power. Pilate's interpreters, by and large, have failed to make it also. Haenchen is typical in this regard. Commenting on this passage, he declares boldly that "Christianity, as the Evangelist understands it, is not a political movement and therefore makes no use of political means."[12] But that is so only if his sovereignty lacks power to effect political change. The truth of which Jesus speaks, the truth which the reader of the Fourth Gospel knows Jesus himself is (14:3), does enjoy such power. And that power is effectively exercised by the one who bears witness to the truth, and thereby makes the connection between the "above" and the "below," between God and the world.

In his essay, "The Hermeneutics of Testimony,"[13] Paul Ricoeur makes two crucial points in this regard. First, he calls attention to the fact that "the action of testifying has an intimate relation to an institution—the judiciary; a place—the court; a social function—the lawyer, the judge; an action—to plead, that is, to be plaintiff or defendant in a trial. Put simply, a "witness" is a political figure, and "testifying" is a political action. Second, Ricoeur observes that "to testify is to attest that . . . But it is also to testify for . . ., or in favor of . . . " "By these expressions our language means that the witness seals his bond to the cause that he defends by a public profession of his conviction, by the zeal of a propagator, by a personal devotion which can extend even to the sacrifice of his life. "The witness is capable of suffering and dying for what he believes. "When the test of conviction becomes the price of life, the witness changes his name; he is called a martyr. "But is it a change of name? *Martus* in Greek means 'witness.' "

The Jesus attested in the Fourth Gospel is such a witness. He bears witness to the truth he himself is, the truth of God. Through his witness to the truth the world in its darkness is illumined, and by that light its darkness is judged.

This is the power of Jesus. In the terms of the Prologue, it is the power of the "grace and truth" which comes to the world through him (1:17), and thus the power to make God known (1:18). This power evidences his authority, and, in turn, confirms sovereignty. The legitimacy of this claim is known only to those who "hear" his voice because they are "of the truth." Jesus confronts Pilate with this claim at his trial, but Pilate, ever the politician, chooses to compromise rather than to decide. Pilate learns, however, that not to decide is to decide. As Alan Culpepper puts it, "Pilate is a study in the impossibility of compromise, the inevitability of decision, and the consequences of each alternative."[14]

And so we have these two claims. We have the claim of Pilate, representing Caesar, to a rightful authority over human life within his jurisdiction. It is a claim which Jesus acknowledges and limits, reminding his judge that his authority as well as that of Caesar is "from above" and thus subject to the Authority which authorizes theirs. We also have the claim of Jesus to represent in the world not an anonymous "above" but the God who reveals himself as the Father through the Son. It is a claim which Jesus evidences by his witness to the truth, inviting Pilate and all others to "hear" his voice and belong to the truth. Pilate declines the invitation because he belongs not to the truth, not to himself, not even to Caesar, but to the crowd in his courtyard. They own him because he fears their

[12]Haenchen, *op. cit.*, p. 179.

[13]Paul Ricoeur, *Essays on Biblical Interpretation*, ed. by Lewis S. Mudge (Philadelphia: Fortress Press, 1980), pp. 119-154.

[14]R. Alan Culpepper, *Anatomy of the Fourth Gospel* (Philadelphia: Fortress Press, 1983), p. 143.

power, people power, the power of the people.

This power is manifested with ferocity in the final scene of the episode. Recognizing Pilate's reluctance to condemn Jesus, the crowd plays its ace. "If you release this man," the people cry, "you are not Caesar's friend; every one who makes himself a king sets himself against Caesar." "The roles are now reversed," C. F. Evans observes. "In place of the Roman governor offering the Jewish people the choice, 'Which will you have, Jesus or Barabbas?' the Jewish people offer the governor the choice, 'Which will you have, Christ or Caesar?' "[15]

For Pilate there can be but one answer, for he has no king but Caesar. The irony is that the leaders of the people who are the people of God join him in his choice. To his question, "Shall I crucify your king?" they respond, "We have no king but Caesar!" "So with splendid irony," Barnabas Lindars remarks, "John makes the Jews utter the ultimate blasphemy in the same breath as their final rejection of Jesus."[16]

As splendid as the irony of the Evangelist may be at this point, it goes even deeper. For in the end we are left with a representative of Caesar who surrenders his authority to the people, and to people who recognize no authority other than that of Caesar. The scene is disquietingly modern. For we live in a world divided by the pretentious claims of the absolute state and the equally vain claims of the absolute electorate.

In such a world Jesus, now through his Church, continues to bear witness to the truth. Government has a Source which transcends the will of the people, and the people have a Sovereign who transcends themselves and their government. That is the truth. But that truth is denied in the trial of Jesus as narrated in the Fourth Gospel. It is denied, speaking anachronistically, by both the State and the Church. And in their denial, both are tried and judged by the truth. In that sense, the trial of the State and the Church continues. At this trial we are called to be witnesses.

[15]C. F. Evans, "The Passion of John," *Exploration in Theology 2* (London: SCM Press, 1977), p. 61.
[16]Barnabas Lindars, *The Gospel of John* (Grand Rapids: William B. Eerdmans, 1972), p. 572.

# Calvin and Melanchthon on Romans 13:1–7

David C. Steinmetz

*Philip Melanchthon has given us a great deal of light by reason of the outstanding character of both his learning, industry, and the skill in all kinds of knowledge in which he excels, in comparison with those who have published commentaries before him. His only object, however, seems to have been to discuss the points which were especially worth noting. He therefore dwells at length on these, and deliberately passes over many matters which can cause great trouble to those of average understanding.*[1]

John Calvin wrote these words on October 18, 1539, and included them in the dedication of his Commentary on Romans, published in Strasbourg in 1540. On the one hand, Calvin confesses his indebtedness to Melanchthon, who has written what Calvin regards as an extremely learned and informative commentary on Romans. On the other hand, he indicates his dissatisfaction with Melanchthon's exegetical method. In Calvin's view, Melanchthon seems content to comment on the great *topoi* or themes in Paul and to leave smaller, but nevertheless puzzling, exegetical details to one side.

Melanchthon is the only commentator from Wittenberg that Calvin cites by name in his preface, though Melanchthon was not the first theologian on the Wittenberg faculty to lecture on Romans. Martin Luther[2] and Johannes Lang[3] had lectured on Romans before him. Their unpublished lectures are interesting as a chapter in the evolution of the new Reformation theology. But it was Melanchthon who served as the principal commentator on Romans at Wittenberg in the formative period of early Lutheranism, even when his reading of Paul differed from Luther's.

Calvin does not tell us which commentary by Melanchthon on Romans he is using. The question is not frivolous. Melanchthon's first commentary was an unauthorized edition, drawn from student notes and published in Nuremberg in 1522 by Luther without Melanchthon's approval under the title, the *Annotationes Phil. Melanchthonis in Epistolas Pauli ad Romanos et ad Corinthios*.[4] Melanchthon's second commentary, his *Dispositio orationis in Epistola Pauli ad Romanos,* was published in 1529 in Hagenau. The *Dispositio* emphasized the rhetorical

[1]John Calvin, *The Epistles of Paul to the Romans and Thessalonians,* translated by Ross Mackenzie, *Calvin's New Testament Commentaries,* edited by David W. Torrance and Thomas F. Torrance (Grand Rapids: Wm. B. Eerdmans Publishing Company, 1961), p. 2. All translations of Calvin are from this edition. I have used the Latin text edited by T.H.L. Parker, *Iohannis Calvini Commentarius in Epistolam Pauli ad Romans,* Studies in the History of Christian Thought 22 (Leiden: E.J. Brill, 1981), pp. 281–85. The Latin text of Melanchthon's 1532 commentary is found in *Melanchthon's Werke, Band 5: Roemerbrief-Kommentar 1532,* edited by Rolf Schaefer (Guetersloh: Guetersloher Verlagshaus Gerd Mohn, 1965), pp. 302–25. Melanchthon's 1556 commentary is cited in the Latin edition found in the *Corpus Reformatorum,* Volume 15, edited by C.G. Bretschneider (Halle: C.A. Schwetschke and Son, 1848), cols. 1009–17. Because it is easy to find one's way in these commentaries and in order to keep footnotes to a minimum, I will cite these commentaries by page number only when it is absolutely necessary.

[2]*Dr. Martin Luthers Werke: Kritische Gesamtausgabe, Vol. 56* (Weimar: Hermann Boehlaus Nachfolger, 1938).

[3]Reinhold Weijenborg, OFM, "Die Wittenberger *Roemerbriefvorlesung* des Erfurters Augustiners Johannes Lang. Erstausgabe nach dem *Vat. Pal. Lat. 132* mit Einleitung und Kommentar," *Antonianum* 52 (1976): 394–494.

[4]For a history of Melanchthon's commentaries see the introduction by Rolf Schaefer to Melanchthon, *Roemerbrief-Kommentar 1532,* pp. 15–24.

rules which Paul used in the development of his themes.

In 1532 Melanchthon lectured once again on Romans. In these lectures from the period following the composition of the Augsburg Confession, Melanchthon attempted to clarify differences between Paul and Augustine (a tension which Luther was always reluctant to mention) and to define more precisely, with the help of Aristotle, the meaning of "righteousness." The 1532 lectures were published in the fall at Wittenberg as the *Commentarii in Epistolam Pauli ad Romanos.* A later edition of this work with a new dedication and various other changes was published in 1540. After the death of Luther and eight years before his own death, Melanchthon returned one final time to Romans, publishing his last commentary on this book, the *Enarratio Eqistolae Pauli ad Romanos,* in 1556.

It seems unlikely that Calvin made use of Melanchthon's last commentary on Romans. While both Melanchthon's commentary and Calvin's final revision appeared in 1556, Calvin completed his revision no later than January 24, 1556 and thus so early in the year that it seems impossible for him to have made use of Melanchthon's *Enarratio*.[5] In all probability Calvin consulted the 1532 commentary by Melanchthon in one of its many printings. It seems likely that Calvin was influenced, if at all, by the mature rather than the young or the aging Melanchthon.

## I

I want to use the assigned text for this symposium (Romans 13:1–7) as focal point for a comparative study of the exegesis of these two seminal commentators on Paul. Do Melanchthon and Calvin read this text in a similar way? How seriously should we regard Calvin's praise of Melanchthon's skill as an interpreter? Does Calvin read this text with spectacles provided by Melanchthon? Or does Calvin's criticism of Melanchthon's method imply a criticism of his substantive comments as well? To what extent can Melanchthon be numbered among Calvin's teachers in the art of biblical interpretation?

Melanchthon cites a wealth of authorities in his exposition of Paul, beginning with the Bible itself: Genesis 9:6, 14, 25, 41:40ff., Deuteronomy 32:35, 2 Chronicles 19:6, Psalm 82:6, Proverbs 8:15, 16:11, Ecclesiastes 8:8, Isaiah 11:9, Jeremiah 29:7, Daniel 2:48, Micah 4:3, Matthew 5:39, 8:10, Luke 3:14, 22:25, Acts 5:29, 10:1ff., 15:10, 28, Romans 12:19, 1 Corinthians 6:7, 13:4–7, Colossians 3:14, 1 Timothy 1:9, 2:1f., and 1 Peter 2:13–18. Among the ancient authors he cites Aristotle, Plato, Xenophon and Herodotus, and alludes to such other classical and historical figures as Alexander the Great and Julian the Apostate. More surprising are his allusions to Roman and canon law. He cites legal texts, ancient and modern, from Canon 12 of Nicaea to the Code of Justinian and from the Decretum of Gratian to the pronouncements of Innocent IV and John XXII. He even refers to such teachers of law as Baldus Ubaldus from the fourteenth century and C. Cassius Longinus from the first. While he does not mention any scholastic theologians except Gerson by name, he does report in a general way on a question disputed by scholastic theology. Apparently, Melanchthon feels it is appropriate to enlist the full range of one's learning in the task of biblical interpretation and to exhibit that learning in the exegesis itself.

Calvin, astonishingly enough, makes few biblical allusions. He seems more interested in uncovering the *Sitz im Leben* of the text than in tracing parallel passages, however appropriate and suggestive. He believes that Paul wrote Romans 13 in order to restrain the "restless spirits" who thought that Christian liberty means the abolition of all earthly powers. Since

[5]For the history of Calvin's commentary on Romans, see T.H.L. Parker, *Calvin's New Testament Commentaries* (Grand Rapids: Wm. B. Eerdmans, 1971), and *Calvini Commentarius,* pp. ix–xvii.

the Roman Empire was involved in the persecution of early Christian communities, it seemed doubly absurd to many Christians to render obedience to authorities who were "contriving to snatch the kingdom from Christ." In Calvin's view it was, therefore, particularly important for Paul to lay great stress on the authority of magistrates. Calvin draws an analogy between the restless spirits of the first century and the malcontents of his own, though the reference is veiled and no group is singled out by name.

Calvin's philological interests in this passage are fairly minor. He appeals to the causative *gar* in Greek (13:3a), mentions the Hebrew usage of the word "praise" (13:3b), and alludes generally and vaguely to the political teaching of "the philosophers" (13:3b). He does not, however, cite a single authority by name, biblical, philosophical, literary, legal or theological. Such citations appear to interfere with the "lucid brevity" for which Calvin is striving.

## II

Several questions trouble both commentators. Who, for example, are the higher powers to whom Christians should be subject? Does Paul have in mind both secular magistrates and ecclesiastical superiors? Do Christians owe such powers unqualified obedience? On what grounds is obedience owed to any human power? May Christians discharge the role of a magistrate with a tranquil conscience? Or does obedience to God inevitably set Christians at odds with the state?

1. *Identity of the Powers.* There is a medieval exegetical tradition that identifies the higher powers to which Christians owe obedience as both secular and spiritual. According to this tradition, when Paul says that the ruler does not bear the sword in vain, he means both the physical sword of temporal magistrates and the spiritual sword of ecclesiastical prelates. Christians owe obedience to both, princes and bishops, and Paul is articulating a principle of universal applicability.

Sixteenth century interpreters of Paul divide on this question and not necessarily along confessional lines. Thomas de Vio Cardinal Cajetan[6] and Girolamo Cardinal Seripando[7] think that Paul is referring solely to secular magistrates. Martin Luther[8] and Jacopo Cardinal Sadoleto[9] do not agree. In his 1515–16 lectures on Romans, Luther argues that Paul had in mind both secular and spiritual authorities. Having made this point, Luther shows very little curiosity about secular rulers, who seem to him to be doing a capable enough job—certainly better than the spiritual authorities whose stewardship of the Church has left it in rags and tatters.

Sadoleto, on the other hand, agrees with Luther's reading of Paul's intention, but not with Luther's criticism of the Church. For Sadoleto the papacy is unarguably the highest of the higher powers. He therefore heaps scorn on the Protestants who grovel before petty German princes (whose title to power is often, to say the least, ambiguous) while rebelling against the spiritual sword held by the Church, given directly to Peter by Christ.

In this dispute Melanchthon and Calvin side with Cajetan and Seripando against Luther and Sadoleto. Paul has in mind only secular magistrates. Whatever needs to be said about offices and order in the institutional Church (and Melanchthon and Calvin agree that a good deal needs to be said) is simply not the subject of this passage. Calvin sums up the views of Melanchthon as well as his own when he writes:

[6]Thomas de Vio Cardinal Cajetan, *Epistolae Pauli et aliorum Apostolorum* (Paris, 1540), pp. 83–85.
[7]Girolamo Cardinal Seripando, *In D. Pauli Epistolas ad Romanos et Galatas Commentaria* (Naples, 1601), 220–24.
[8]*WA* 57.476–82.
[9]Jacopo Cardinal Sadoleto, *In Pauli Epistolam ad Romanos Commentariorum,* Opera omnia IV (Verona, 1738), pp. 307–12.

> The whole of this discussion concerns civil government *(de civilibus praefecturis)*. Those therefore, who bear rule over men's consciences attempt to establish their blasphemous tyranny from this passage in vain.[10]

2. *Grounds for Obedience.* Melanchthon offers two grounds for the Christian's obedience to the magistrate. The first ground is reason and natural law. The gospel, after all, does not teach political science or offer a divinely sanctioned pattern for the state. The positive laws of the state are derived from the principles of natural law which are prehensible to human reason. Not every society views the fundamental principles of law in exactly the same way and there are legitimate differences between the polity of the Saxons and the French. When Paul urges every Christian to be subject to the higher powers, he does not expect Saxon citizens to obey the laws of France or the French to obey the laws of England. Nor does Paul expect all Christians to model their polity on the law codes of Moses. Indeed, in matters of polity the law codes of Moses are binding on Christians only to the extent that they conform to the principles of natural law.

On the other hand, reason has its limitations. It does not see that there is a second ground for Christian obedience in God's own ordination of the state and the rule of law. The state and the political order are ordained by God, not as an unavoidable evil that must be tolerated, but as a good that should be reverenced and celebrated. The state protects the bodily life of its citizens and promotes the welfare of the human race. The magistrate must be obeyed, not only because the rule of law is better for human life than anarchy, but because God has made such obedience mandatory. To disobey the state in those matters in which the state licitly commands is to commit mortal sin and put oneself in danger of eternal damnation.

There are, of course, objections that can be raised against this view. While Melanchthon only lists monks as critics who have misunderstood the intention of Paul in this matter, it is clear from the way in which he echoes the common objections of the Anabaptists to civil power that he has them in mind also. There are three objections which these critics lodge: (1) that the gospel commends nonresistance to evil; (2) that Christians are called to a higher moral standard than the law codes of the Roman Empire; and (3) that Christians cannot serve as magistrates.

The first objection is the one that seems to concern him most. Melanchthon repeats themes from Luther's social ethic when he distinguishes between public vindication of the law and private vengeance and between what one may do as a public officer of the state and as a private individual.[11] The gospel clearly forbids vengeance by private individuals. There is no divine sanction for blood feuds or mob justice. The right to reward the good and punish the wicked has been given by God to public officials who may wield the sword and shed human blood in the discharge of their public office. Kings have no more right to murder private enemies than do peasants. But unlike peasants they can execute criminals who have broken the laws and violated the just order of the state.

The second objection, that Christians are called to a higher moral standard than the minimal righteousness enforced by the law, is conceded. What Melanchthon denies is that commitment to a higher righteousness necessarily puts Christians in conflict with the requirements of the state. Melanchthon seems to see the higher justice of the Chrisian community as a completion or perfection of the lower justice of the state rather than as a dissent from it. Grace perfects nature; it does not abolish it.

[10]Calvin, *Romans and Thessalonians*, p. 283.

[11]On this question see my essay, "Luther and the Two Kingdoms," in *Luther in Context* (Bloomington: Indiana University Press, 1986).

The third objection, that Christians cannot be magistrates, is met by a flat denial. God has ordained this work, reason demonstrates its utility, and therefore Christians ought not to shrink from its demands. The service of the state is Christian service and the magistrate, the living law, is the highest embodiment of the political order. While Melanchthon does not call princes *Wunderleute* or disparage lawyers and law books in favor of the political institutions of princes, as Luther sometimes does, he clearly regards the magistrate as more than a bureaucrat who applies society's rules to society's ills in a mechanical and unimaginative way. The magistrate is not a law clerk. The magistrate directs public affairs, inspires other public officials in the discharge of their duties, and even leads armies into battle. The task is as complex as the tangled affairs of human life to which it responds. Christians ought to be grateful for the state with its magistrates, laws, and judgments, and to give the state the reverence, honor and support which is its due.

At this point Melanchthon launches a fairly long discussion of several matters, not all of which have been brought up by Paul, but all of which are implicit for Melanchthon in the Christian acceptance of a stable political order: namely, taxes, private property, enforceable contracts, and litigation. What Melanchthon wants to show, over against Anabaptist criticisms of the political order, is that all of these matters are licit for the Christian. If the Anabaptists reject private property in favor of communal, if they refuse to pay war taxes, if they suggest that Christians may not sue Christians in court, they are in fact rejecting the higher powers to whom Paul commands all Christians to render obedience.

Calvin takes a somewhat different attitude about the state and its polity, though he agrees with Melanchthon about a number of issues. He agrees, for example, that the state has been ordained by God for the well-being of the human race and not as a punishment to afflict it. He agrees that the magistrate has a legitimate right to collect taxes, though he adds the caveat, missing from Melanchthon, that taxes are public property to be used in the promotion of the public good rather than private funds to be squandered by rulers in the gratification of their own lusts. He even agrees with Melanchthon that the magistrate has been given by God the right to shed human blood in the public interest.

But the tone of Calvin's exposition is quite different. There is less of a polemical edge, less inclination to bring up matters not explicitly brought up by Paul. Furthermore, whereas Melanchthon, breathing out counter-revolutionary sentiments, stresses the dark side of state power (such as its right to punish criminals and wage war), Calvin emphasizes the positive side of political order (such as the promotion of domestic peace and the prevention of armed conflict).

They even differ in their starting-points. While Melanchthon grounds the state in both human reason and divine ordination, Calvin stresses divine ordination alone. It is vain curiosity to ask by what right rulers rule. For Calvin it is enough that they rule by divine ordination. To despise human government is to despise the providence which set that government in place. Rulers must be obeyed, not on the grounds of human necessity, but on the grounds of obedience to God.

Having taken this position, however, does not prevent Calvin from discussing the utility of the magistracy as an instrument for the promotion of the public good and the restraint of human wickedness. Sin is such a dangerous reality that anyone who opposes the legitimate functioning of the state marks himself out as an enemy of the human race. Wicked rulers are to be obeyed and even rulers who have no power to enforce their will on their subjects. Both Melanchthon and Calvin agree that there is no tyranny so vile that it lacks all semblance of justice. The duty to obey does not rest on the goodness of princes or on their power but on the commandment of God. Indeed, Calvin even ventures the uncomfortable suggestion that God may from time to time send malicious and tyrannical rulers to Christians as a just punishment for their sins.

3. *Limits of Obedience.* Since Melanchthon and Calvin have taken such a strong stand on the duty of Christians to obey magistrates, it will come as no surprise that they have very little to say about legitimate restrictions on that obedience. Melanchthon approaches the question from the perspective of the subject. While Christians ought not to value their own judgments more than the judgments of their magistrates (and thus give those magistrates the benefit of any doubt), they cannot and should not obey princes or governors who command them to act against God or the laws of God. What Melanchthon seems to have in mind is civil disobedience rather than any form of armed rebellion. Still he does allow for passive disobedience.

Calvin, on the other hand, focuses on magistrates and the inherent limitations of their power. Magistrates are servants rather than lords. Their power is restrained and limited by what promotes the common welfare of their people. They are ministers and stewards of God and therefore answerable to God for abuses of their power. Calvin even suggests that dictatorships are not ordained governments, though he does not amplify what he means by that remark. We know from other contexts that Calvin does allow lesser magistrates the right to act in concert against the abuse of power by a despotic ruler. But since there is nothing in Paul's text on the subject of civil disobedience, Calvin does not bring the matter up.

Calvin may also ameliorate the absolute and unqualified nature of Paul's injunction to obey magistrates by his comments on the original setting of the text. Paul spoke so absolutely because he had to put an end to the fanaticism that believed that redemption in Christ placed one outside the civil order. Even unchristian governments have their legitimate rights and are owed honor, obedience, and taxes from their Christian subjects. Nevertheless, it is clear from what they say that both Calvin and Melanchthon are uneasy with Paul's unqualified endorsement of the rights of the magistrate and wish to soften it with themes drawn from elsewhere in the Bible.

It is also worth noting that Melanchthon's most enthusiastic endorsement of state power comes in the period immediately following the Peasants' Revolt and the Diet at Augsburg. The reformers at Wittenberg had good reason to be grateful to Protestant princes for their protection and optimistic about the benign influence of state power in furthering the cause of the Reformation. By 1556 Melanchthon's early optimism has waned. In his final commentary on Romans he presses the point that pastors have the right to rebuke princes and to be obeyed in those matters that touch the ministry of the gospel. Whoever disobeys the divine commandments that sound from the pulpit commits mortal sin. As an example of what he has in mind, Melanchthon cites the excommunication of the emperors Theodosius and Valens by Ambrose and Basil. For old Melanchthon the Church has once again become a buffer against the unbridled power of the state.

## III

It would be a mistake to draw large conclusions from such a relatively small sample of the biblical exegesis of Calvin and Melanchthon. Nevertheless, there are some observations that we can make.

1. At first glance Calvin and Melanchthon seem to form a common front on the question of the power and legitimate functions of the state. However, when we look more closely at them we find there are in fact a great many differences between their views, not all of

which are attributable to differences in method. It may, of course, be a difference in method that prevents Calvin from talking about many of the questions concerning property, contracts and litigation that seem to trouble Melanchthon. Calvin usually reserves lengthy discussions of related issues to the pages of the *Institutes,* where they do not interrupt the flow of biblical exegesis.

Less easy to categorize as a difference of method is Calvin's dismissal of Melanchthon's view of the role of reason and natural law in providing a foundation for the political order. Calvin does not, of course, contradict Melanchthon's arguments or mention him by name. But he does relegate Melanchthon's carefully articulated position to the realm of vain curiosity. Vainly curious questions are questions that it is neither necessary nor useful to ask. They are, generally speaking, the kinds of questions scholastic theologians are inordinately fond of asking. Calvin, however, wants to follow in his exegesis the simplier structure of Paul's argument. It is enough for him to know that the political order in Strasbourg (and later in Geneva) is an order ordained by the providence of God.

2. Calvin and Melanchthon are both uneasy about the absolute endorsement of state power that Paul seems to offer. Each tries in characteristically different ways, to soften that endorsement. Melanchthon appeals to the right of passive disobedience by ordinary Christians and the duty of pastors to confront the established powers in the name of the gospel. Calvin calls attention to the original setting of this passage and reminds rulers that the only legitimate state power is power directed toward the welfare of their subjects.

Still it does not appear that Calvin and Melanchthon have altogether escaped a reading of Paul that provides an ideological justification in religion for the power and privileges of the ruling classes. Melanchthon in particular lays such heavy emphasis on the rights and privileges of magistrates that Christian subjects are given almost no leverage against wicked and unjust rulers. Even the right of pastors to rebuke the powerful and defend the defenseless does not have the same force or reliability as a constitutional restraint. Will pastors protest in time? Will princes listen? Are ordinary Christians willing to suffer the grisly penalties of civil disobedience?

On the other hand, if Calvin and Melanchthon offer little in the way of restraint on the powerful, Paul offers even less. His statement is absolute; theirs at least is qualified. Both commentators have softened the seemingly harsh character of Paul's dictum by introducing qualifications not found in the text. Perhaps Calvin is right when he argues that Paul is combatting a tendency toward an illegitimate freedom in the Roman Christian community. That is certainly the interpretation that Cajetan also embraces. Perhaps (as Calvin does not suggest) Paul is only articulating an interim ethic to describe Christian conduct in the brief period before the Lord's return. Whatever is the case, Paul provides the text which Melanchthon and Calvin must interpret and which they cannot escape.

3. Confronted as we are by worldwide abuses of civil power, it is very difficult for us to see with Melanchthon and Calvin the state and the magistracy as good gifts of God. Understandably, our generation has been more interested in rediscovering the biblical underpinning for political dissent than in re-evaluating the biblical basis for civil obedience. It may therefore be appropriate for us to engage in an experiment in thought, to look at government and political power with the eyes provided by these sixteenth century commentators on Paul, to see the tolerably just state once again as a gift of God for the benefit of the human race. Anarchy does not provide the conditions necessary for the orderly development of human life and even revolutionary governments must build roads and bridges, regulate medications, grade meat, pay pensions, put out fires, arrest criminals, educate children, provide water and sewers, certify drivers, collect customs duties and taxes, provide health care

for the indigent and elderly, combat acid rain, protect endangered species, rescue flood victims, provide temporary shelter for the homeless, and defend the safety of its citizens.

Of course, we cannot and should not substitute the exegesis of Melanchthon and Calvin for our own. We stand in different circumstances and must discharge our theological task in the light of the Church's knowledge at the present time. We can, however, learn from Melanchthon and Calvin what we can no longer so readily learn from each other, that a tolerably just political order enhances human life and that Christians have legitimate reason to be grateful for it.

# The Prophetic Critique of Kings

Patrick D. Miller, Jr.

Prophets and kings belong together. At least they did in ancient Israel. The relationship was an uneasy one. Prophets feared for their lives at the hands of the kings of Israel and Judah. Less noticed perhaps is that the kings had even more to fear from the prophets. Some of them in effect lost their heads by the word of the prophets.

Still, go together they did, and neither position or role was viable or understandable apart from the other. Prophecy, in effect, was an outgrowth of the state, a direct result of the formation of the nation state and a *sine qua non* for its continuing and effective existence. As the Old Testament records the story, prophecy began with kingship and in effect disappeared with it, though there are some of the minor prophets whose precise historical context is difficult to determine. At the beginning the primary relationship of the prophets, and in some sense their sole relationship, was to the political ruler. The rise of prophecy as a divinely authorized check or control on the human king by the divine king is clear and does not need to be recapitulated here.[1] We are more interested in exploring the substance and content of that check.

To be sure the prophets did not confine their message to the rulers of Israel and Judah. Increasingly they found themselves sent with a word of the Lord to other religious and political leaders and to the people as a whole. John S. Holladay has suggestively related the increasing tendency of the prophets to address the people from the eighth century on to changing patterns of Assyrian statecraft.[2] Even so the king remained a primary focus of the prophetic word early and late. The ruler's activities, conduct, and administration were virtually the only concern of such early prophets as Nathan, Gad, Ahijah, and Micaiah and to a large extent Samuel, Elijah, and Elisha. Even after the exile Haggai is explicitly introduced as "the prophet to Zerubbabel the son of Shealtiel, governor of Judah, and to Joshua the son of Jehozadak the high priest." (Hag.1:1). In between there were prophets who were closely tied to the court, for example, Isaiah, and others who were unconnected to the king, but still prophesied to and about the king, for example, Amos.

The royal acknowledgment of the divine direction and control through the prophets is apparent at many points. I Kings 22 is an obvious demonstration of the royal readiness and even desire to have the prophetic word from the Lord. There seems to be, however, a gradual change in how kings reacted to the prophet's presence and word, though this may be primarily a reflection of how different kings responded, or are remembered as having responded, to different prophets. What we do see in the beginning is an immediate acceptance by Saul and David of the prophetic critique and word of judgment, even though in one case it meant the loss of the throne (1 Sam. 15: 24–31) and in another the loss of a son and future tragedy and shame in the royal house (2 Sam. 12:7–15). The "good" kings of Judah as described in the books of Kings seem to have sought the prophetic word and accepted it, whatever its content, e.g. 1 Kings 22: 5,7 (Jehosaphat); 2 Kings 19–20 (Hezekiah); 2 Kings 22: 14–20 (Josiah).

The "bad" kings, i.e. those upon whom the Deuteronomistic Historian placed a negative judgment, tended to resist in various ways the prophet and the word the prophet brought.

[1]See, for example, G. E. Wright, "The Nations in Israel's Prophecy," *Encounter*, 26 (1965), pp. 225–37; and F. M. Cross, *Canaanite Myth and Hebrew Epic* (Cambridge: Harvard, 1973), pp. 219–29.

[2]J. S. Holladay, "Assyrian Statecraft and the Prophets of Israel," *Harvard Theological Review* 63 (1970), pp. 29–51.

Jeroboam I at first attempted to seize the anonymous prophet who condemned the altar he had built at Bethel (1 Kings 13:4) but then sought the prophet's favor and prayer to God to restore his suddenly withered hand (1 Kings 13: 6–7) and later sent his wife in disguise to Ahijah to obtain word about the prospects for his sick son and received a word of judgment against his whole house. Ahab called Elijah "troubler of Israel" (1 Kings 18:17 and "my enemy" (1 Kings 21:20) but humbled himself when he received the prophetic word of judgment against himself, his wife, and his house. Yet on another occasion he indicated his unwillingness to inquire of the Lord through Micaiah because Micaiah always brought bad news. Indeed Ahab threw Micaiah in jail when the prophet again gave a bad report (1 Kings 22). Ahaz did not threaten Isaiah but refused to receive his word (Isaiah 7).

Jehoiakim, king of Judah near the time of its downfall, represents the extreme example of royal disdain for the prophetic criticism and thus a dismissal of the word of the Lord that comes to him. He calmly cut off strips of the scroll of Jeremiah's prophecies as it was read to him and threw them in the fire. The text (Jer. 36:20 26) explicitly notes the absence of fear on the part of the king and his servants and their failure to rend their garments in the face of the divine word of judgment (in contrast, by the way, to Ahab when he received a similar word at a much earlier time [1 Kings 21:27]). Instead Jehoiakim tried to arrest Jeremiah and Baruch, "but the Lord hid them" (Jer. 36:26). Zedekiah, the last of the kings of Judah, vacillated between seeking a divine word from Jeremiah while protecting him and turning him over to the princes for execution. It is clear, therefore, that by the end of the monarchy royal power no longer could be presumed to place itself under the control of the word of the Lord as conveyed by "his servants the prophets," Josiah being a notable exception. By this time, and indeed well before, the king's resistance was matched by that of his courtiers, royal officials, princes, and priests. Not just the ruler of the state but its officialdom in seats of power, prestige, and wealth joined with the king and in some cases outdid him in seeking to suppress the prophetic critique (for example, Jeremiah 27–28).

In his recent *Old Testament Theology in a Canonical Context* Brevard Childs has written: "The Old Testament has no concept of the state either in the Greek sense or according to modern theory. There was also no clear separation between the civil and religious spheres of life. The term 'Israel' designated the covenant people . . ." (p. 178). The fact is that whatever conceptual undergirding it may or may not have had, a state did exist in Israel beginning around the tenth century. Its formation included the creation of the office of king, the development of a court and a system of royal appointees or officials to oversee various aspects of the government and the nation's life. A standing army was developed as well as a system or systems of taxation to support the national government. The nation state was recognized by other nations, exchanged ambassadors of various sorts, and entered into alliances and treaties with other nations.

It is true, however, that there was, as Childs says, no clear separation between civil and religious spheres. The term Isreal was the name of a nation state and in fact became the name of one part of the original state, but it was first the name of a people whose existence was created by a covenant with the God Yahweh. The term was understood primarily as a kinship and religious designation—a people who traced their lineage back to the eponymous ancestor Jacob-Israel and who understood themselves also to be "the people of Yahweh." In their early history they went into war under this rubric rather than as the army of Israel. They were, to the extent such a governmental form is possible, truly a theocracy. Nor was that self-understanding simply set aside when monarchy and state came into being, a state of affairs that created a serious tension in the socio-political structure.

Even, if not especially, at the ideological level shifts had to be made, shifts that are reflected in the royal ideology. What is most interesting in the relationship between prophets and kings is that the prophets not only made their peace with the royal *ideology* but contributed significantly to its development. At the same time they vigorously criticized the *practice* of monarchy. For this reason it is possible to some extent to distinguish between what I would call *normative*[3] texts, that is those that set the norm for the conduct and character of the king, (e.g. Isa 9:1–6 [Eng. 9:2–7]; 11:1–9; Jer. 21: 11–12; 22:1–4; 23:3–6; 33:14–16; Ezek. 34:23–24; Micah 5:1–3.) and *critical* texts, that is those that criticize the practice of a particular king or kings and/or announce judgment against the king, (e.g. 1 Sam. 15; 2 Sam. 12:1–23; 1 Kings 12:29–40; 13:1–10; 17–18; 20:35–43; 21; 22; 2 Kings 22:16–20; Isa. 7:3–17; Jer. 21:3–7; 22:5–9, 11–12, 13–19, 20–30; 23:1–2; 36:27–31; Ezek. 34:1–10; Hos 13:4–13; Amos 7:7–9). The distinction between these two categories is not always sharp and in some instances a normative text becomes a critical text or vice versa, but the distinction alerts us to both the positive and the negative function of the prophet in the politics of God. There are of course prophetic words that are not formally addressed to the king that deal in a rather direct fashion with the conduct of king and state, and these also belong to the prophetic critique of the kings.

One such text (Amos 7:10–17), between prophet and priest rather than prophet and king, identifies sharply the issues raised by the turn toward monarchy and the development of the state. How could a covenant people become a nation state? Or how could a people who understood themselves to be brought into being by divine gift and who saw their destiny as wholly shaped and led by God, their true king, function as a national state led by a permanent human king with the power of government fully in his hands? What did the term "Israel" primarily designate—a covenant people in obedience to the will and purpose of the God of Israel as discerned and proclaimed by its leaders or a nation among the nations vying for power, wealth, and security? The confusion about this is readily apparent in the conversation between Amaziah the priest and Amos the prophet:

> Then Amaziah the priest of Bethel sent to Jeroboam king of Israel saying, "Amos has conspired against you in the midst of the house of Israel; the land is not able to bear all his words. For thus Amos has said,
> "Jeroboam shall die by the sword, and Israel must go into exile away from his land."
> And Amaziah said to Amos, "O seer, go, flee away to the land of Judah, and eat bread there, and prophesy there; but never again prophesy at Bethel, for it is the king's sanctuary, and it is a temple of the kingdom."
> Then Amos answered Amaziah, "I am no prophet, nor a prophet's son; but I am a herdsman, and a dresser of sycamore trees, and the Lord took me from following the flock, and the Lord said to me, 'Go, prophesy to my people Israel.'
> "Now therefore hear the word of the Lord.
> You say, 'Do not prophesy against Israel,
> and do not preach against the house of Isaac.'
> Therefore thus says the Lord:
> 'Your wife shall be a harlot in the city,
> And your sons and your daughters shall fall by the sword,
> and your land shall be parceled out by line;
> you yourself shall die in an unclean land,
> and Israel shall surely go into exile away from its land.' "

While much attention to this passage has been focused on Amos' self-understanding as a prophet, described in vv.14–15, the larger reality of the text is a *conflict of perspectives*. The protagonists in this conflict are identified immediately. On the one side is Amaziah, priest

[3]I prefer the term "normative" to "ideal" because the latter suggests the prophets were indicating the way kingship in Israel should be but never could be. In fact they were giving very specific words about the divine intention for the human ruler.

at the national shrine at Bethel, and the king Jeroboam II, to whom he reports; on the other side is Amos, sometime prophet from the south, and Yahweh, the God of Israel, who has sent Amos. The conflict can be presented rather sharply in schematic fashion:

| Amaziah's perspective (vv.10–13) | vs. | Amos's perspective (vv.14–17) |
|---|---|---|
| –*Jeroboam* is King | | –The *Lord* is king |
| –"Thus *Amos* has said" (vs.11) | | –"Thus says *the Lord*" (v.17) |
| –"Jeroboam shall die by the sword" (vs.11) | | –"I (the Lord) will rise against the house of Jeroboam with the sword" (v.9) |
| –"*Amos* has conspired against you" (v.10) | | –"*The Lord* took me . . . and *the Lord* said to me, 'Go, prophesy' (v.15) |
| –"house of Israel" (v.10) | | –"my people" (v.15) |
| –Amaziah claims authority over Amos | | –"The Lord took me . . . and the Lord said to me, 'Go prophesy . . ." (v. 15) |
| –Amos should prophesy in *Judah* (v.12) | | –"Go prophesy to my people *Israel*" (v.15) |
| –Bethel is the king's sanctuary and a temple of the kingdom (v.13) | | –"Bethel is the Lord's sanctuary (implicit) |
| –Amaziah threatens Amos (flee) (v.12) | | –Amos announces judgment on Amaziah (vv.16–17) |
| –Amaziah said to Amos, 'Go' " (v.12) | | –The Lord said to me, 'Go' " (v.15) |

The two perspectives are that of the state and that of the covenant people. Amaziah's words present a view of the northern kingdom totally as a nation state whose ruler is the king. Amos speaks of and to a covenant people whose ruler is understood to be in fact the Lord. Although Amaziah is chief priest at the principal place where the Lord was worshipped in Israel, his total concern is not for the will and worship of the Lord but for the safety and preservation of the king and the state. He thus perceives Amos' oracles condemning the national life and announcing judgment on king and people as a threat to the welfare of king and state rather than words from the Lord. He sees Amos not as emissary of the Lord but conspirator against the king, a legitimate concern for a protector of the throne if one looks back on the history of prophecy in the northern kingdom and the role of various prophets in dethroning kings. Amos has indeed announced Jeroboam's violent death and the imminent exile of the people. But in his concern for king and state Amaziah has "de-theologized" Amos' words and ignored their origin ("Thus says Amos" not "Thus says the Lord"). Preservation of the "house of Israel" is the issue not the obedience of "my people Israel." The religious leadership has become an establishment of the state whose primary concern is to avoid rocking the boat, particularly the ship of state. The temple of the Lord has become the temple of the kingdom, a royal chapel whose modern day equivalent is perhaps best seen in the occasional use of the East Wing of the White House as a presidential chapel where application of that same plumb line of justice and righteousness that Amos saw or pronouncement of equally harsh words of judgment would also be seen as a threat to the state and resisted rather severely. Even as Ahab failed to see that his designation of Elijah as "troubler of Israel" was more appropriately applied to himself, so Amaziah as guardian of throne, state, and national-royal sanctuary has given his allegiance so thoroughly to king and state that he does not perceive that it is he, Jeroboam, and the royal and wealthy establishment in Samaria who threaten the future of Israel.

The encounter between Amaziah the priest and Amos the prophet is, therefore, a reminder of the fact that the prophetic critique of the kings and their administration of the kingdom is not confined to those texts that speak to or about kings. The criticism of officials, princes, priests, and false prophets or prophets of "good" is a part of the critique of the monarchy. Relatively few of the oracles of Micah and Hosea, or even Isaiah and Amos deal directly with the king, but they do speak to and about rulers, leaders, officials of Samaria and Jerusalem who were a part of the royal establishment and the apparatus of the state (for example, Amaziah, or prophets who give the king the good prophecy he seeks) or had access to king and court and thus to wealth and the use of both wealth and influence to increase their personal worth, property, and capacity for a luxurious life, early examples in a long tradition of which Michael Deaver is only the latest example.[4] Then as now the activities of such persons and groups was often legal but, according to the prophetic indictment neither just nor right.[5] In ancient Israel societal life was sufficiently less complex than our own that the way in which this was done legally but at the expense of the less well off was fairly well exposed whereas in contemporary society that is often hidden and more indirect.

There is another feature of this story that is of note for thinking about the prophetic critique of kings, and that is the question of the *locale* of the prophetic ministry. Amos gives us an example of a prophet sent by the Lord from his own land to go preach a word of criticism and judgment in another territory. This is not an incidental fact in Amos' prophecy, as the narrative makes clear. For Amaziah's command to Amos is essentially: If you want to prophesy and criticize, then go back home and do it *there* (the Hebrew is emphatic at this point); but don't do it here in our territory. The passage, therefore, is most interesting for the issue of whether or not it is legitimate to utter a prophetic word in someone else's back yard or must it always be in one's own. Judah was in sad shape at this time also. Isaiah makes that very clear. There was a prophetic role in Judah that Amos could have assumed, and there were other prophets in the northern kingdom roughly contemporary with Amos. Yet God does not tell Amos to prophesy in Judah. Rather the Lord tells this southerner to leave home and go into strange territory, the north, and utter the divine word of judgment there. These circumstances suggest that the prophetic critique was not to be understood as parochial or provincial. No area was excluded from the word of judgment and no individual precluded from being the Lord's messenger. The issue was not whether someone had a right to utter a prophetic word in a particular context but whether the people of God would listen, repent, and obey.

The substance of Amos' critique against the northern kingdom was the absense of justice and righteousness in the land. But the substantial issue that is central to his encounter with Amaziah is *the authority of God over the state and the responsibility of king and leaders to be obedient to the word and will of the Lord.* In this instance, the "Thus says the Lord" that introduced Amos' oracles was no longer being heard. It was not the word and will of the Lord that Amaziah was concerned to preserve but the state and the state religion represented in the person of the king and the structure of the state sanctuary ("temple of the kingdom"). Amaziah is apparently chief priest, one set apart to the Lord. In fact he is set apart rather to Jeroboam and the state. The problem was not *a priori* the state, but its existence under a ruler with full power and large economic resources created the situation in which authoirty came to be seen as absolute. The danger and ultimate damnation for king and subordinates was

[4]In *Jesaja und die Politik* (Munchen: Chr. Kaiser Verlag, 1976) Walter Dietrich elaborates at length the relationship of the development of the state and the monarchy to the social sickness of eighth century Judah and its class society that was attacked by Isaiah (pp. 25–37) and suggests reasons why that being the case, more of the prophetic indictments are not aimed directly at the kings themselves (pp. 36–37).

[5]On the conflict between legality and righteousness see the important article by J. L. Mays, "Justice: Perspectives from the Prophetic Tradition," *Interpretation*, 37 (1983), pp. 12–14. This article has contributed much to my thinking about this topic.

that they would forget who was true Lord of the nation and what their proper obedience was, centering their efforts not on heeding the divine word but on preserving the state, its institutions, and the status quo.

The resistance of the king to the authority of God and the direction of the prophetic word of the Lord was thus a significant aspect of the prophetic critique. It is reflected generally in several accounts of the efforts of kings to stop the prophetic word. One thinks, for example, of Jehoiakim's disdainful cutting and burning of the scroll of Jeremiah's oracles. *Disobedience of the divine instruction* is specifically the substance of the prophetic critique in two cases where judgment is announced upon kings, both of them having to do with the stipulations of holy war. In 1 Samuel 15 Saul is denounced for having failed to carry out the *ḥērem* against Amalek as instructed. Saul acknowledges that the issue is obedience when he says that he has "transgressed the commandment (lit. "mouth") *of the Lord* and your words, because I feared the people and *obeyed their voice*." (v.24). The prophetic judgment speech specifically identifies obedience as the delight of the Lord more than sacrifice and rebellion and stubbornness as the equal to divination and idolatry. Saul's punishment corresponds to his sin.[6] The one who rejects the word of the divine king is rejected as human king. This is more than just an example of poetic justice, which indeed it is. Proper functioning in the role of the human ruler depends entirely upon the guidance and direction given by the divine ruler, through torah or prophetic word. Disobedience of the rules of holy war is also the grounds for the sentence of death pronounced on Ahab (1 Kings 20:42). Once again failure to obey the divine command to carry out the *ḥērem* (Deut. 20:16–18) produces talionic punishment, as king and people must take Ben-Hadad's place under the ban.

It would not take many other examples to underscore the way in which the matter of royal disdain for or disobedience of the lord's instruction is fundamental to the prophetic critique of the kings. As in the two examples just cited, 1 Samuel 15 and 1 Kings 20, one discerns also that the specifics of royal misconduct evoking prophetic condemnation tend to fall into certain categories. The one just described has to do with the *conduct of war.* Contrary to contemporary sensibilities but consistent with Deuteronomic law, the prophets criticize the kings for merciful acts of accommodation toward captured kings and armies who were to have been utterly destroyed. While we might be inclined to change the rules, we must not fail to see that the conduct of war was not haphazard under the divine government, that there were rules and directions for its conduct to which the human ruler was subject. The oracles of Amos against the neighboring states of Israel (Chs. 1 and 2) are [entirely] (apart from the Judah oracle) indictments against those nations for brutality, betrayal, and harsh conduct against Israel *and other nations* in military conquests.

The conduct of war by the kings, however, is part of the larger sphere of international relations and politics, and prophets addressed kings in other facets of this area of their responsibility as well. The classic case is that of Isaiah *vis a vis* Ahaz and Hezekiah during the time of the Syro-Ephraimite coalition (Ahaz) and later when Sennacherib moved against the western part of his empire, including Judah (Hezekiah). The encounter with Ahaz in Isaiah 7 sets the tone that sounded consistently throughout this prophet's career. The Judaean king, fearful at the move of the kings of Syria and Israel against Jerusalem to force Judah to join it against Assyria and to replace Ahaz with a king of their own choosing, decided to call for help from the Assyrian king, Tiglath Pileser III. The divine word through the prophet was that this move would be first of all bad faith (vv. 4–17) and secondly bad politics (vv.18–25). The king is spoken of (v.2) and addressed (v.13) as "house of David," a title that implies all that is carried in the Davidic promises, God's promise to maintain

[6]Cf. P. D. Miller, Jr. *Sin and Judgment in the Prophets* (Chico, California: Scholars Press, 1982), pp. 85–86.

the throne of David forever. With Isaiah in the encounter is his son Shear-yashub, whose presence is a sign to Ahaz that by his actions he has the power to settle the ambiguity of the child's name, whether it will be a name of judgment, that is, "Only a remnant shall return," or a name of hope, "A remnant shall return." In sarcastic tones the doom of Damascus and Ephraim and their kings is announced, and Ahaz is called to trust in the power of the Lord and demonstrate the spiritual courage and fearlessness necessary if king and nation are to endure the machinations and international politics of the states around them (vv.4 and 9).

In this case the prophet initially simply set the divine assurance before the Davidic ruler, who had no guarantee of continuing survival and rule except the promises of God given long ago and reconfirmed in the words of the prophet. The prophetic message is consistent with the instruction that came to earlier leaders of the people: Faith is directed toward the promises of God. It called for an action that seemed to the king noncoordinate with the circumstances (but see below). It was ultimately a call to Ahaz to declare who was his God. His only security was in regarding the Lord as secure and in manifesting a corresponding human courage. The decision before him was to put aside his trust in Assyrian power and trust in the power that had guided this people throughout its history.

The essential word of this prophet to both Ahaz and Hezekiah was that Judah was not to play the game of power politics, finding its salvation in alliances with one or more powers against another power. The nation's only hope lay in the Lord. The word of the Lord to Isaiah made it clear that going to Egypt or Assyria for help and binding Judah in military alliances was not only bad faith but also bad politics. To call for help from Tiglath Pileser against Syria and Israel was like letting a lion in the house to save oneself against the wolf. The two smaller nations confronting Judah would go under before Assyrian might, but Assyria's presence on the scene was an even greater threat. Clearly it was possible to view the political scene differently. The king and his counselors did so consistently. But the prophetic word was both right and wise. When Ethiopian and Egyptian ambassadors came to Jerusalem for discussion about an alliance against Assyria at the time of the rebellion of Ashdod in 713 B.C., the prophet declared in word (18:1–6) and symbolic action that such an alliance was the way to destruction, for the Egyptians and Ethiopians would end up in exile.

In Isaiah 28, 30, and 31 the prophetic word sounds the same note when Judah was faced with the threat of Sennacherib in 705–01 B.C. The problem was twofold: a.) king and counselors did not look to the Lord for help but relied upon their own plans and the military equipment of other nations; and b.) the help of Egypt was "worthless and empty" (30:7), bringing "neither help nor profit but shame and disgrace" (30:5).[7] Isaiah's demand was not for a passive inactivity and acceptance of one's fate, but a genuine trust in the deeds and purposes of the Lord. It was not in all the frantic political activity and intrigue, which was ultimately futile for that little country, that Judah could find her salvation but in returning to the Lord, that is, in seekng the Lord's will and in confident trust in the Lord rather than the purposes and power of other nations. Otto Kaiser suggests quite forthrightly that this call to trust in the Lord's word and way is consistent with a political realism:[8] "Isaiah shows that trust in God and clear, sober political thought are not irreconcilable, and that the person who takes God into account in good and ill can assess reality."[9]

[7]It is interesting to see in the Rabshakeh's address to Jerusalem at the time of Sennacherib's siege that he also posed the issue in terms of trust (the verb *bāṭah* and its cognates appear six times in his speech) and claimed with the same vigor as Isaiah that Egypt was a weak reed (2 Kings 18:19–35).

[8]On the various points of view in the history of modern scholarship about whether Isaiah's word was realistic or utopian from a political perspective, see Dietrich, *Jesaja und der Politik*, pp. 247–55.

[9]O. Kaiser, *Isaiah 13–39* (Philadelphia: Westminster), p. 286.

A similar criticism of the resort to international alliances is sounded by Hosea in the northern kingdom and often on similar grounds[10] (e.g. 5:8–6:6, 7:11–12, 15–16; 8:8–10). As a spokesman of the Lord he condemned their resort to international intrigue as a way to solve their problems rather than turning to the Lord of Israel. He saw the conflicts between Judah and Israel as a violation of the kinship and covenantal relationship. The abandonment of a generally neutral stance and an unwillingness to risk dependence on the Lord's protection as the nations fought around and over them became a betrayal of the relationship with their God and a sure sign of the coming of divine judgment.

The responsibility of the kings for *providing security and safety* for their people was crucial and a part of the definition of kingship in the more normative texts (e.g. Jer. 23:4–7; 33:14–16; Psalm 72:1–7; see below). Indeed it was generally a characteristic of the ideal of kingship in the ancient Near East. From the prophetic perspective, that security was not found in building up arms and armies or in various kinds of international alliances. Indeed the prophets were critical of both. The prophets who spoke most about international alliances, Isaiah and Hosea, condemned them at every point and on several grounds. The development of a strong military power and fortifications was not a part of the prophetic norm for kingship, and efforts in that direction were criticized in scathing and sarcastic terms usually because they reflected, in human terms, a failure of nerve and, in theological terms, a lack of trust. Isaiah best represents this perspective, as the following quotations suggest:

> In that day you looked to the weapons of the House of the Forest, and you saw that the breaches of the city of David were many, and you collected the waters of the lower pool, and you counted the houses of Jerusalem, and you broke down the houses to fortify the wall. You made a reservoir between the two walls for the water of the old pool. But you did not look to him who did it, or have regard for him who planned it long ago (22:8b–11)

> You said, "No! We will speed upon horses,"
> therefore you shall speed away;
> and, "We will ride upon swift steeds,"
> there your pursuers shall be swift. (30:16)

> Woe to those who go down to Egypt for help
> and rely on horses,
> who trust in chariots because they are many
> and in horsemen because they are very strong,
> but do not look to the Holy One of Israel
> or consult the Lord (31:1)

In the famous swords into ploughshares speech of Isaiah 2 and Micah 4 the prophetic insistence on not relying on arms is stated positively, and eschatologically. The weapons of war have no place in the kingdom of God.

The narrative of Micaiah ben Imlah's prophecy to the kings of Israel and Judah is instructive for separating royal military enterprises and coalitions from the security and place of the people. The true prophecy of Micaiah was a word of judgment and doom against the king of Israel. Its result, however, was the return of the people to their land in peace (1 Kings 22:17). The destinies of king and people were not always separable, but in this case they clearly were. Ahab's death was a judgment for his violation of the ancient and covenantal canons of justice in the Naboth affair. The defeat and death of the unjust king cut the people loose from the death and destruction of war to go home in peace.

It is clear from the prophetic texts as a whole, the more critical and the more normative, that security and safety for the people were brought about by a different kind of royal activity

[10]See the comment of J. L. Mays: "Neither prophet had any patience with the frantic plots and conspiracies by which the reigning kings sought to save themselves" (*Hosea* [Philadelphia: Westminster, 1969], p. 289).

altogether. The key to security in the land was *the maintenance of justice and righteousness*, a responsibility that fell first and foremost upon the king (e.g. Ezek. 34:1–6). This more than resistance to foreign kings was the way to shalom. Prophets spoke out against oppression from outside and announced the judgment of God against those rulers of other nations who oppressed Israel. Their cry, however, was justice within more than liberty from outside forces. The latter is clearly there either implicitly or explicitly, for example, Isaiah 58:6, but in this as in other instances the issue was more internal oppression and bondage than liberation from external oppressors. It was after the destruction of Jerusalem, when the monarchy was no more, that the note of liberation from foreign rule sounded with some force.

Three texts clustered together in Jeremiah's prophecies illustrate the primacy of justice and righteousness in the king's responsibilities:

> And to the house of the king of Judah say, "Hear the word of the Lord, O house of David! Thus says the Lord:
>
> 'Execute justice in the morning,<br>
> and deliver from the hand of the oppressor<br>
> the one who has been robbed,<br>
> lest my wrath go forth like fire,<br>
> and burn with none to quench it,<br>
> because of your evil doings.'<br>
> (Jer. 21:11–12)
>
> Thus says the Lord: "Go down to the house of the king of Judah, and speak there this word, and say, 'Hear the word of the Lord, O king of Judah, who sit on the throne of David, you and your servants, and your people who enter these gates. Thus says the Lord: Do justice and righteousness, and deliver from the hand of the oppressor the one who has been robbed. Do no wrong or violence to the alien, the fatherless, and the widow nor shed innocent blood in this place. For if you will indeed obey this word, then there shall enter the gates of this house kings who sit on the throne of David, riding in chariots and on horses, they, and their servants, and their people. But if you will not heed these words, I swear by myself, says the Lord, that this house shall become a desolation.' " (Jer. 22:1–5)
>
> Woe to the one who builds his house<br>
> by unrighteousness,<br>
> and his upper rooms by injustice;<br>
> who makes his neighbor serve him for nothing,<br>
> and does not give him his wages;<br>
> who says, 'I will build myself a great house<br>
> with spacious upper rooms,'<br>
> and cuts out windows for it,<br>
> paneling it with cedar<br>
> and painting it with vermilion.<br>
> Do you think you are a king<br>
> because you compete in cedar?<br>
> Did not your father eat and drink<br>
> and do justice and righteousness?<br>
> Then it was well with him.<br>
> He judged the cause of the poor and needy;<br>
> then it was well.<br>
> Is not this to know me?<br>
> says the Lord.<br>
> But you have eyes and heart<br>
> only for your dishonest gain,<br>
> for shedding innocent blood,<br>
> and for practicing oppression<br>
> and violence." (Jer. 22:13–17)

These texts are criticisms of the monarchy for two failings that are really sides of a single coin: a.) economic exploitation and oppression and b.) failure to support and give justice to widow, orphan, resident, alien, and the needy. In his seminal study of justice in the prophetic tradition James Mays has pointed to the centrality of the economic issue, centering around access to land and its productivity, in the prophetic message. What the prophets attacked was the accumulation of landed estates and the wealth derived therefrom in an increasingly upper class.

> Those who lost their land were deprived of status and material support. They had to become slaves or wage laborers to live. The leverage employed was the administrative apparatus of the monarchy and of the courts where all social conflict in Israel was settled. The rights of the widow, the fatherless, and the weak to protection against the economic process were widely ignored. The result was a growing differentiation between rich and poor.[11]

The bases for this "early capitalism" were laid or institutionalized with the monarchy and the social and administrative structure that grew up with it.

> Kings had appropriated land for the partial support of this administrative class, but they were left to some degree to manage their own support. They needed a basic capital to allow them to serve the crown. As officials they also had the opportunity to gain from international trade. Their emergence created a group who had a vested interest in the accummulation of land and goods as capital. They were not originally an economic class, but they soon became one.[12]

The direct involvement and responsibility of the king for such an economic state of affairs is signalled by Jeremiah, who clearly labeled it oppression (21:12; 22:17; cf. 21:3) and regarded it as a violation of the norms of kingship (22:15) as well as the contributing reason for the kings' downfall (21:12c; 22:15c and 16b; cf 22:4–5). The *tôb* or "good" of the king depended not upon administration, in the sense of management, but upon the administration and maintenance of justice, particularly in the economic sphere.

The Naboth story in 1 Kings 21 is the classic case of monarchical arrogance and the uses of the justice system by the state to do personal and economic violence to its citizens. Several interpreters have pointed out how the story has uncovered the issue of *adjacency* as an incentive to greed and the assumption of special rights on the part of the powerful. The significance of the ancient (or contemporary) landmarks fades before the sense of a special claim or right, "a first option," on adjacent territory because it will make a better vegetable garden. Jezebel expresses the royal arrogance explicitly when she says to the king: "You now are the one who exercises kingship over Israel. Go eat, and let your heart be cheerful. *I* will give you the vineyard of Naboth the Jezreelite" (1 Kings 21:7). Isaiah saw the extension of the adjacency factor into a general tendency when he cried:

> "Woe to those who join house to house,
> who add field to field" (Isaiah 5:8)

as did Micah:

> "They covet fields and seize them;
> and houses and take them away;
> they oppress a man and his house,
> a man and his inheritance" (Micah 2:2)

Jezebel's kangaroo court demonstrates in dramatic fashion the royal manipulation of the system of justice for economic gain and oppression. The prophetic word is pointed: "Thus says the Lord, 'Have you killed [The commandment against murder is in view here.] and

[11]Mays, "Justice," p. 9.
[12]*Ibid.* pp. 9–10.

also taken possession?' " Violence in pursuit of economic gain, the subordination of the judicial process to the interests of the rich and powerful, chief of whom is the king—this is what Jeremiah and his prophetic compatriots inveighed against. In the Deuteronomistic History the Naboth story is the classic illustration of royal injustice and the triumph of power over law, of economic oppression over social good.

Naboth is one of the few names preserved to us of the victims of royal power cut loose from God's demand for righteousness and justice as the political norm for the kingdom God rules.[13] Few others are named but their status is often indicated. They are those who cannot take responsibility for power because they do not have power. They are the widow, the orphan, the resident alien, and the poor. It is salutary to have the Naboth incident in the record as a reminder that *any* citizen was subject to royal injustice, but the Jeremiah texts quoted above indicate clearly who are the primary victims of the development of a class society as an outgrowth of a state system where economic rather than justice factors are the touchstone of those in power. Both the tradition of Israelite law reaching back to its earlier stages (e.g. Exod. 22:21–22, 25–26; 23:6–12) and the nature of Israel's God as one who heard the cries of the weak and powerless and in compassion came to their aid (e.g. Exod. 2:23–25; 3:7–8; 22:23–24, 27; Amos 7:2–3, 5–6; Psalm 82; the lament psalms, Isa 5:16 etc.) place conduct toward widow, orphan, sojourner, and poor as a fundamental criterion for the practice of righteousness and a just society. Such normative prophetic texts as Isaiah 9:7 and 11:3–5 join the prophetic critique in identifying justice and righteousness, particularly for the poor, as a sine qua non for the practice of kingship.[14] That such persons as these—widow, orphan, resident alien, and poor—are the primary victims of economic injustice and disparity is signalled not only by the witness of Scripture but equally dramatically by statistics from our own wealthy, democratic society established on biblical principles of justice. These categories or their contemporary equivalents continue to be the economic victims in society and in fact meld together. It is the widow (= single woman/mother), orphan (= fatherless child) and resident alien (Hispanic[15]) who make up the poor and live as victims of individual and systemic acts of economic oppression.[16] In such a context a

[13]Paul Lehmann has aptly articulated the interrelationship between God's intention and the work of those who have responsibility for power: "This *righteousness* or justice—in the reciprocity of word and deed (i.e. praxis)—is the making room in this world for the faithfulness of God in being present to and in the midst of human life as help and salvation (deliverance). The righteousness of God *so practiced* effects the displacement of enmity by reconciliation and of oppression by justice." ("The Metaphorical Reciprocity between Theology and Law," *The Journal of Law and Religion*, 3 [1985], p. 189).

[14]One should take note of a similar understanding of kingship in the texts from Ugarit where Danel, the king, administers justice to widow and orphan and Yassib asks his father, Kirta, to step down from the throne because he is no longer able to give justice to such persons.

[15]Both history and present practice suggest that many blacks find themselves in the sojourner-alien-stranger category.

[16]The following quotation from Ruth Sidel, *Women and Children Last* (New York: Viking, 1986), which appeared in a recent issue of *The Charlotte Observer*, gives the devastating statistical facts: Of poor people in the United States today, the vast majority are women and their children. According to the Census Bureau, in 1984, 14.4% of all Americans—33.7 million people—lived below the poverty line. From 1980 to 1984 the number of poor people increased by 4.5 million. For female-headed households in 1984, the poverty rate was 34.5%, a rate five times that for married-couple families. The poverty rate for white female-headed families was 27.1%, for black female-headed families, 51.7%, and for Hispanic families headed by women, 53.4%. The poverty rate for the elderly, most of whom are women, was 12.4% in 1984. Two out of every three poor adults are women, and the economic status of families headed by women is declining.

The impact of women's poverty on the economic status of children is even more shocking. The poverty rate for children under 6 was 24% in 1984; in other words, nearly one out of every four preschool children lived in poverty. In the same year the poverty rate for children living in female-headed households was 53.9%. Among black children, the poverty rate was 70.5%.

national ruler who says, "I don't believe that there is anyone that is going hungry in America simply by reason of denial or lack of ability even. It is by people not knowing where or how to get this help,"[17] sounds like those leaders and officials of Jeremiah's time who said "Peace," "Peace," when there was no peace and sought to heal the wound of God's people lightly (Jer. 6:13–14; 8:10–11).

The normative prophetic texts identify the kings' primary responsibility as the provision among the people of security and shalom wrought out of justice in the land rather than foreign alignments or resistance to foreign rule. (Isa. 9:5–6; 11:1–9; Jer. 23:5–6; 33:15–16). It was only as the weaker members of society were carefully provided for that peace and prosperity could be genuine possibilities. Nowhere is that more directly stated than in Psalm 72 where the prayers for justice and righteousness on the part of the king and peace and prosperity for land and people are all bound up together (vv 1–7). Indeed the very grounds for worldwide acknowledgment of the king's rule are found in the fact that he helps the poor and needy and redeems them from oppression and violence (Psalm 72:12–14; note the casual "for" at the beginning of verse 12).

Particularly in the Deuteronomistic History prophetic voices, who sometimes are mouthpieces for the Deuteronomistic perspective, criticize the king also for *religious faithlessness*, a turning to other gods and forgetting that the Lord alone is God of Israel (1 Kings 11:31–39; 13; 18:18; 2 Kings 21:10–15).[18] In the writing prophets this critique is tied up with the failure to turn to, call upon, and consult the Lord in affairs of state generally (for example, Hosea 7–9; 14: 2–3). The prophets seem to have understood what the kings forgot—Josiah being a notable exception—that the monarchy was a political instrument of the divine rule, the kingdom of God. Its *raison d'etre* was not self-generated or justified by the analogy of other nations. The prophets understood the monarchy as a very penultimate reality whose existence and purposes were to be understood in terms of means rather than ends. Turning away from its ground, monarchy could not and did not long endure, whether such turning was to other nations or to other gods. The ambiguous view of the monarch found in the account of its beginnings (for example 1 Samuel 8:7–8) is reflected in the prophetic indictment of king and people for turning away from the Lord and grounding their confidence in other divine and human kings. Not coincidentally the Deuteronomistic association of royal oppression with royal apostasy is reflected in the accounts of several kings such as Solomon, Ahab, and Manasseh.

Two points in the prophetic critique remain to be identified. Both are to a large degree facets of problems already discussed. One of these is the issue of *example and leadership*. Isaiah's challenge to Ahaz (Isaiah 7) is in a basic way a call to the kind of leadership that is reflected in spiritual courage. Saul in his response to Samuel's judgment speech says: "I have sinned; for I have transgressed the commandment of the Lord and your words, because I feared the people and obeyed their voice" (1 Sam. 15:24). Again the king's weakness is a lack of the courage of leadership and a hesitancy to trust the word of the Lord when it cuts against the grain of human desires and expectation.

One of the ways in which this issue is addressed is with the prophet's frequent use of *shepherd* imagery to speak about the realities and expectations of royal leadership (Micah 5:4; Jer. 10:21; 22:22; 23:1–4; Ezekiel 34). The shepherd is a widespread image for kingship in the ancient Near East. Its use accomplishes two things. It suggests a *pastoral* definition of royal leadership, that is, the responsibility of the ruler to guide, care for, and protect the

[17]This is a statement made by President Reagan to a group of high school students in the summer of 1986.

[18]Huldah's positive prophecy about Josiah because of his penitence and obedience should be included in this list also.

flock, the king's subjects. The imagery also is an effective vehicle for identifying the relationship between the quality of rule or leadership and the consequences for the welfare of the flock (especially Jer. 23:4 and Ezek. 34:2–6).

The matter of royal leadership and example is also at the center of the Deuteronomic law of the king in Deuteronomy 17:14–20,[19] a text either directly under prophetic influence or consistent with that tradition. Three things are to be noted about this text. It places a clear limitation on power to avoid tyranny and the danger of the king assuming the Lord's rule of the people. The perquisites of power—wealth, wives, and military might—are explicitly denied. Royal responsibilities are limited and separated from important functions carried by others. Secondly, all of these restrictions and injunctions also serve to enjoin a full and undivided allegiance to the Lord. Finally, the law of the king places upon that figure the obligations that were incumbent upon every Israelite. The king is to be the model Israelite. That is seen especially in the fact that the essential responsibility of the king is to read and study the law constantly (cf. 6:7 and 10:19) "that he may learn to fear the Lord his God, by keeping all the words of this law and these statutes, and doing them" (v. 19). This is the word that Moses constantly places on all Israel throughout his speeches. The warning "that his heart may not be lifted up" echoes the same warning to Israel in 8:14 even as the prohibition against multiplying silver and gold (v. 17) is reminiscent of the words of 8:13–17 about Israel doing the same thing and then forgetting that it is the Lord who has given the wealth. So also the warning not to "turn aside from the commandment, either to the right and or to the left" is the same as or similar to words addressed to each Israelite (cf. 5:32, 11:28; 17:17; 28:14, 31:29; Josh 23:6) or to other leaders (e.g. Josh 1:7). The fundamental task of the leader of the people, therefore, is to exemplify and demonstrate the true obedience to the Lord for the sake of the well-being of both the dynasty and the kingdom. King and subject share a common goal: to learn to fear the Lord (v. 19).

Related to the question of royal leadership and example is the prophetic critique of the *personal moral behavior of the king*. That is reflected in various ways in the public actions of the kings already discussed, such as, for example, Ahab's "legal" lynching of Naboth. The classic case, however, is David's adultery with Bathsheba and his "military" murder of Uriah, her husband. No more powerful prophetic judgment speech is recorded in the Deuteronomistic History than Nathan's indictment and judgment of David. It is even couched in a parable that speaks of the actions of the rich and powerful against the poor. The tragic events that coursed through the rest of David's story were not the outcome of military events or incompetence. They were the direct result of the moral delinquency of the king. The private morality of the monarch was not a matter of indifference to the prophets or the God who sent them. Exemplary conduct was expected in personal life as much as obedience to the Lord's instruction in public life. As Deuteronomy insisted in conjunction with the prophets, *all* the commandments were enjoined upon the king as much as upon any other citizen.

Despite what has been said above about the close ties between prophecy and kingship—if not always between actual prophets and kings—ties that continue even into the post-exilic period to some degree, it must be recognized that with the fall of Judah and the monarch, voices began to be heard anticipating a future under the rule of the Lord but without king or state. Norbert Lohfink has argued the case for seeing in Dtr I, the primary and pre-exilic edition of the Deuteronomistic History, a view of the history of Israel that largely accepted

[19]On this text in its context see the following studies by Norbert Lohfink: "Die Sicherung der Wirksamkeit des Gotteswortes durch das Prinzip der Schriftlichkeit der Tora und durch das Prinzip der Gewaltenteilung nach den *Ämtergesetzen des Buches Deuterononium (Dt 16, 18#18,22)*, "*Testimonium Veritati: Festschrift fur Bischof Wilhelm Kempf*, hrsg. H. Walter, S. J. (Frankfurt: Verlag Joseph Knecht, 1971), pp. 143–55; *Great Themes of the Old Testament* (Chicago: Franciscan Herald Press, 1982), pp. 55–75.

king, state, and royal ideology without debate while Dtr II, in light of the experience of the downfall of Judah and the exile, placed everything in question without flatly rejecting monarch and state.[20] Instead Dtr II proposed in the Deuteronomic laws of the officials (Deut. 16:20–18:22) as well as 1 Samuel 12 a divine administration that was mediated through the torah and the prophets to those under God's rule, which included both king and people.

While the prophetic voice as a means of divine administration over the human king was surely an early part of the politics of the Israelite state, Lohfink is correct in suggesting a heightening of the critique of monarchy and state in the exile and on the part of Dtr II. He further suggests that a final retouching of the Deuteronomistic History took place in the last years before Cyrus, recognizable most clearly in Deut 4:1–40 and 30:1–10 but also discernible probably in the late insertions in 2 Samuel 7 (vv. 7, 10, 23–24) and 1 Kings 8 (vv. 52–53, 59–60).[21] Here one finds an anticipation of the future but a future that included neither king nor state.

Such a hope was shared by other post-monarchy theologians such as the Priestly writer, the Jeremianic Deuteronomists (so Lohfink) who spoke of the promise of a new covenant (Jer. 31:31–34), and Deutero-Isaiah, who announced that the Davidic prerogatives were handed over to collective Israel (Isa 55:3). One might add to this list exilic sections of Ezekiel, such as 34:11–16. The reality of king and state was not an assumption that all the prophets and writers of later Israel carried into the future. Indeed it became increasingly tenuous, and the voices of those who foresaw a return to the direct rule of Yahweh (e.g. Isaiah 56–66) or a divine rule mediated through a priestly rather than royal line (e.g. Ezekiel 40–48) grew ever louder.

[20]N. Lohfink, *Rückblick im Zorn auf den Staat: Vorlesungen zu ausgewählten Schlüsseltexten der Bücher Samuel und Könige* (Frankfurt am Main: Hochschule Sankt Georgen, 1984).

[21]*Ibid.* pp. 190–95.

# First Corinthians 6:1–11
# An Exegetical Paper

Reginald H. Fuller

1 Τολμᾷ τις ὑμῶν πρᾶγμα ἔχων πρὸς τὸν ἕτερον κρίνεσθαι
ἐπὶ τῶν ἀδίκων καὶ οὐχὶ ἐπὶ τῶν ἁγίων; 2 ἢ οὐκ οἴδατε ὅτι οἱ
ἅγιοι τὸν κόσμον κρινοῦσιν; καὶ εἰ ἐν ὑμῖν κρίνεται ὁ κόσμος,
ἀνάξιοί ἐστε κριτηρίων ἐλαχίστων; 3 οὐκ οἴδατε ὅτι ἀγγέλους
κρινοῦμεν, μήτιγε βιωτικά; 4 βιωτικὰ μὲν οὖν κριτήρια ἐὰν ἔχητε,
τοὺς ἐξουθενημένους ἐν τῇ ἐκκλησίᾳ, τούτους καθίζετε; 5 πρὸς
ἐντροπὴν ὑμῖν λέγω. οὕτως οὐκ ἔνι ἐν ὑμῖν οὐδεὶς σοφός, ὃς
δυνήσεται διακρῖναι ἀνὰ μέσον τοῦ ἀδελφοῦ αὐτοῦ; 6 ἀλλὰ ἀδελ-
φὸς μετὰ ἀδελφοῦ κρίνεται, καὶ τοῦτο ἐπὶ ἀπίστων; 7 ἤδη μὲν
ὅλως ἥττημα ὑμῖν ἐστὶν ὅτι κρίματα ἔχετε μεθ᾽ ἑαυτῶν. διατί
οὐχὶ μᾶλλον ἀδικεῖσθε; διατί οὐχὶ μᾶλλον ἀποστερεῖσθε; 8 ἀλλὰ
ὑμεῖς ἀδικεῖτε καὶ ἀποστερεῖτε, καὶ τοῦτο ἀδελφούς. 9 ἢ οὐκ
οἴδατε ὅτι ἄδικοι θεοῦ βασιλείαν οὐ κληρονομήσουσιν; μὴ πλα-
νᾶσθε· οὔτε πόρνοι οὔτε εἰδωλολάτραι οὔτε μοιχοὶ οὔτε μαλακοὶ
οὔτε ἀρσενοκοῖται 10 οὔτε κλέπται οὔτε πλεονέκται, οὐ μέθυσοι,
οὐ λοίδοροι, οὐχ ἅρπαγες βασιλείαν θεοῦ κληρονομήσουσιν. 11 καὶ
ταῦτά τινες ἦτε· ἀλλὰ ἀπελούσασθε, ἀλλὰ ἡγιάσθητε, ἀλλὰ
ἐδικαιώθητε ἐν τῷ ὀνόματι τοῦ κυρίου Ἰησοῦ Χριστοῦ καὶ ἐν τῷ
πνεύματι τοῦ θεοῦ ἡμῶν.

*Initial Translation from Nestle*

(1) Does any(one) of you dare, when he has a case against another, to go to law before unrighteous persons rather than before the saints? (2) Or do you not know that the saints shall judge the world? And if the world is (to be) judged by (lit. in) you, are you unworthy (to judge) the pettiest of lawsuits? (3) Do you not know that we shall judge angels, to say nothing of matters pertaining to *this* life? (4) If therefore you have lawsuits pertaining to mundane matters (things of this life) are you appointing (making to sit, presumably in judgment) those of no reputation in the church? (5) I say this to put you to shame. Does this mean that there is no wise person among you who will be able to pronounce judgment between his brother (sic)? (6) But brother goes to law with brother, and that in the presence of unbelievers? (7) The very fact therefore that you have lawsuits at all with one another shows there is something wrong with you. Why not rather put up with injustice? Why not rather allow youselves to be defrauded? (8) But you do wrong and defraud, and your brothers at that. (9) Surely you know that the unrighteousness will not inherit the kingdom of God? Do not deceive yourselves; neither fornicators nor idolators nor adulterers nor catamites nor homosexuals, nor covetous persons, not drunkards, not slanderers, not extortioners, shall inherit God's kingdom. (11) And some of you were people of those kinds. But you got yourselves washed, but you were sanctified, but you were justified in the name of the Lord Jesus and in the Spirit of our God.

*Textual Problems*

VERSE 1. *ex* Alexandrinus, P (a later Alexandrian text), and a few minuscules. External evidence suggests this is a later elucidation; it makes no difference in the meaning.

VERSE 2. *ē* (or) at the beginning of the verse is omitted by Claromantanus, Rhegius and the majority of Greek minuscules. Its inclusion seems original and its omission later, despite Vischer's claim that "Es sprechen ebenso gute Gründe für wie wider die Ursprünglichkeit."

*Krinousin*. There were no accents in the earlier MSS (p. 46, Sinaiticus and later Alexandrian texts). However the second hand of Vaticanus accented it as a present tense (*Krínousin*). But the sense seems to require its accentuation as a future (*Krinoûsiv*), since the reference is to future-eschatological judgment. After all, it would be unrealistic to assert that the saints are even now judging the world. Moreover, the future would be in accord with Paul's general apocalyptic orientation in this context.

VERSE 5. Vaticanus has *lalō* in place of *legō*. Vischer reasonably attributes this to assimilation to 1 Corinthians 15:34. In any case no difference of meaning is involved.

*eni* (same verse) Claromontanus, Boernerianus, and two miniscules have *estin* instead of *eni*. External evidence is in favor of the rarer *ouk eni* which does however occur three times in Gal. 3:28 (cf. the ? deutero-Pauline Col. 3:11) and is not un-Pauline.

*oudeis* is apparently omitted by $P^{11}$ (a later papyrus, 7th century) also by the original reading of Claromontanus and by two minuscules. One would suppose that a later scribe balked at the double negative. However, according to Vischer (Nestle is silent on this point) *oudeis* appears in different places: Before *sophos* (Vaticanus, Sinaiticus, three later Alexandrian MSS, Augustine, and Ambrosiaster); after *sophos* in the third hand of Claromontanus, Rhegius, and a few church fathers; while in some texts it is written *oude heis*. All of this makes it probably that *oudeis* was not in the original text.

The phrase *ana meson tou adelphou* while normal in Greek, is difficult if not impossible in other languages and the Vulgate, Boharic and Peshitta add "and (the) brother." The English versions have to resort to various paraphrases. To make some alterations is an exigency of translation.

VERSE 7, $P^{46}$ omits *oun*, as does the original reading of Sinaiticus and of Claromontanus plus some miniscules. It appears in $P^{11}$ (apparently), in the first corrector of Sinaiticus and in the majority of minuscules. Nestle prints it in square brackets. In my opinion the external evidence gives the omission a slight edge, but the phrase *men oun* is common and has a specific meaning (see below).

The singular *krima* is read by Sinaiticus. This changes the meaning from "lawsuits" (a sense which according to BAGD is not otherwise attested) to "sentence." The lack of evidence for the meaning lawsuit is probably the reason for the change to the singular.

VERSE 8. While the early MSS read *touto*, the majority have *tauta*. The external evidence favors the singular.

VERSE 10. *oute* before *methusoi* has earlier attestation ($P^{45}$ and Vaticanus). But Sinaiticus, later Alexandrinus, Claromontanus, and minuscules have *ou*. No difference of meaning is involved whether one reads "nor" or "not."

*ou* is added before *klēronomēsousin* in the majority of MSS, but $P^{46}$, Vaticanus and Sinaiticus make strong evidence of its omission. In any case a double negative would not change the meaning.

VERSE 11. *hēmōv* is added after *kuriou* in Vaticanus, two other later uncials, plus more than eight minuscules, and the Latin, Syriac and Bohairic versions. The addition would conform to the standard liturgical formula and will therefore be secondary. In sum, the variants are of minor significance and do not affect the exegesis.

The problems of punctuation are greater. Do verses 4 and 8 end with periods or with question marks? Editors and commentators vary in their decisions, and exegetical decisions are involved. These will be discussed below.

*Larger Context*

Our pericope occurs in that part of 1 Corinthians where Paul is dealing with oral information which has reached him from Corinth. In chapter 7 he will start to deal with the information brought in a letter from the Corinthians. In this part of the letter he is dealing with more discreditable phenomena at Corinth: factions, sexual immorality, and now litigiousness. Whether all these matters were brought to him by Chloe's people, who reported on the factiousness (1:12) is uncertain. The only connection between our passage and the preceding topic of incest (5:1–5) is the verbal one of *krinei* (5:13)–*krinesthai* (6:1). The ensuing section (6:12–20) also deals with another sexual problem, viz., that of temple prostitution. One would therefore have expected 6:12–20 to follow immediately after 5:13, thus our passage is an interruption of the discussion of sexual problems. For this reason some have taken the *pragma* of v. 1 to involve a marital dispute. But since F. C. Baur[1] an inner connection has been seen between the three sections. All deal with the bad impression the Corinthians are making on their pagan neighbors.

Barrett and Nestle divide the passage into two paragraphs, vv.1–8 and 9–11; Vischer argues for a threefold division, vv. 1–6, 7–8, and 9–11, and RSV 1973 agrees. A two fold division however is preferable. In vv. 1–8 Paul begins by stating the problem at Corinth, viz. litigousness, manifested particularly in their having legal disputes arbitrated by non-Christians (v.1). In 2–3 he explains why such conduct is unworthy of Christians, and then proceeds to offer two alternative methods of handling the situation in v. 5 and v. 7, and after each alternative suggestion he returns to complain of their current behavior (vv. 6 and 8). In the second section the Apostle reminds the Corinthians that all immoral conduct, litigousness included, excludes from the kingdom of God and is inconsistent with their present eschatalogical status. Thus vv. 1–8 deal with the issue in hand, vv. 9–10 put that issue in the broader context of unethical conduct.

We will now discuss the passage verse by verse.

*First Section*

Verse 1. *Tolma*. Bauer gives two meanings for this verb. The first is the ordinary sense of "to dare," the second is "to presume to do something" and for this passage he suggests "can any of you bring himself to . . .?" I would suggest, "Has any of you the gall to . . ." As Barrett observes, it is a strong expression, and as Paul is going to say in v. 5, he is trying to create in the Corinthians a sense of shame at their conduct.

*pragma echein pros* is according to Vischer a technical expression, "to have a lawsuit with someone." According to Bauer it is found in this sense in Oxyrrhynchus papyrus 743:19 (dated 1st century B.C.E.), and according to Vischer *"ist in der Profanliteratur* mehrmals belegt."

The *adikoi* and the *hagioi* are respectively unbelievers and church members. Neither word is intended in a moralizing sense. The *adikoi* are those who have not responded in faith to the Gospel, are not justified by the grace of God and therefore are outside the eschatological community of faith. The *hagioi* are consecrated to God in baptism and therefore are members of the eschatological community. The *heterovn* is obviously a fellow-member of

[1]F. C. Baur, *Theologische Jahrbücher* (1852), 9, cited by Vischer.

the congregation. The Corinthians are washing their dirty linen in public! *Krinesthai* in the middle or passive means "to go to law"—but whether this actually means to go before a pagan court in our present context must be decided from the meaning of *kathizesthai* in v. 4.

VERSE 2. With the opening phrase, "Do you not know," Paul reminds the Corinthians of an item in which they had been instructed in their catechesis, viz., that at the End the eschatological community will participate with the Son of man in the last judgment as judges over the unbelieving world (*kosmos*). This belief was taken over from Jewish apocalyptic into early Christianity. For the presence of this expectation in pre-Christian Judaism see Dan. 7:22 *kai to krima edōkev hagiois* and Wisd. 3:8, *krinousin ta ethnē* and cf. Enoch 38:5 etc. (Billerbeck 3:365 *ad loc.*). For NT parallels, indicating that this was a feature of early Christian teaching, see: Matt. 19:28 and Luke 22:30, where the Twelve will judge the twelve tribes of Israel. 2 Tim. 2:12 says that the believers will reign with the Messiah in the end-time kingdom, while similar ideas appear in Revelation (2:26–27; 20:4). *Shpht* means both "to judge" and "to reign." But, as Vischer pertinently observes, only in Paul and only here does this future hope have consequences in the present: Christians have the authority to judge within the community already here and now. *Kosmos* here denotes the nations of the unbelieving world. *ev humin*. The *en* is characterized by Conzelmann as a "forensic *en*" and he cites from Ditt., *Syll* 1:195, lines 57–59, the phrase *krinesthō en Athenaiois*, "Let him be judged *by* the Athenians." From this it would seem that Vischer's assertion that the use of *ev* as an equivalent of *hypo* in a sense *"sonst nicht gebräuchlich"* is not correct. Bauer gives two alternative translations for *anaxioi*: "not good enough" or "not competent." The second is to be preferred here. Bauer translates the rest of the clause: "to settle trivial cases." "To settle" is not in the Greek, but it adequately expresses the sense of the genitive. Although *kriteriov* normally means court or tribunal, it has the same meaning as it has in v. 4, namely, "lawsuit" (Vischer). We shall however argue that here it is not an actual lawsuit in a recognized state court but only private, informal, though binding, arbitration. *Elachistōv* "trivial" or "petty" suggests that the cases involved were not sexual transgressions, but cases involving money matters, such as uncollected debts. In Judaism a distinction was drawn between such matters and more serious crimes, the latter being submitted to qualified judges (see below). It is trivial money matters that were a stake at Corinth.

VERSE 3. This enhances the eschatological situation depicted in v. 2. The believers will judge not only the unbelieving nations but even angels. Some commentators have taken angels here to mean the angels of the nations, often understood in a demonic sense. This is one of the passages on which Karl Barth built up his peculiar doctrine of the state and which O. Cullmann modified.[2] Taken in this way, it could have direct connections with the pagan courts to which the Corinthians are supposedly having recourse: so far from submitting to pagan courts, the believers will actually be judging the demonic powers that lie behind them and control them. But Vischer's criticism of this interpretation is pertinent: *"Wenn aber Paulus daran gedacht haben sollte, hätte er seinen Gedanken deutlicher zum Ausdruck bringen müssen."* Neither in pre-Christian Judaism nor in the NT itself is there any evidence for the belief that the eschatological community will judge the angels. However, the OT, intertestamental apocalyptic and the NT know of the idea that the (fallen) angels will be judged.[3] Also, Jesus' promise to the "little flock" (Luke 12:32) implies the picture painted here by Paul: the community will share the judging functions of the Son of Man at the end.

*biotika* are cases involving money and property. Such cases, as we have already mentioned, were distinguished in rabbinic Judaism from capital cases. The former could be arbitrated

[2] O. Cullmann, *Christ and Time*, Tr. F. V. Filson: Philadelphia, Westminster, 1960, 191–210, esp. 199, 202.
[3] Vischer cites Apoc. Bar. 51:12; Jub. 1:24f., and finds the same idea behind 1 Pet. 1:52; Eph. 3:10; 1 Cor. 2:8.

either by three persons, or by a single qualified judge acting alone, or even by a single lay person when both parties agreed beforehand to abide by the decision. On the other hand, a capital process required a formal session of twenty-three authorized judges. It is clear from this that the type of case envisaged at Corinth falls into the first of these two categories. *elachistōn* in v. 2 refers to the same category. T. W. Manson[4] reasonably suggests that the objections to the use of pagan arbitrators emanated from Jewish Christians who were familiar with synagogue practice. This would suggest also that the offenders were Gentile Christians. *Mētige*, which had originally meant, "not alone," "much less," had by NT times developed the meaning of "not to mention" (Liddell-Scott-Jones).

VERSE 4. When you have cases involving matters of money or property, suggests Paul, the procedure you are following is to "appoint" those of "least regard in the church." There are several problems here. First, should the sentence conclude, as in Nestle with a question mark? Is it a statement of what they are actually doing? Or is it an imperative: this is what you ought to be doing? The decision on this question involves also the meaning of *exouthenē menous ev ekklēsia*. If the sentence is interrogatory, then it will mean: are you appointing non-Christians, people whom you otherwise despise, as arbitrators? The sense is, do you have nothing better to do than that (Vischer)? There are two difficulties here. Would Paul refer to pagans as "those who are despised," held in contempt by the church? Second, can *kathizein* mean "appoint to an office not already held," and if so, could Christians so "appoint" pagan officers? If it is a question, it must mean Gentiles, for Paul would not ask them whether they are doing something which from verse 1 we know they are not—the judges or arbitrators to whom they were resorting were *adikoi* i.e., Gentiles. Can we then take it as an imperative? If we do, then *exouthenēmenous* will have to be taken in the sense of despised members of the Christian community. But this would fly in the face of Paul's constant theme in 1 Corinthians, namely that all members of the body, however different their functions and status, are equal in dignity (1 Cor. 12:4–31). If we take it as a statement, then again it must refer to what they are actually doing, viz., resorting to pagans to judge their cases. In deciding the correct meaning we have to bear in mind that according to the next verse Paul is saying something which will make them ashamed of their conduct (v.5). Probably the best procedure would be to take it with Nestle as an interrogative sentence and understand it to mean: "Are you actually appointing to adjudicate your cases the very people whom as church people you otherwise hold in contempt?"

A further problem is the meaning of *kathizete*. Properly it should denote "make to sit," and therefore appoint to an office, which is what Bauer suggests here, "appoint as judge." But that would be too formal. Christians are hardly nominating pagans for a judicial office which they did not have before. In that case it might be equivalent to "resort to" judges already appointed by the (pagan) state, an interpretation which would indeed have far-reaching implications for the problem with which we are concerned in this symposium, that of Church and state. It would, however, bring it into conflict with the positive doctrine of the state in Rom. 13. It is this problem that led Stein[5] to take *kathizete* in the sense of "to appoint not an already acting judge, but appoint a *Jewish* lay person," i.e., resorting to the synagogue and its existing provisions for arbitration. I do not think that this is possible, and Conzelmann *ad loc.* rejects it out of hand. However, Stein may have a valid insight into what was going on at Corinth. This, I suggest, is that the (Gentile) Christians were resorting to their pagan neighbors (not officially appointed judges) and inviting them to act as arbitrators. That is, they were following something like the Jewish practice noted

[4]"The Cephas party speaking from the Jewish Christian standpoint." Manson, 198.
[5]Stein, 89.

above, but using pagan lay persons rather than Jewish ones. Paul is putting them to shame by reminding them that the very people they were resorting to were of low account for the particular task which they were expecting of them since, in the coming eschatological judgment, they would themselves be judging these very same lay people. This interpretation removes our passage from any negative assessment of the Roman judicial system, and therefore keeps it from conflicting with Romans 13.

VERSE 5. After saying that he has written the previous verse to shame them, Paul proceeds to give the first of two suggested solutions. This is that they should appoint a *sophos* from among their own number as arbitrator. The word *sophos* ironically recalls the Corinthian boast about their *sophia* in chapters 1–4. Paul recommends setting up the same procedure in the Corinthian congregation as had been customary in the synagogue. A *sophos* then would be the Christian equivalent of a rabbi or as Barrett suggests, a *hakam*, a scholar less qualified than a rabbi. This strengthens our interpretation of verse 4. In neither verse is Paul envisaging a formal judicial process, whether pagan or Jewish, or intra-Christian. In both cases he has in mind private arbitration, only prefering that the arbitrator(s) chosen should be Christian rather than pagan, *hagioi* rather than *adikoi* (v. 1) or *apistoi* (v.6). Jewish practices in such matters will be indicated in an excursus from Vischer at the end of this paper.

VERSE 6 serves as a bridge to Paul's second and preferred alternative solution. It repeats the point already made in verse 1 but emphasizes that what they are doing pits brother against brother, Christians against fellow Christians.

VERSE 7. *ēdē mei oun holōs* is well translated by Barrett: "In fact, (*men ouv*) it is already (*ēdē*) nothing but (*holōs*). . . . " *hēttēma* can mean either a defect, a deficiency, or a defeat. Conzelmann takes it to mean "fault" (i.e., defect). W. B. Harris, quoted by Barrett (cf. Bauer) prefers "defeat": "from the truest Christian standpoint you have already lost the case by bringing it in to the courts at all" (Harris, cited by Barrett, cf. Moffatt). The very fact that you have such conflicts about money matters shows that you are not living up to the highest standard of the Christian ethic: "Why do you not rather put up with injustices, why do you not rather allow yourself to be defrauded?" (7bc). Paul clearly echoes the teaching of the Sermon of the Mount (Matt. 5:39–42), but as usual he does not quote directly from the Jesus tradition. Why not? The reason for this has been detected by John Piper:[6]

> The paraenetic tradition of the early church does not employ these sayings of Jesus (viz., Matt. 5:39–42) directly. His commands were so specific that they were apparently unsuitable for moral instruction in the congregation. Even so, his commands control the development of the paraenesis . . . Suffer wrong and be defrauded rather than go to court, especially with a brother (1 Cor. 6:7).

VERSE 8 also serves as a bridge to the next section, which draws further upon catechetical material.

VERSE 9. "Do you not know" indicates that Paul is here calling to mind something they already knew. E. Dinkler has pointed out the probability that in this section Paul is drawing upon a primitive pattern of catechesis used in the baptismal practice of the early Hellenistic communities. He finds the clue to the understanding of this section in the *locus classicus* for the Pauline treatment of baptism in Rom. 6:3–11. *Adikos* is used here in a moral sense (contrast v. 1): the difference indicates Paul's use of a source. It is further to be noted that the term "kingdom of God" is rare in Paul, usually occurring in paraenetic passages where the Apostle is citing catechetical material (see Rom. 14:17; Gal. 5:21). This is an entry saying.[7] Conzelmann states that "the original apocalyptic sense of the concept 'kingdom of

[6]Piper, 59.

[7]On the entry sayings see H. Windisch, "Die Sprüche vom Eingehen in das Reich Gottes," *ZNW* 27 (1928), 163–92.

God' is maintained." Even if we agree with recent British scholarship that the concept "kingdom of God" is not of apocalyptic origin[8] it clearly refers to an eschatological future here, though in the baptismal catechesis the vices here indicated (a list which also most probably came from the baptismal catechesis) would have had to be surrendered at baptism. Accordingly, in the pre-Pauline source the term kingdom of God would have contained an element of realized eschatology. Baptism is a proleptic entry into the kingdom of God and the entry conditions have to be fulfilled at that moment. *Mē planāsthe* is an instance of diatribe style (Vischer): "make no mistake about it." In the list of vices Paul once more draws upon pre-Pauline catechetical lists. Ten vices are listed. The first five are sexual and not directly relevant to the present discussion (though they have bearing on the wider context, in chapters 5 and 6:12ff.). The items in the second group however are directly relevant, particularly *pleonektai*, and it will be for the sake of this that Paul will have quoted the list. Its implication that works, rather than faith, decide our admission into or rejection from the kingdom of God is another indication of the use of traditional materials rather than of Pauline composition. It is not necessary for our purpose to discuss the other vices.

VERSE 11. "Such were some of you." Paul here stops quoting the baptismal catechesis and addressed the Corinthians directly. *ēte* denotes that Paul is speaking of "some" (NB not all) who had lived in these pagan vices (is he differentiating between former pagans and former Jews?) before their conversion and baptism. Dinkler however takes this phrase differently. *"Mit dem* kai tauta tines ēte *spielt hier Paulus nicht auf die vorchristliche Existenz an, denn wäre auch das einschränkende* tines *kaum motiviert, sondern er meint die vor heidnischen Gerichten prozessierenden Christen in Korinth."*[9] But the imperfect tense of *ēte* clearly rules out this interpretation as also does the contrast *ēte . . . alla* (cf. Col. 3:5, 8, a contrast schema also denoting a baptismal transition). Paul is speaking of what obtained in the past before their baptism. Those Corinthians who are resorting to pagan arbitrators are in danger of lapsing back into their pre-conversion condition and of forfeiting their entry into the Kingdom of God at the End.

The middle *apolousasthe* is not reflexive. Baptism was never self-administered, for it was primarily an act of God. Rather it means "you submitted to baptism" (*ihr habt euch abwaschen lassen*, Vischer). The other two verbs are in the passive, referring to what God did in, with, and under the baptismal rite: *"Man darf sie nicht vom ersten trennen; alle drei beziehen sich auf die Taufe"* (Vischer). In the age of Protestant orthodoxy theologians were puzzled at the word order, sanctification coming before justification, not *vice versa* as in dogmatic soteriology. However, like most of the soteriological vocabulary in the Pauline epistles, whether Paul's own, or as here, pre-Pauline, the terms can be used equally in a past, present, and future sense. Salvation including sanctification is decisively inaugurated at baptism, it involves a present process (hence the baptismal event is here the ground of Christian ethical obligation) and will be consummated at the End. Baptism was performed in the name of the Lord Jesus Christ. This is evidently a pre-Pauline formula. Paul himself would have written *into* (*eis*, 1 Cor. 1:13) the name. The difference is important. For Palestinian Christianity baptism was performed *under the authority* of the Lord Jesus Christ. For the Hellenistic and Pauline churches it made one over into the Lordship of Jesus.[10] This formula does not state explicitly that the Spirit was *conveyed* in baptism. Still less does it tie the conferral of the Spirit to an additional ceremonial act of anointing or laying on of hands which did not develop

[8]B. Chilton, *God in Strength* (SUNT 5); Linz: Plöchl, 1979.

[9]Dinkler, 190, n. 1.

[10]This distinction has been brought out for the first time by Michel Quesnel, *Baptises dans l'Esprit* (LD 120; Paris: Cerf. 1985), pp. 79–119.

until the subapostolic period. (Heb. 6:2; Tit. 3:5). Paul, however, clearly understood baptism as the moment of sealing with the Spirit (2 Cor. 1:22), the reception of the Spirit of adoption whereby we cry Abba, Father (Gal. 4:6; Rom. 8:15). Paul's concern here however is not to comment on the baptismal rite, although he is apparently quoting from a baptismal liturgy (Vischer). He is concerned rather to ground the radical Christian ethic in baptism and therefore in soteriology and eschatology.[11] In the new Being which we receive at baptism and which will be consummated at the End there is no place for the kind of *pleonexia* the Corinthians are showing by seeking pagan arbitrators for their quarrels over money matters. Rather they should live out the radical obedience of the Sermon on the Mount as the *hagioi* they are through their baptism: *werde das, was Du bist!* To which Paul would add: *sei das, was Du sein wirst.* Do not look out for pagan arbitrators. If you must seek arbitration, keep it within the community. Better still, suffer injustice and fraud among yourselves.

*Concluding Reflections*

Paul is here concerned with the basic issue of the relation between the church and world. No conduct on the part of Christians must obscure the fact that they belong to the eschatological community and are therefore "saints." If our exegesis is correct, Paul says nothing about pagan law courts as such, negative or otherwise. He is only concerned with the impression about their holiness which individual Christians as makers of the holy community make on individual pagans if they seek out such pagan individuals (whether bearing judicial office or not) to arbitrate their trivial quarrels about money matters. Such individual impressions will reflect on the whole community.

*Appendix: Judicial Practice in Judaism*[12]

Cases involving financial transactions as well as other matters of law, unlike capital cases, as noted in the text, could be decided by three judges. They did not even need to be authorized jurists. Even lay persons could make valid judicial decisions. Sanhedrin I:1; III:1; Jabamoth XII:1; Bahamezia fol. 32a (bab. Talmud, ed. Amsterdam, 1644). It was also possible for a learned person, an officially empowered judge, to decide a case involving property alone when, for example, he was the only authorized judge resident in a particular locality. "Lawsuits involving financial matters are for three judges. But when there is (only) one authorized person present, he can sit in judgment alone." Rabbi Nahman († 320) says: "exactly as I judge alone on money matters . . ." Sanhedr. 4b (bab. Talmud ed. Amsterdam, 1644). But even a single nonauthorized judge could pronounce valid legal decisions if both parties agreed to recognize his judgment or to accept him as their arbitrator. In the same passage we read: "If anyone has received no authority, then his legal decision (which he has pronounced alone) is no legal decision!" Mar Zutra ben Nahman (ben Jaacob, c. 320) had (as a single judge in a financial suit) made a legal decision and in doing so had committed an error. (Was he obligated to pay damages?) He appeared before Rabbi Joseph († 333). The latter said to him, "If both parties accept you as judge, you need not pay any damages. But if they do not, go and pay up!" From that it may be inferred that although he had received no official authorization, his judgment was nevertheless valid. Cf. Pal. Talm. Ned. 10:42b; Hag. 1:76c, 56 (ed. Cracow, 1609). Paul is evidently thinking of such judges sitting as sole arbitrators.

Occasional reference is made in the Jewish sources to the advantages of legal arbitration. Rabbi Simeon ben Gamaliel says: a legal judgment (sentence?) is for three, an arbitration

[11]On this point see Lohse, 321–22.
[12]Vischer, 16.

for two judges. The force of an arbitrator's decision is greater than that of judge. For when two pronounce judgment, the parties in conflict can refuse to accept their judgment. But when two arbitrators settle a conflict, then the parties cannot withdraw from their judgment (J. Lighfoot, *Horae Hebraicae*, Leipzig, 1679). "Wise man" (*sophos*) is an occasional designation for an authorized judge. Tosephta Ned. V:5, p. 281 (Zuckermann), cf. Billerbeck 3:364f.

*Final Paraphrase*

Can it be that some of you actually have the gall to go to your pagan neighbors and ask them to arbitrate when you have a dispute over money matters with one of your fellow Christians? Surely you remember what you were taught in your catechetical instruction, that in the eschatological judgment we Christians, God's holy people, will sit on the bench with Christ, judging the pagan world. If we are to judge pagans at the End, then surely you are competent to arbitrate among yourselves quarrels involving petty squabbles about money without going outside the Christian fellowship. After all, we shall even be judging angels at the last judgment. If then you have legal disputes involving mundane trivialities like dollars and cents why do you go to your pagan neighbors—people whom we as Christians otherwise hold in contempt? (I wouldn't say that normally, but I am saying it now in order to make you ashamed of yourselves). Why can't you Christians at Corinth, who boast so much of your wisdom, find one of your own members—someone wise enough and expert enough (like a rabbi in the Jewish community) to arbitrate in disputes with your fellow Christians? That is the very least you could do. But the very fact that you resort to arbitration however shows that you have lost your case already and there is something radically wrong. Indeed there is a higher way, the way Jesus taught us in the Sermon on the Mount when he said, "Love your enemies." That is, to put up with injustice and allow yourselves to be defrauded. Turn the other cheek! Yet there you are, not only putting up with it when other Christians defraud you, but actually wronging and defrauding one another!

As you remember from your catechetical instruction, unethical behavior excludes us from the kingdom of God. Make no mistake about it. There is a whole list of vices in the catechism which exclude us from that kingdom: sexual promiscuity, pagan worship, matrimonial infidelity, homosexual practices, both active and passive, money grabbing (that strikes home!) drunkenness, slander, extortion. Some of these vices were not unknown to some of you before you became Christians. But then you came forward for baptism, the sacrament which was administered in the name of Jesus and in which the Holy Spirit was at work. Then you became what you ought to *be* in your daily lives, people who are distinct from the world and who are right with God.

## Books and Articles consulted

C. K. Barrett, *A Commentary on the First Epistle to the Corinthians*, London: Black, 1968.

W. Bauer, *A Greek-English Lexicon of the New Testament*, Tr. and ed. F. W. Gingrich and Frederick Danker; Chicago University Press,² 1979.

H. Conzelmann, *A Commentary on the First Epistle to the Corinthians*, Tr. J. W. Leitch; Hermeneia Commentaries; Philadelphia: Fortress 1975.

E. Dinkler, "Zum Problem der Ethik bei Paulus: Rechtsnahme und Rechtsverzicht (1 Kor. 6, 1–11)," *ZThK* 49 (1952), 167–200.

E. Lohse, "Taufe und Rechtfertigung bei Paulus," *KuD* 11/4 (1967), 308–24.

T. W. Manson, "The Corinthian Correspondence (1)" in *Studies in the Gospels and Epistles*. Ed. M. Black; Manchester: University Press, (1962), 190–209.

J. Piper, *'Love your enemies,'* SNTSMS 38; Cambridge, University Press, 1979.

A. Schlatter, *Paulus der Bote Jesu: Eine Deutung seiner Briefe an die Korinther*, Stuttgart: Calwer Verlag, 1956.

A. Stein, "Wo trugen die Korinthischen Christen ihre Rechtshändel aus" ZNW 59 (1968). 86–90.

L. Vischer, *Die Auslegungsgeschichte von 1. Kor. 6, 1–11*. Tübingen: Mohr (Siebeck), 1955).

# Toward a Biblical Theology of Litigation: A Law Professor Looks at I Cor. 6:1–11

Robert D. Taylor

## A. Introduction

At present, in this country, we sue one another without a moment's hesitation. Doctoral candidates sue their dissertation advisors; children sue their parents; wives, their husbands; parishioners, their pastors; and Christians haul other Christians into court without the slightest tremor of conscience. And so trial dockets bulge as courts give cognizance to causes of action unrecognizable in the past. Even the Honorable Warren Burger, Chief Justice of the U.S. Supreme Court, laments publicly over the tragedy of our "excessive litigiousness"[1] and our "litigation neurosis."[2] Strangely enough this proclivity to sue is limited to Western societies in general and American society in particular. But in the Orient, by contrast, legal process is employed with extreme reluctance, and then only with a deep sense of abiding shame and remorse.[3] For while an oriental regards litigation as a symptom of societal illness rather than an index of social health, an occidental, in contrast, will boast of going to court with his attorney almost as fondly as he speaks of undergoing analysis with his psychotherapist.

With this disconcerting state of affairs in mind and in preparation for a course which I teach at the law school, a course entitled "Law and Religion: The Quest for the Spiritual Foundations of Law," I turned to an examination of I Cor. 6:1–11 and the literature interpreting it.[4] For it is in this epistle that St. Paul advances two positions; first, that Christians should practice renunciation of their legal rights; and second, that Christians should practice mediation of disputes between themselves within the Christian community exclusively.

Now with these two principles of St. Paul, an antilitigation principle and a promediation principle, the floodgate opens to a deluge of questions; for example: What theological rationale might be proffered for these Pauline views? Why is litigation cast in a negative light but mediation in a much more favorable one by St. Paul? How would those who are St. Paul's interpreters answer these questions? What understanding of litigation and mediation, whether explicit or implicit, do the interpreters of St. Paul entertain? Do the exegetical positions clustering about I Cor. 6:1–11 contain any material which might be useful for constructing a Christian biblical theology of litigation? Would this Christian biblical theology of litigation have anything to say to our contemporary hyperlitigious society where Christians sue Chris-

[1]Warren Burger, "Isn't There a Better Way?", *A.B.A. Journal* 68 (1982), p. 275.

[2]*Loc, cit.*

[3]Leonard L. Riskin, "Mediation and Lawyers," *Ohio State Law Journal* 43 (1982), pp. 29–30.

[4]Far too frequently that literature, particularly that literature dealing with Pauline ethics, acted as if I Cor. 6:1–11 had suddenly been expunged from the canon of sacred scripture. It was as if the highly charged sexual matters of I Cor. 5:1–13 and I Cor. 6:12–20 had obliterated the dreary legal matters of I Cor. 6:1–11: a case of *eros* swallowing *nomos*. Perhaps the psychoanalytic recognition by St. Paul and his interpreters that legal controversy or litigation should be fruitfully understood as a kind of perverse sexual struggle.

tians without experiencing the slightest qualm? And why is it better for Christians to lay down their rights and suffer injury rather than to litigate? In short, why shouldn't Christians sue one another and what's wrong with litigation?

In the course of finding answers to these questions, it became increasingly apparent that the implicit criticism of litigation and the consequent endorsement of mediation contained within the exegetical material on I Cor. 6:1–11 corresponds in a surprisingly substantial way to the thinking of law professors, jurists, and lawyers who are proponents of what has become known as the Alternative Dispute Resolution (hereinafter referred to as ADR) movement within the law. The ADR movement has emerged in the 1970's and

> has provided the setting for a remarkable series of developments that are changing the way in which Americans settle disputes. A variety of dispute settlement institutions and practices have emerged as alternatives to the formal, adversary relations that characterize adjudication. The emergence of conciliation and mediation centers and the extension of conciliation and mediation to the settlement of disputes heretofore left to other processes are, perhaps, the most dramatic of these developments. *This phenomenon represents a return, in part, to the more modest modes of dispute settlement of an earlier epoch.*[5] (italics supplied)

Much of the particular content of this movement as a return to earlier modalities of dispute resolution corresponds to many of the exegetical observations used to justify the Pauline positions set forth in I Cor. 6:1–11. And so it appears that biblical exegetes and professors of jurisprudence have much to share with each other in attempting to understand something about the nature of litigation and mediation.

The consensus of scholarly thought establishes that the First Epistle to the Corinthians was authored by St. Paul, probably in Ephesus, near the middle of the sixth decade of the first century C.E. and was written to a Christian fellowship in Corinth, a cosmopolitan seaport, commercial center, and the seat of the Roman governor of the province of Achaia which embraced southern and central Greece. While the socio-economic, religious and philosophical makeup of the congregation has received diverse treatment by scholars, there is nonetheless virtually universal agreement that in this epistle, St. Paul is addressing very specific matters pertaining to the life of this community; and one of these matters involves litigation between Christians before a public, pagan tribunal. It is this matter which elicits I Cor. 6:1–11 along with its vociferous antilitigation and promediation posture.

Additionally, the interpreters of the present passage are virtually of one voice in asserting that St. Paul lays down two principles regarding controversy between Christians. First, Christians should not take their disputes before judicial tribunals presided over by those who are not followers of Jesus Christ; instead they should employ a mechanism of internal dispute resolution within the Christian community itself. Secondly, and more trenchantly, St. Paul concludes that it would be better for Christians to renounce their own rights and to absorb injury even though they have just cause. In other words, the rule of law for a Christian, so to speak, is not to push forward one's rights, but voluntarily to renounce those rights and personally to absorb any and all injuries that otherwise would be amenable to legal remedy and redress.

But even given these Pauline jurisprudential principles, why should we turn to this passage in the expectation of finding hints for a biblical theology of litigation? We do so prompted by the fact that in I Corinthians St. Paul, as in no other epistle, is "practicing applied theol-

[5]David N. Smith, "A Warmer Way of Disputing: Mediation and Conciliation," *American Journal of Comparative Law* 26 (1978), p. 205.

ogy, so to speak."[6] This feature of the epistle has been ably described by C. K. Barrett who affirms:

> There is scarcely a paragraph in the epistle that does not bear historical witness to what was happening at Corinth, and theological witness to the positive and creative criticism of this that Paul believed was applied by the Gospel. It is this fact that gives I Corinthians its unique importance within the New Testament. . . . [I]t has the great value of showing theology at work, theology being used as it was intended to be used, in the criticism and establishing of persons, institutions, parties, and ideas.[7]

So, if St. Paul is practicing a kind of applied theology in this epistle, is he not in I Cor. 6:1–11 implicitly bringing to bear upon litigation a criticism from within the framework of the gospel?

But, can one not object that St. Paul is himself silent as to the reasons why he arrives at his antilitigation and promediation position? Indeed, St. Paul may have been silent, but his interpreters have not been. Throughout the history of the interpretation of I Cor. 6:1–11, abundant justifications have been suggested as the biblical-theological rationale for St. Paul's position.[8] It is to these exegetical justifications that we must now turn.

## B. The Schemes of Justification

In the history of interpretation, the various rationales that have been offered for St. Paul's position on litigation worked out in I Cor. 6:1–11 are found within three traditional theological loci. These loci are, in the order of their treatment, the christological, the anthropological-moral, and the ecclesial-eschatological. Of course, these categories are not hermetically sealed but they do provide a reasonable and useful arrangement for a presentation of representative and illustrative material. Along with each presentation of material under each of these loci, we shall attempt to trace the view of litigation that is entailed within each one of them; and we do so in order to compare the understanding of litigation held, either explicitly or implicitly, by the interpreters of St. Paul with those views advocated by the proponents of ADR.

### 1. The Christological Scheme of Justification

Now the first scheme of justification which is used to account for St. Paul's antilitigation posture in general, and his advocacy of a Christian's renunciation of one's rights in particular, is the christological. This scheme brings forward either the teachings of Jesus himself and/or his own nonretaliatory manner of comporting himself in a violent, hostile, and unjust world. Both *what Jesus said* and *what Jesus did* are proposed as sources for the Pauline norm concerning a Christian's renunciation of pushing forward his rights by means of litigation.

In the Christian West, St. Augustine was the first systematic thinker of record to appeal to the teaching of Jesus as authority for the Pauline norm in I Cor. 6:1–11. He found that authority in the Sermon on the Mount.[9] In that "Sermon" Jesus commanded

[6]Hans Conzelmann, *A Commentary on the First Epistle to the Corinthians,* trans. James W. Leitch (Phila.: Fortress Press, 1975), p. 9.

[7]C. K. Barrett, *A Commentary on the First Epistle to the Corinthians* (N.Y.: Harper & Row, 1968), p. 27.

[8]For a history of interpretation of I Cor. 6:1–11 see Lukas Vischer, *Die Auslegungsgeschichte von I Kor. 6, 1–11* (Tübingen, J.C.B. Mohr, 1955).

[9]St. Augustine, *Enchiridion* (Phila.: Westminster Press, 1955) LCC VII, pp. 386–87.

> . . . do not resist one who is evil. But if anyone strikes you on the right cheek, turn to him the other also; and if anyone would sue you and take your coat, let him have your cloak as well . . . (Matt. 5:39–41)![10]

And so following St. Augustine, a host of interpreters have employed his scheme of justification for I Cor. 6:1–11, some with complete assurance and others with accustomed scientific caution or caveat![11] One contemporary exegete of Matt. 5:39a even argues that this Matthean passage deals exclusively with the issue of protest and litigation; and so he offers as a paraphrase of Jesus' teaching the following: "Do not protest against the wrongdoer. Don't file a (legal) complaint, don't make a court case of it, don't seek damages."[12] In short, Jesus taught his followers to forego attempting to procure their legal remedies in order to vindicate their legal rights, and it is this teaching of Jesus which grounds I Cor. 6:1–11.

Another variation of the christological scheme of justification for I Cor. 6:1–11 refers not to the teachings of Jesus, but Jesus' own nonresisting and nonretaliatory way of life. Accordingly, some exegetes of I Cor. 6:1–11 point to I Peter 1:23 which poignantly reminds us that "[w]hen he was reviled, he did not revile in return; when he suffered, he did not threaten; but he trusted him who judges rightly."[13] It does give one ample pause for reflection to imagine our Lord surrounded by a bevy of attaché case-carrying attorneys zealously striving to procure from Rome and the Sanhedrin every legal remedy, if any, to which the Crucified One arguably would have been entitled.

Now the German jurist, Rudolf Von Ihering, vociferously rejects any position that would encourage one to renounce his rights. As his interpreter suggests:

> To fight and sue in courts is a legal, moral, and social duty. We should praise those who turn the other cheek, the Bible tells us. . . . The Holy Scripture is incorrect! The category of people who prefer peace over struggle, who are prepared to relinquish their rights rather than to fight, that category of people should be ostracized . . . One who gives in to others, or gives up his just struggle for his violated rights is a coward and social misfit![14]

According to Von Ihering it is a moral obligation to fight for one's legal rights. Nonetheless, the christological scheme of justification for I Cor. 6:1–11 speaks to the contrary and is ultimately predicated upon the notion of *imitatio Christi,* that is to say, the renunciation of rights by a Christian roots in a "hard saying" of Jesus (Matt. 5:38ff) which in turn roots in the "hard doing" of Jesus' own praxis. The implication is that since Christ himself did not resist or retaliate neither should his followers, even in the face of physical onslaught.

Now this christological scheme offered as justification for St. Paul's position in I Cor. 6:1–11 is predicated upon an understanding of litigation which regards it, at best, as a species of self-defense or retaliation, or at worst, as a kind of violence. In fact, this is precisely how

[10]It should be noted that this passage addresses both bodily injury as well as litigation concerning property (personaliy), just as does I Cor. 6:7b, 7c.

[11]The following are some of those who refer in varying degrees to the teaching of Jesus contained in Matthew 5:39ff as a possible basis for St. Paul's position in I Cor. 6:1–11:

William Baird, *I Corinthians* (Atlanta: John Knox Press, 1980), p. 26; C. K. Barret, *A Commentary on the First Epistles of Corinthians* (N.Y. Harper and Row, 1968), p. 139; F. Godet, *Commentary on St. Paul's First Epistle to the Corinthians,* (Edinburgh, T. & T. Clark, n.d.), tr., p. 294; Jean Hering, *The First Epistle of St. Paul to the Corinthians* (London: Epworth Press, 1962), tr. p. 41; Jerome Murphy-O'Connor, *I Corinthians* (Delaware; Michael Glazier, 1979), p. 47; William F. Orr and James Arthur Walther, *I Corinthians* (Anchor Bible, 1976), p. 197; Archibald Robertson and Alfred Plummer, *A Critical and Exegetical Commentary on the First Epistle of St. Paul To The Corinthians* (Edinburgh: T. & T. Clark 1914), p. 117.

[12]Stuart D. Currie, Matthew 5: 39a—Resistance or Protest," *Harvard Theological Review* 57 (1964), p. 145.

[13]I Peter 2:23 is employed by, among others, Hèring, *The First Epistle of St. Paul to the Corinthians,* p. 41, and also by Orr and Walther, *I Corinthians,* p. 197.

[14]Mieczyslaw Maneli, *Juridical Positivism and Human Rights* (N.Y.: Hippocrene Books, 1981), p. 91.

Karl Barth understands the position underlying I Cor. 6:1–11![15] According to the christological scheme of justification for I Cor. 6:1–11, a trial is a kind of counter-violence to an initial violence, although a counter-violence in the controlled setting of the court room, a species of regulated warfare, so to speak. And the argument runs thus: What a Christian cannot do directly when injured, namely, employ physical violence, he should not then be able to do indirectly by employing the impersonal instrumentality of the judicial system of the state. John Howard Yoder gives succinct articulation to this position when he writes:

> The very nature of the state is force, and the Christian has committed himself to have no recourse to force, not only in his own interest but even for the sake of justice![16]

So the modality of litigation, while it regards itself as a surrogate for violence, is looked upon christologically as a form of counter-violence. This rather jarring theology of litigation, implicit within the christological scheme used to justify I Cor. 6:1–11, does cause us to confront a question only recently being asked by some more enlightened jurists; namely, what aspects of violence do we come across in a trial?

In order to sketch an answer to this question, it is necessary to turn to that recent literature in law which proposes alternative dispute resolution devices in place of litigation. The ADR literature does indeed uncover possible dimensions of violence in the litigation process itself; and, it is for these and other reasons that the process of mediation is vigorously proposed as an alternative to litigation.

In the first place, litigation, even though controlled and concealed as it is in a highly stylized ritual, nevertheless remains a form of combat involving an "exercise of sovereign force;" while mediation, to the contrary, is a dialogue of "moral persuasion."[17] So while litigation is premised upon the state's monopoly in the use of force, and thus, at best, is a fist wrapped in a judicial gown, mediation, to the contrary, is an experience, not in winning or losing in consequence of force, but of mutual communication and understanding. Indeed, litigation contains an implicit assumption that human understanding and communication are well nigh impossible![18] While the metaphors appropriate to mediation are those analogous to *paideia,* those associated with litigation often betray their ancient origin in trial by battle, ordeal, and fire. Indeed, lawyers frequently refer to themselves as "hired guns," or "professional knife throwers," or "hit men." Litigation is a fight unto death in which irreparable harm (economic, psychological, and spiritual) is done to parties; but mediation, by contrast, makes room for compromise and mutual growth.

A second dimension of violence, not unrelated to the first, results from the concealing or "masking over" of the reality of persons which the legal system fosters.[19] The view of the human being which is operative in litigation is a highly truncated one. The human being is regarded as a skeleton with rights hanging from its limbs like ornaments from a Christmas tree. This abstract and denatured view of the person leads to devastating consequences where courts and lawyers tend to respond to litigants as legal objects rather then

[15]See Karl Barth, *Church Dogmatics* (Edinburgh: T & T Clark, 1961), III-4, §55, pp. 429ff. According to Barth, "those involved in an ordinary lawsuit . . . plaintiffs as well as defendants [are] excluded from the kingdom of God as heathen and unrighteous by the mere fact that they go to law against one another," p. 429.

[16]John Howard Yoder, *The Christian Witness to the State* (Newton, Kansas: Faith and Life Press, 1964), p. 7.

[17]For a thorough comparison of litigation and mediation see Leonard L. Riskin, "Mediation and Lawyers," *Ohio State Law Journal* 43 (1982), p. 29ff.

[18]William Simon, "The Theology of Advocacy: Procedural Justice and Professional Ethics," *Wisconsin Law Review* (1978), pp. 53–56 and fn 56.

[19]Refer to John T. Noonan, Jr., *Persons and Masks of the Law* (N.Y.: Farrar, Straus and Giroux, 1976), for a thorough treatment of the masking of personhood within the legal system.

full human beings.[20] Furthermore, those third parties (lawyers and judges), who control the dispute "discuss" the dispute through an obtuse, abstract, and often fictional network of language which radically attenuates or reduces the controversy by cutting it down to "legal" proportions; but this reduction cuts away at far too many aspects of the self. In Martin Buber's well-known language, the adversary system converts "I-Thou" relationships into "I-It" relationships. Or to use biblical language which is receiving new potency by contemporary biblical exegetes,[21] litigation is an arena in which the "principalities and powers" are operative along with their attendant damage to human dignity, freedom, and responsibility.

A third possible dimension of violence which resides in litigation is uncovered when it is realized that litigation attempts to right a wrong by doing an additional one. That is, by exclusively focusing attention on restoring wholeness to the aggrieved plaintiff, it thus overlooks the harm which accrues to the defendant who loses; for example, the defendant's own economic defeat.[22]

Summing up these suggested dimensions of violence which occur in litigation, it is evident why the old Hungarian maxim, "may you have a lawsuit in which you believe you are right," is regarded as a curse. And we are certainly left to ask why a follower of Jesus Christ would activate this kind of litigational machinery in order to prevail over another Christian or, for that matter, any other human being?

## 2. The Anthropological-Moral Scheme of Justification

The second scheme of justification offered in support of St. Paul's position as contained in I Cor. 6:1–11, the anthropological-moral, unlike the first, focuses neither upon Jesus Christ's teaching nor upon his existential comportment; instead it justifies St. Paul's principle of Christian renunciation of rights and his antilitigation/promediation position by primarily considering the impact of litigiousness upon the litigants, particularly upon the moral or relational life of the litigants. The ablest representative of this scheme of justification is John Calvin (1509–1564).[23] Calvin treats of I Cor. 6:1–11 both in his commentary, *The First Epistle of Paul the Apostle to the Corinthians,* and in his *Institutes of the Christian Religion.* Because Calvin was himself a student of law, which he studied at Orleans and Bourges, his treatment of I Cor. 6:1–11 is penetrating and cogent. He possesses the incisivness of a lawyer in grappling with the Pauline text.

Calvin refuses to adopt St. Paul's position in a literal way, and yet he does not avoid its rigor. He rejects a position which would absolutely bar access to the law courts by Christians; and likewise, he repudiates a theology which would offer no scriptural-theological perspective on litigation whatsoever. In the first place, according to Calvin, St. Paul could not have completely rejected access to courts by Christians in an absolute sense since he himself utilized legal process (Acts 16:37; 22:1,25).[24] Secondly, courts are not to be rejected

[20]See Richard Wasserstorm, "Lawyers as Profssionals: Some Moral Issues," Human Rights 5 (1975), pp. 15–22.

[21]This is so in the extraordinarily original mutli-volumed work by Walter Wink, *Naming the Powers: The Language of Power in the New Testament* (Phila.: Fortress Press, 1984).

[22]This feature is coming more to the fore as certain classes of defendants—anaesthesiologists, orthopedic surgeons, midwives, and more recently municipalities—abandon their traditional activities due to rising insurance costs occasioned by litigation. Also, in a more abstract way, huge awards in products liability cases harm smaller manufacturers and also foster inflation.

[23]A neoplatonic variation of this anthropological-moral scheme can be found in the *Miscellanies* (Stromata) of Clement of Alexandria (150–215 C.E.), particularly in book VII, chapter XIV, where he expounds upon I Cor. 6:1–11. Also, the *Didascalia Apostolorum* (Syrian version) sets forth a similar treatment in Chapter XI.

[24]John Calvin, *Institutes of the Christian Religion* (Phila.: Westminster Press, 1960), trans. by Ford Lewis Battles, IV, xx, 19 p. 1507.

outright by Christians because courts are themselves a gift from God and their judges are "minister(s) of God for our good."[25] Calvin clearly wishes to reject what he regards to be the anarchical radicalism of the Anabaptists who would abolish civil government altogether as completely opposed to God's purposes.[26] Likewise, Calvin rejects a kind of Christian hyper-spiritualism which looks upon the legal realm as a profane object unworthy of theological reflection.[27] But how then does Calvin understand litigation given the Pauline imperatives in I Cor. 6:1–11?

What concerns Calvin is the interior disposition with which a Christian enters and leaves litigation. Accordingly, Calvin constructs a Christian theology of litigation based both upon his understanding of I Cor. 6:1–11 and upon his personal knowledge of litigation and of the juridical. Calvin asserts that, for the most part and for most of the time, there are two particular moral-psychological states of affairs which are catalytic for activating litigational-judicial machinery. The first state, presumably in a cause of action involving property, is "greed."[28] The second motivational factor in a lawsuit, obviously in a cause of action sounding in torts, is the vice of "impatience,"[29] understood as a failure to "bear injury patiently."[30] Additionally, says Calvin, a lawsuit agitates most litigants to such a degree that "their minds are inflamed far too much by wrongful greedy desires, and they are not prepared for calmness of mind and endurance of wrongs, according to the commandment of Christ."[31] So Calvin takes St. Paul in I Cor. 6:1–11 to mean that although lawsuits are not wrong *in se* they are wrong to the degree that litigation is "bound up with improper attitudes of mind" *(pravi affectus.)*[32] And Calvin is quick to add that such attitudes are "the inevitable accompaniment of most lawsuits."[33]

So Calvin's approach to justifying I Cor. 6:1–11 is to work out a table of vices which are likely either to motivate litigation or are to come into play as the trial runs its procedural course. These vices are as follows: greed *(avaritia)*;[34] impatience *(impatientia)*;[35] revenge *(ulciscendi libido)*;[36] hostility or anger *(inimicitia)*;[37] and obstinacy *(pertinasia)*.[38] Succinctly put, litigation will most probably wreak havoc with the virtue of long-suffering love by which a Christian is to respond to injury as Jesus Christ himself taught.[39] So Calvin adopts the position that a Christian's adverting to judicial process and litigation should be an instrument of the very last resort. And because litigation is very likely to injure love, Calvin concludes that St. Paul, in I Cor. 6:1–11, is essentially correct for the lamentable reason that

> Christians ought indeed so to conduct themselves that they always prefer to yield their own right rather than go into court, from which they can scarcely get away without a heart stirred and kindled to hatred of their brother.[40]

[25]John Calvin, *Institutes,* IV, xx, 17, pp. 1506–07. Here Calvin relies upon Romans 13:4.

[26]Calvin, *Institutes,* IV, xx, 1, p. 1486.

[27]Calvin, *Institutes,* IV, xx, 2, p. 1487.

[28]Calvin, *The First Epistle of Paul the Apostle to the Corinthians* (Grand Rapids: Wm. B. Eerdmans, 1960), trans. by David W. and Th. F. Torrence, p. 117.

[29]Calvin, *First Corinthians,* p. 122. Calvin also refers to impatience as "lack of endurance," p. 121.

[30]Calvin, *First Corinthians,* p. 122.

[31]*Loc. cit.*

[32]*Loc. cit.*

[33]*Loc. cit.*

[34]Calvin, *First Corinthians,* p. 117.

[35]Calvin, *First Corinthians,* p. 122.

[36]*Loc. cit.*

[37]*Loc. cit.*

[38]*Loc. cit.*

[39]Calvin, *First Corinthians,* p. 121. Here Calvin relies upon Matt. 5:44 and Rom. 12:2.

[40]Calvin, *Institutes,* IV, xx, 21, p. 1509.

Now Calvin is quite aware, throughout his reading of I Cor. 6:1–11, that a "good litigant," i.e., one who is "free from and innocent of every unworthy attitude of mind," is a rarity.[41] And so Calvin warns that if a Christian is unable to remain of right heart, motive, and comportment, and as a result love is thereby ever so slightly damaged, then "*the whole court action of even the most just cause cannot be but impious*" (underline supplied).[42] One must suffer all things rather than be carried away by enmity toward the injuring party.

So Calvin's view of litigation which is utilized in his understanding of I Cor. 6:1–11 is quite trenchant. Litigation is so very deadly for Christians because it is a breach of love which smacks of retaliation, revenge, or "returning evil for evil."[43] Litigation, then, is not a morally neutral event as legal positivism so often asserts; it is, to the contrary, a moral transaction which will most likely impact in a catastrophic way upon the moral or relational life of the parties to the dispute. As a result, it is more than probable that the proper relationship of love which is to be normative for and between Christians will be damaged.

But, unfortunately, the anthropological, social, and psychological dimensions of litigation have received attention in legal literature only quite recently. This is so because law professors and lawyers have traditionally had an aversion toward these dimensions; toward the psychological, because of law's purported objectivity; toward the moral, because of legal positivism's claim that legal education and the law itself must be value-free and value-neutral. So the law is studied, and regrettably also practiced, in a moral-psychological vacuum, and only recently has this vacuum been abhorred by the advocates of alternative dispute resolution devices.

This ADR literature acknowledges and demonstrates that a litigant or litigants are psychologically harmed by litigation.[44] In fact, litigation, held in play as it is by adversariness, produces its own forms of cruelty and agitating circumstances for litigants.[45]

If, as Calvin interprets the Apostle Paul, St. Paul recognized the moral-psychological harm of litigation to the litigants, so too, did the late Lon Fuller, Professor at Harvard Law School. He was well aware that litigation ruptures relationships, and accordingly he explored in depth the process of mediation whose central quality is

> its capacity to reorient the parties toward each other, not by imposing rules on them, but by helping them to achieve a new and shared perception of their relationship, a perception that will redirect their attitudes and dispositions toward one another.[46]

Mediation, unlike litigation, lets the disputants control their own dispute, not third parties (judges and advocates); it aims at restoration of relationship and not at winning; and it allows mutual understanding to emerge rather than imposing the burden of *a priori* rules upon the disputants.[47]

Now to break through to the understanding of litigation as a psychological moral-event (and the likely superiority of mediation as measured by these criteria) wil require, of course,

[41]Calvin, *First Corinthians,* p. 123.

[42]Calvin, *Institutes,* IV, xx, 18, 1506–07.

[43]Calvin, *Institutes,* IV, xx, 19, 1507.

[44]See Robert S. Redmount, "Psychological Discontinuities in the Litigation Process," *Duke Law Journal* (1959), pp. 571ff.

[44]See Marvin E. Frankel, *Partisan Justice* (N.Y.: Hill and Wang, 1980) and William S. Simon, "The Ideology of Advocacy: Procedural Justice and Professional Ethics," *Wisconsin Law Review* (1979), p. 29ff, for an understanding of these matters.

[46]Lon L. Fuller, "Mediation—Its Forms and Functions," *Southern California Law Review,* 44 (1971), p. 325.

[47]For a nontechnical understanding of the contrast between litigation and mediation refer to Jack Etheridge's article "Mending Fences: Mediation in the Community," *Trial* (Oct., 1985), p. 31ff.

a radically different orientation in law schools.[48] Instead of being trained exclusively as a professional troublemaker, the lawyer will now need to add to his repertoire of skills that of peacemaker, and needless to say, this new role will elicit from clients a vastly different understanding of dispute resolution than that prevailing in an exclusively adversary system. Different mechanisms of dispute possess different moral-psychological climates and different understandings of the human being. A Christian who would develop a theology of litigation must reflect upon and arrive at an understanding of these nuances and variations.

### 3. The Ecclesial-Eschatological Scheme of Justification

The two schemes of justification for Paul's position on litigation—the christological and anthropological-moral—have focused on the individual litigant and upon the litigational relationship respectively. The third scheme of justification, however, transcends both these limits by focusing upon larger entities; namely, upon the community of faith and the context of the world understood as a "sphere elevated into a power over against God by the unbeliever."[49] This third scheme of justification holds within its embrace two emphases; namely, the missionary task of the *ecclesia* and its eschatological context.

With the first emphasis, the stress falls upon the impact of litigation upon the missionary task of the believing community. The exegetes who employ this scheme of justification do so by suggesting that St. Paul's position in I Cor. 6:1–11 was partially motivated by his thought that it would most assuredly harm Christian missionary work to air one's "dirty linen"[50] before unbelievers by taking a dispute involving Christians before pagan legal tribunals. Such disputation and contentiousness before a public tribunal would render unpersuasive a gospel whose message stresses reconciliation and forgiveness. Christian lawsuits before public forums would show to the world that Christians say and think one truth but really live out another. As one exegete put it,

> [A] united community in which love dominates is the existential affirmation of the truth of the gospel. A community which contains within itself the divisions which characterize the 'world' has no power to transform its environment because the contradiction between theory and practice is too evident.[51]

Litigation between Christian disputants wreaks havoc with the ecclesia's missionary (and we might add catechetical) task.

In order to avoid this result, it is hypothesized that St. Paul made a concession to the community at Corinth by proposing an internal-ecclesiastical, alternative dispute resolution process. Authorities are in disagreement as to the actual source for this Pauline proposal—whether from Judaism at large, or the Essene community at Qumran, or some pagan analog.[52] Be this as it may, T. W. Manson is quick to add that St. Paul's real intention is that

[48]For a discussion of these requirements, see Leonard L. Riskin, "Mediation and Lawyers," *Ohio State Law Journal* 43 (1982), pp. 43–51.

[46]Erich Dinkler, "Zum Problem der Ethik bei Paulus: Rechtsnahme und Rechtsverzicht" (I Kor: 6, 1–11) in *Signum Crucis* (Tübingen: J.L.B. Mohr, 1967), p. 207 (translation my own).

[50]This metaphor is employed by C. K. Barrett in *A Commentary on the First Epistle to the Corinthians* (N.Y.: Harper & Row, 1968), p. 135. For the Jewish roots of this idea see T. W. Manson, *Studies in the Gospels and Epistles* (Phila.: Westminster Press, 1962), p. 197ff. Also see Calvin J. Roetzel, *Judgment in the Community* (Leiden: E. J. Brill, 1972), pp. 126–27.

[51]Jerome Murphy-O'Connor, *I Corinthians* (Delaware: Michael Glazier, 1979), p. 47.

[52]For the Jewish background see Manson's *Studies in the Gospels and Epistles,* pp. 197–198. For a discussion of the Qumran influence see Mathias Delcor, "The Courts of the Church of Corinth and the Courts of Qumran," in *Paul and Qumran* (Chicago: Priory Press, 1968), pp. 69ff. For the pagan analogs refer to Plato's *Gorgias* 509c, Epictetus' *Discourses,* Chapter 5, and Marcus Aurelius' *Meditations* 2.1.

while "Christian cases should be tried by Christian courts . . . *[t]here should be no cases: Christian courts should have perpetual white gloves"* (underline supplied.)[53] This state of affairs will be the prevalent one because Christians are to renounce their legal rights as we have seen above, and so the internal resolution processes would have nothing to process.

It is to be noted that the implicit understanding of litigation which is contained within the scheme of justification is that litigation is a species of worldly dirt, soil that should not stain the pristine faith community and thus render its witness unpersuasive. Litigiousness between Christians is a defect (I Cor. 6:7) and indicates a defeat in both a legal as well as a moral sense.[54] This understanding of litigation approximates that of oriental cultures;[55] and it is based on the recognition that litigation is a manifestation of an absence of community, not only between the disputants but as a support for the disputants as well. As one jurist was fond of telling lawyers, "We only sue one another because we are strangers to and among one another."[56]

Do we not encounter here a troubling and paradoxical feature of law itself; namely its limits?[57] That is to say, when law is seemingly effective in holding a community together it is really not needed; and when it is needed to restore a disintegrating community, it is actually ineffective. This suggests that communal bonding (*Gemeinschaft* as opposed to *Gesellschaft)* cannot be created by law, but that law itself derives or borrows its efficacy from preexisting bonding of all sorts: familial, religious, vocational, ideological, etc.

Also, with this third scheme of justification we are brought face to face with the question of how alike and how different from the world are Christians to be in all the multifarious transactions which constitute our life? As a partial answer to this question, it must be noted that St. Paul does not advocate what many of the "Christian Right" desire; that is, the construction and employment of a body of "Christianized" law to replace or compete with the body of pagan law.[58] Instead, as we have shown, St. Paul regards the pushing forward of rights to be a form of self-assertion which a Christian is voluntarily to surrender for the reasons suggested above. It is here that we come across the second emphasis of the third scheme of justification; namely, the eschatological.

The most trenchant formulation of the meaning of eschatology for St. Paul is this:

> No longer is the world the means whereby man attempts to create his own life. No longer is the world seen as the sphere of human self-assertion.[59]

Or again:

> The destiny of those who belong to Christ, therefore, is discovered not from speculation about the future of salvation, but from the recognition that already in the present their lives are determined by the lordship of Jesus . . . and no longer by the schemes of the world.[60]

So the Church is the sphere of Christ's lordship, a lordship that even addresses the issue of the destiny of a Christian's litigiousness. That lordship exposes litigation as a species of self-assertion, a causing-to-be rather than a letting-be which remains open to Him who

[53]Manson, *Studies in the Gospels and Epistles,* p. 198.

[54]Barrett, *A Commentary on the First Epistle of Corinthians,* pp. 138–39.

[55]See footnote 3 and associated text.

[56]The late Honorable Louis Mandarino, Justice of the Supreme Court of Pennsylvania.

[57]There is not jurisprudential work that seriously explores the limits of law; perhaps this is due to the fact that theology has only recently been regarded by law as a dialogue partner.

[58]Erich Dinkler, "Zum Problem der Ethik bei Paulus," p. 212.

[59]Darrell J. Doughty, "The Presence and Future of Salvation in Corinth," *Zeitschrift für die Neutestamentliche Wissenschaft* 66 No. 1/2 (1975), p. 72.

[60]*Ibid.,* p. 78.

will judge rightly (I Peter 2:23).[61]

But what does the eschatological perspective—the perspective that the Christian is no longer under the power of the world but the lordship of Christ—offer in the way of a theological understanding of litigation?

In the first place, by setting our disputatiousness within a larger jurisdiction, the jurisdiction of the end-time, it relativizes our litigiousness. This is all to the good in that it cuts across the grain of our present thinking where we act as if every human problem has a legal solution and that only the legal solution is the really efficacious one; i.e., we do not have the feeling that anything is settled until a court has spoken on the matter. In short, the eschatological perspective converts law as an ultimate into law as a penultimate.

In the seond place, by going against the grain of our forensic reductionism, the eschatological perspective invites the telling of human stories in a more robust perspective than that of rights, duties, and privileges. The truth of this last sentence is a *raison d'etre* of mediation centers, based as they are on the

> recognition that an individual may simply want an opportunity to tell the story about his or her life condition, of which the stated dispute is only a part.[62]

We need to ask with more care the question just why it is that people bring their disputes to courts. As such, a Christian theology of litigation cannot stress often enough that litigation fosters "I-ness" as opposed to mediation's attempt to recover and reaffirm our "we-ness."

Finally, it is to be noted in passing that the eschatological emphasis of the third scheme of justification, unlike the first two schemes, turns our attention away from the litigants and toward that of the activity of judging itself (I Cor. 6:2–4). The eschatological question for the judge is: What realities will the judge let speak in the course of the dispute? What will be allowed to count in telling forth the controversy? This exposes the power of the judge in a very raw way: a linguistic police officer who establishes, by allowance and disallowance of certain perspectives, the way the litigants are able to talk about their own controversy. And eschatology, by reminding us that God is to be the ultimate judge of one's cause, judges the activity of judging itself.

From the perspective of the eschatological, the juridical framework is shattered, so that, to extrapolate from St. Paul's own thinking, "let those who litigate do so as though they were not. For the form of this world is passing away" (see I Cor. 7:29–31).

## C. Conclusion

I Cor. 6:1–11 addresses the matter of a Christian suing another Christian. But what about suing a non-Christian? What about suing more abstract entities such as a corporation, a governmental agency, or a municipality? Also, what about suits on behalf of third parties, trusteeships for example? Here we are left in the dark. These more complex matters will have to be approached only after there has been hammered out a theology of litigation for the simpler situations. What a biblical theology of litigation has offered us so far is a fuller, richer understanding of what a dispute is. It is a christological, moral, emotional, and communal event which has to be examined from an ultimate perspective. From this per-

[61]For a discussion of the regrettable centrality of self-interest involved in legal consciousness see Leonard L. Riskin. "Mediation and Lawyers," *Ohio State Law Journal* 43 (1968) p. 47 and fn 111.

[62]David N. Smith, "A Warmer Way of Disputing: Mediation and Conciliation," p. 208.

spective, we learn that a dispute is far more than something which courts and its officers (attorneys) adminster; it is rather an event that requires that

> we walk together, listen together, and even love one another, in our curiosity about what justice is and where justice comes from. . . . It is from Torah and Gospel . . . that we are most likely to be able to sketch out radical alternative to the law's response to disputes. As a matter of fact, our religious culture contains both a theoretical basis for these alternatives and a way to apply theory to disputes.[63]

[63]Andrew W. McThenia and Thomas L. Shaffer, "For Reconciliation," *Yale Law Journal* 93 (1984), p. 1665.

# Praying for Kings: The Place of Human Rulers in the Divine Plan of Salvation

Geoffrey Wainwright

The New Testament texts assigned to me for interpretation in this symposium on Church and State are 1 Peter 2:11–17, 1 Timothy 2:1–8, Titus 3:1–2, and Revelation 13:1–10. They all raise the question of the place of the civil ruler in God's plan of salvation. Taken in themselves or in literary context, all four raise also questions concerning the content of salvation, its extension, and the nature of the Church. The civil ruler has to be seen in relation to these other matters. The first three texts envisage a benign role for the civil ruler in the larger drama; the fourth text, with perhaps an anticipation in the penumbra of the third, presents an altogether darker picture. The themes of worship and prayer are present or close to all four passages. That will not be surprising if we hold, with the Westminster Catechism, that "man's chief end is to glorify God and to enjoy him for ever."

1 Peter 2:17 reads: "Honor all men. Love the brotherhood. Fear God. Honor the king." This single verse thus brings into play the nature of the right relationship to God; it broadens the human horizon to universal dimensions; it characterizes the life of the Church as a community of love; and it hints that the civil ruler has somehow a contribution to make to the proper state of affairs.[1] The passage from which it comes is therefore a good starting-point for our considerations.

## I

> 11Beloved, 1 beseech you as aliens and exiles to abstain from the passions of the flesh that wage war against your soul. 12Maintain good conduct among the gentiles, so that in case they speak against you as wrongdoers, they may see your good deeds and glorify God on the day of visitation. 13Be subject for the Lord's sake to every institution, whether it be to the King as supreme, 14or to governors as sent by him to punish those who do wrong and to praise those who do right. 15For it is God's will that by doing right you should put to silence the ignorance of foolish men. 16Live as free men, yet without using your freedom as a pretext for evil; but live as servants of God. 17Honor all men. Love the brotherhood. Fear God. Honor the king.
>
> (1 Peter 2:11–17, RSV, reading *king* for *emperor*)

Most modern commentators appear to recognize baptismal associations to 1 Peter. There is no need to follow in detail either the Anglo-Catholic reconstruction of F. L. Cross or the German Protestant reconstruction of H. Preisker.[2] Admitting the futility of such attempts to reconstitute from 1 Peter a primitive baptismal liturgy and even to distribute passages in the epistle to places in the rite, it is nevertheless hard to miss the echoes that the letter

[1]It will be seen that, with the overwhelming exegetical tradition, I take 1 Peter 2:17 as four distinct clauses, rather than allowing the first clause to govern the other three, as the new English Bible does ("Give due honor to everyone: love to the brotherhood, reverence to God, honor to the sovereign").

[2]F. L. Cross saw in 1 Peter an incomplete text of the celebrant's part in the paschal vigil service of baptism (*I Peter, a paschal liturgy*, London: Mowbray, 1954). In his revision of H. Windisch's commentary on the Catholic Epistles, H. Preisker detected in 1 Peter the elements of a baptismal service composed largely of hymns, prayers and sermons.

makes to the process of initiation. The Christians who receive the epistle have heard "the preaching of the good news" (1:12,25). They "have been born anew through the living and abiding word of God" (1:23), "begotten again to a living hope through the resurrection of Jesus Christ from the dead" (1:4). They have tasted the kindness of the Lord"(2:3). "Like living stones," they are to "be built into a spiritual house, to be a holy priesthood, to offer spiritual sacrifices to God through Jesus Christ" (2:5). As "a chosen race, a royal priesthood, a holy nation, God's own people," they are to "declare the wonderful deeds of him who called [them] out of darkness into his marvellous light" (2:9).[3] There is no knowing how active a missionary proclamation this was to be: it may be that the simple telling and showing of God's praises by God's people will be testimony enough, so that a doxology aimed directly at God will indirectly serve to invite other people into the praising community. [4]The persecution under which the addressees of 1 Peter were suffering may have hampered their ability to spread the good news. In the Soviet Union, where the churches are forbidden by the civil rulers to evangelize, the radiant witness of the liturgy is attracting people to the Christian faith.

Coming specifically to our appointed text, we find the writer first characterizing his addressees as "aliens and exiles." Similar terms are found elsewhere in the New Testament designation for the faithful "in this world": Eph. 2:19; Heb. 11:13; cf. 1 Peter 1:1,17. The primary and contrasting reference point is their implied eschatological citizenship in the kingdom of God: Phil. 3:20; Heb. 13:14; cf. Ep. ad Diognetum, 5:9. Persecution will doubtless heighten their present sense of being aliens and exiles. The author of 1 Peter draws consequences for behavior: "Abstain from the passions of the flesh . . . Maintain good conduct . . ." (cf. 4:1–3).

It is "among the Gentiles" that the Christians are to maintain good conduct. The first thought of 2:12 in this connection appears to be the eschatological confusion of the heathen, their conviction at the last judgment for having failed to recognize the true quality of Christians (cf. 4:4–5). Other New Testament texts suggest the possibility that unbelievers may, through the ethical testimony of Christians, be converted in time. Thus Matthew 5:16, a sentence used at the alms-giving in the Anglican communion service according to the Book of Common Prayer: "Let your light so shine before men, that they see your good works, and glorify your Father which is in heaven." This more generous outcome—the bringing of converts to the worship of God—may even be at the back of the writer's mind when he comes, in 1 Peter 2:13–17, to locate Christian conduct in relation to civil society.

What, theologically, can be the ground of the injunction to "honor all men" (v.17) other than the fact that humankind is made in the image of God, and that the Creator offers a chance of salvation to all (cf. perhaps 4:19 and 4:6)?[5]

According to verse 16, the liberty brought by the gospel does not carry antinomianism as a concomitant. As the Anglican collect puts it, it is in "the service of God" that we find our "perfect freedom".[6] Such free service bears implications for our relations to fellow

[3]"Enlightenment" was an early term for baptism: Justin, Apology I, 61; cf. Eph. 5;14, Heb, 6:4, 10:32.

[4]Behind *ex-angello* at 1 Peter 2:9 stands the Old Testament *higgid* (from *ngd;* LXX *an-angello, ap-angello),* which is used for a solemn declaration, a recitiation of faith before God (Deut. 26:3–10), a publication of God's name and deeds among the nations (Ps. 9:11, 40:5 etc.). In the New Testament, *kat-angello* is used for proclaiming Christ (Acts 17:3; Phil. 1:17–18; Col. 1:28), the gospel (1 Cor. 9:14), the word (Acts 13:15, 15:36, 17:13); at 1 Cor. 11:26 it refers to the eucharistic proclamation of the Lord's death until he come.

[5]"*Honor all men*—As being made in the image of God, bought by His Son, and designed for His Kingdom" (John Wesley, *Explanatory Notes upon the New Testament,* ad loc.). Wesley takes "the day of visitation" in v. 12 as "the time when God shall give them fresh offers of His mercy."

[6]The second collect of morning prayer: "O God, who art the author of peace and lover of concord, in knowledge of whom standeth our eternal life, whose service is perfect freedom . . ." The sources in the Gelasian and Gregorian Sacramentaries even use the formulation "cui servire est *regnare.*"

human beings. In Luther's words: "Ein Christenmensch ist ein Herr über aller Dinge und niemandem untertan. Ein Christenmensch ist ein dienstbarer Dinge und jedermann untertan."[7] Towards Christians it appears that kings and governors still have the divinely given function—which is why *they* are to be "honored" as institutions—that they have towards humankind at large: "to punish those who do wrong and to praise those who do right" (vv.13–14). Thus civil law, benignly understood, is a guide and encouragement also to Christians.

By "doing right," the Christians will "put to silence the ignorance of foolish men" (v.15). As Luther recognized, along with other expositors of the Lord's Prayer, the first way to "hallow God's name" is to cease profaning it by blasphemies, lies, and evil deeds. The positive way is to speak and do God's praises.[8] It may be that by their worship and by the witness of their good deeds, Christians will bring at least *some* others to glorify God.

"Fear God" (v.17) is a reminder that God is God. The noun "fear" occurs also at 1:17, where the Christians are told that the God they invoke as Father remains universal Judge. God is judge, even of the Church (4:17a), from which he requires a holiness corresponding to his own (1:15–16). Some, perhaps even Christians, may finally fail salvation:

> What will be the end of those who do not obey the gospel of God? And "if the righteous is scarcely saved, where will the impious and sinner appear?." (4:17b–18)

Yet the dominant note of the epistle is the comfort, hope and joy that come from the redemption God has given and the glory he will bestow. These are for believers (1:7–9, 21; 5:9), and there is no reason to think that their number may not be increased.

In reference to our special theme of Church and State, a special question remains regarding the respect enjoined toward king and governor at a time of persecution. Several historians have argued that the civilian authorities would have been likely to investigate Christianity only if popular hostility could cast the Christian community in the light of a disturber of the public peace. If Christians were brought before the magistrates, their case would be improved, 1 Peter seems to argue, if their conduct were such as rightfully to win the praise of properly constituted authority; nevertheless, the possibility of unjust suffering is not excluded, any more than it was for Christ (3:14–18; 4:12–16). Even the closing (and perhaps later) reference to "Babylon" (5:13) is not yet evidence that the Roman emperor has forfeited his divine commission to rule.

## II

> 1First of all, then, I urge that supplications, prayers, intercessions, and thanksgivings be made for all men, 2for kings and all who are in high positions, that we may lead a quiet and peaceable life, godly and respectful in every way. 3This is good, and it is acceptable in the sight of God our Savior, 4who desires all men to be saved and to come to the knowledge of the truth. 5For there is one God, and there is one mediator between God and men, the man Christ Jesus, 6who gave himself as a ransom for all, the testimony to which was borne at the proper time. 7For this I was appointed a preacher and an apostle (I am telling the truth, I am not lying), a teacher of the Gentiles in faith and truth.
>
> 8I desire then that in every place the men should pray, lifting holy hands without anger or quarrelling . . . (1 Timothy 2:1–8, RSV)

In his commentary on the Pastoral Epistles, G. Holtz finds extensive traces of eucharistic liturgy in the letters. He considers 1 Tim. 2:1–7 to contain quotations from prayers at the

[7] Luther, WA 7, 21 (1–4).
[8] Luther, Large Catechism, first petition of the Lord's Prayer.

eucharist.[9] More modestly, A. T. Hanson heads the section "How to conduct public prayer."[10] The passage is invoked by "the whole tradition" as the scriptural foundation for the "universal prayer" that figures in the patristic liturgies between the reading and exposition of Scripture and the eucharist proper.[11] The first formulator of the *lex orandi, lex credendi* principle, Prosper of Aquitaine (*c.* 440), appeals to our passage to make a precise point against semi-pelagianism: the apostolic injunction to *pray* for the whole human race—which the Church obeys in its intercessions at Mass—proves the obligation to *believe* that all faith, even the beginnings of good will as well as growth and perseverance, is from start to finish a work of grace.[12] On tabulating the results of his examination of the "universal prayer" *(oratio fidelium)* in the Latin rites up to the sixth or eighth century, P. de Clerk shows that prayer for "emperors and kings," especially with an eye to peace, is, with prayer for the Church and clergy, the most frequently recurring of all themes: it figures in nine cases out of ten, whereas prayer for "pagans" sinks to two.[13]

Our passage begins with the exhortation to pray,[14] and give thanks, "for all men." What is the sense of *hyper?* For the benefit of? On account of? In place of? The question pales when we look ahead at what verses 4–6 say precisely about "all": God "desires all men to be saved," and Christ "gave himself as a ransom for all." Believers may not only "pray" but also even "give thanks" for all precisely as all are the objects of God's saving love;[15] they are thus hastening and anticipating the day when they will no longer need to speak vicariously for a world that, as Karl Barth says, "is not yet" ready and willing for God.[16] That God desires all to be saved is not, except in a Calvinistic universe, a guarantee that all will in fact let themselves be saved; but then, Calvinists do not like 1 Tim. 2:4–6. At least for an apostle (v.7), the mission is an active one of preaching and teaching.

Next, prayers and thanksgivings are to be made "for kings and all who are in high positions." In an article of 1933, and written while he was still a Lutheran, Heinrich Schlier pointed out that such prayer is both a recognition of the *divine source* of civil authority—and thereby of the limitations of that authority also.[17] The civil authority is not autonomous, and its task is restricted to ensuring a civic peace in which a pious and moral life is possible. An interesting shift takes place in 1 Clement 61:2, where it is prayed that the rulers may "piously administer in peace and mildness the authority granted them by thee." There remains cause to pray for bad rulers, as Calvin argues:

> If the question is raised whether we ought to pray for kings from whom we do not receive these advantages [mentioned in 1 Timothy 2:2], my answer is that we ought to pray that, under the

[9] G. Holtz, *Die pastoral briefe* (theologischer Handkommentar zum NT 13), Berlin: Evangelische Verlagsanstalt, 1965, pp. 52–63, 95.

[10] A.T. Hanson, *The Pastoral Epistles* (New Century Bible Commentary), Grand Rapids: Eerdmans, 1982, p. 66. In *Studies in the Pastoral Epistles* (London: SPCK, 1968, pp. 62–64), Hanson argues in mroe detail that our passage provides an "outline," almost a "blueprint," perhaps rather a "common tradition," on which 1 Clement 59–61 drew for a full text of apparently public prayer.

[11] Paul de Clerck, *La "Prière universelle" dans les liturgies latines anciennes* (Liturgiewissenschaftliche Quellen und Forschungen 62), Münster: Aschendorff, 1977, p. 4.

[12] G. Wainwright, *Doxology,* New York: Oxford University Press, 1980, pp. 224–227.

[13] P. de Clerck, op. cit., pp. 298–302. Whereas the earliest texts were "très universalistes, suite à 1 Tim. 2:1, d'ailleures," the later formularies "reflètent un monde clos." "On constate, plus on avance dans le temps, un rétrécissement des perspectives . . . On perçoit l'effondrement culturel de l'époque" (p. 302).

[14] Most commentators take *deēseis, proseuchai,* and *enteuxeis* as virtually synonymous, despite nuances.

[15] "We may *give thanks for all men,* in the full sense of the word, for that God 'willeth all men to be saved,' and Christ is the Mediator of all" (John Wesley, *Explanatory Notes upon the New Testament,* ad loc.).

[16] K. Barth, *Prayer,* Philadelphia: Westminster, 2nd edn 1985, pp. 44, 65.

[17] H. Schlier, "Die Beurteilung des Staates in Neuen Testament," reprinted in his *Die Zeit der Kirche,* Freiburg: Herder, 1956, p. 1–16, in particular pp. 11 and 13.

guidance of the Holy Spirit, they may begin to grant us these blessings they have up till now failed to provide. Thus we should not only pray for those who are already worthy, but we should ask God to make wicked rulers good. We must always hold to the principle that magistrates are appointed by God for the protection of religion and of the public peace and decency, just as the earth has been ordained to produce food.[18]

At times, the motivation for praying for civil rulers has taken on a sharper formulation than the peace and quiet needed for a decent life. In face of the charges of political disloyalty made against the "atheistic" Christians for not praying to the Roman gods, Tertullian replies—and indeed with appeal 1 Timothy 2:2—that Christians do in fact pray for regular civic peace, not least for the sake of their own tranquillity; and he continues:

> There is also another and a greater necessity for our offering prayer in behalf of the emperors, nay, for the complete stability of the empire, and for Roman interests in general. For we know that a mighty shock impending over the whole earth—in fact, the very end of all things threatening dreadful woes—is only retarded by the continued existence of the Roman empire. We have no desire, then, to be overtaken by these dire events; and in praying that their coming may be delayed, we are lending our aid to Rome's duration.[19]

Or, more tersely:

> We pray, too, for the emperors, for their ministers and for all in authority, for the welfare of the world, for the prevalence of peace, for the delay of the final consummation.[20]

Whatever may be the apocalyptic calculations that occupy part of the background to this argument,[21] there need be no conflict here with O. Cullmann's rather less outlandish exegesis of 2 Thessalonians 2:6-7: "what is delaying" the End is—in extension and transformation of the Jewish notion that the delay in the Messiah's coming is due to "the still unfulfilled repentance of Israel"—the missionary preaching of the gospel to the Gentiles (cf. Mk 13:10; Matt. 24:14); the interval is a time of God's patience and grace.[22] Now this would fit nicely with the idea, as old as Origen and Eusebius, of the *pax Romana* as providential circumstances for the spread of the gospel.[23] The connection of political peace with the spread of the gospel was maintained by the classical Protestant Reformers: they expected the princes to provide "room" for the gospel to have free course.[24] The "political use" of the law—to check the ravages brought by sin to the social life—belonged to the order of preservation,

[18]Calvin, ad 1 Tim. 2:2 (English translation from D.W. Torrance and T.F. Torrance, eds., *Calvin's Commentaries: The Second Epistle of Paul the Apostle to the Corinthians and the Epistles to Timothy, Titus and Philemon,* Grand Rapids: Eerdmans, 1964, pp. 206–207).

[19]Tertullian, Apology, 32 (PL 1, 508–509)

[20]Apology, 39 (PL 1, 532). See also Tertullian, *Ad Scapulam,* 2 (PL 1, 778). But contrast *De oratione,* 5 (PL 1, 1261), where Tertullian opposes those who "pray for some protraction of the age, when the kingdom of God, which we pray may arrive, tends unto the consummation of the age. Our wish is that our reign be hastened, not our servitude protracted."

[21]L.G. Patterson comments that "Christians had always shared with Rome itself, albeit on somewhat different grounds, the view that Rome [was] the last of the world empires" *(God and History in Early Christian Thought,* New York: Seabury, 1967, p. 60). "Quando cadet Roma, cadet et mundus" (Caractarus). Christians looked on Rome as the fourth and final kingdom of the prophecy in Daniel 2. In *De resurrectione carnis,* 24 (PL 2, 874–877), Tertullian takes the Roman state to be the obstacles that, according to 2 Thessalonians 2, is for the moment holding back the appearance of the Antichrist before "the day of the Lord."

[22]O. Cullman, *Christ and Time,* Philadelphia: Westminster Press, revised edition 1964, pp. 164–166; or, in more detail for the second century, "Wann kommt das Reich Gottes?", reprinted in *Ocasr Cullmann: Vorträge und Aufsätze 1925–1962, Tübingen: Mohr, 1966, pp. 535#547.*

±÷*Origen, Contra Celsum* II. 30; Eusebius, Demonstration of the Gospel III. 7, 30–35. See E. Peterson, "Der Monotheismus als politisches Problem," reprinted in his *Theologische Traktate,* Munich: Kösel, 951, pp. 45–147, in particular pp. 83–93. like Schlier, Peterson converted to Roman Catholicism. This essay dates from 1935.

[24]See, for example, H. Schmid, *Zwinglis Lehre von der göttlichen und menschlichen Gerechtigkeit,* Zürich: Zwingli Verlag, 1959.

which itself was a divine "holding operation" to maintain fallen humanity in earthly existence with a view to bringing it from sin to salvation.

In 1 Timothy 2:8 we see the Church at its liturgical duty and delight—lifting holy hands in prayer.[25] The phrase "in every place" recalls Malachi 1:11, whose "pure oblation" is applied by several early Christian writers to a eucharist that is offered *semper et ubique*.[26] As 1 Timothy 2:8 says the worshippers should be "without anger or quarrelling," so Didache 14:2 enjoins fraternal reconciliation, "that your sacrifice may not be defiled." The Church is a community reconciled in God's love; and the entail of that, as 1 Peter 2:17 said, is "love the brotherhood."

## III

> Remind them to be submissive to rulers and authorities, to be obedient, to be ready for any honest work, to speak evil of no one, to avoid quarrelling, to be gentle, and to show perfect courtesy toward all men.
>
> (Titus 3:1-2, RSV)

Looking ahead to verse 5 ("God saved us . . . by the washing of regeneration and renewal in the Holy Spirit"), H. Schlier argues that obedience to civil authorities is here grounded in regeneration.[27] The rebirth into Christ, which baptism signifies, relativizes the old creation and allows, even requires, submission to earthly rulers as conduct appropriate in a world that is for the moment still being divinely preserved although its form is passing. Believers know themselves to be in the hands of God, come what may; they draw their true life from a new world and belong to a city which they do not themselves have to build (Schlier, op. cit., 8). Schlier argues that Romans 13 is similarly governed by Romans 12:1-2, and that obedience to the civil authorites in 1 Peter 2:13-17 instantiates the general principle of abstinence from the passions of the flesh (v.11) that is appropriate to eschatological "aliens and exiles" (Schlier, *op. cit.*, p.7).

We notice that this passage, again, urges at least "courtesy toward all men."[28] In the previous chapter it has been declared that "the grace of God has appeared for the salvation of all men" (v.11).

A. T. Hanson argues that Titus 3:1–2 is embedded in liturgical, specifically baptismal, material that deliberately opposes Christianity to the imperial cult (2:11–14; 3:3–7), and that the insertion may be a way of implying "You must not join in emperor worship, but that does not mean that you should not be obedient to the emperor."[29] Hanson's notes on the vocabulary of the imperial cult and the Pastoral Epistles are certainly interesting:

> One can find in the Pastorals a whole battery of terms which were also used in the imperial cult: *sōtēr* ("savior"), *epiphaneia* ("appearance", "epiphany of a god"), *makaria elpis ("blessed hope"), megas theos* ("great god"), *philanthrōpia ("humanity"), chrēstotēs* ("kindness"), the suggestions that with the advent of the god a new aeon has begun for mankind—all these features of the Pastorals can also be paralleled in the imperial cult . . . Most of all when we read Titus are we driven to conclude that the author was trying to counter the imperial cult. Such phrases as *hē Gaiou Kaisaros charis* ("the grace of Gaius Caesar"), and *tou epilampsantos hēmin epi sōtērai tou pantos anthrōpou genous euergetou* ("he who has lightened upon us, the benefactor for the salvation of the entire human race"), which [was said] of the

[25]In 1 Tim. 2:8 "men," by way of exception, means males. Here the author is being guided by Jewish practice in public prayer. There is no reason to think that the "good deeds" expected of pious women in vv. 9–10 are restricted to females.

[26]Didache 14:3; Justin, Dialogue with Trypho, 41:2–3; etc.

[27]H. Schlier, op. cit., p. 8.

[28]"Even those who are such as we were [cf. v. 3]" (John Wesley, *Explanatory Notes upon the New Testament,* ad loc.).

[29]A.T. Hanson, *The Pastoral Epistles,* pp. 183–193; cf. *Studies in the Pastoral Epistles,* pp. 78–96.

> emperor Galba (who ruled only three months), make it seem very probable that the author of the Pastorals was consciously attempting to present Christ as the true savior of the human race over against the false savior Caesar . . . Coins from Crete dating from Domitian's reign bear the image of his baby son, who died in AD 83 and was immediately deified.[30]

With that, we come very close to the fourth and last of our scriptural texts.

## IV

> [1]And I saw a beast rising out of the sea, with ten horns and seven heads, with ten diadems upon its horns and a blasphemous name upon its heads. [2]And the beast that I saw was like a leopard, its feet were like a bear's and its mouth was like a lion's mouth. And to it the dragon gave his power and his throne and great authority. [3]One of its heads seemed to have a mortal wound, but its mortal wound was healed, and the whole earth followed the beast with wonder. [4]Men worshipped the dragon, for he had given his authority to the beast, and they worshipped the beast, saying, "Who is like the beast, and who can fight against it?"
>
> [5]And the beast was given a mouth uttering haughty and blasphemous words, and it was allowed to exercise authority for forty-two months; [6]it opened its mouth to utter blasphemies against God, blaspheming his name and his dwelling, that is, those who dwell in heaven. [[7]Also it was allowed to make war on the saints and to conquer them.] And authority was given it over every tribe and people and tongue and nation, [8]and all who dwell on earth will worship it, every one whose name has not been written before the foundation of the world in the book of life of the lamb that was slain. [9]If any one has an ear, let him hear:
>
> [10]If any one is to be taken captive,
> to captivity he goes;
> if any one slays with the sword,
> with the sword must he be slain.
>
> Here is a call for the endurance and faith of the saints.
>
> (Rev. 13:1–10, RSV).

The exegesis of the Book of Revelation is notoriously difficult, and its results are correspondingly varied.[31] I will largely follow another powerful and poignant essay by Heinrich Schlier, written in 1935.[32]

Satan stood on the sea shore (Rev. 12:17), and the beast which arises from the waters (13:1) is Satan's reflection, given its power, rule and authority by him, the old dragon (13:2b; cf. 12:9). The sea is in the West, where Rome lies. For the seer's generation of Christians, which believed itself to be the last, the Roman Empire had become the manifestation of the Antichrist. But it is the whole human history which is in fact being uncovered and judged in Revelation.[33] "Men *worshipped* the beast" (13:4), and "all who dwell on earth [except for the saints] *will worship it*" (v.8): "The beast claims the obedience of everybody at all times. The worship of the beast is universal in time and place" (Schlier, p.25). The beast is, as Schlier wrote in the previous essay, "der Grenzfall des möglichen Staates, . . . die äusserste Möglichkeit der selbstherrlichen Welt" (p.14–15).

Let us with Schlier look more closely at the rule exercized, and the worship claimed, by this mythical beast, concretely identified at the end of the first century with the Roman Empire, and the perennial limit-possibility of an autonomous world. First, at the level of

[30]A.T. Hanson, *The Pastoral Episles,* pp. 187–188;

[31]Unfortunately, John Wesley, following Bengel and the earlier Protestant tradition, identifies the beast with the Hildebrandine papacy. These days, it is probably only liberal Roman Catholics who identify the Pope with Antichrist.

[32]"Vom Antichrist. Zum 13. Kapitel der Offenbarung Johannis," in H. Schlier, *Die Zeit der Kirche,* pp. 16–29.

[33]See also H. Schlier, "Zum Verständnis der Geschichte nach der Offenbarung Johannis," written twenty years after the former article and first published in *Die Zeit der Kirche* (1956), pp. 265–274. Imperial Rome is precisely the "Weltstadt": "Im Rom der Cäsaren ist eine grausame und trunkene Welt-Polis aller Zeiten abbildbar und erkennbar" (p. 267).

words: the beast arrogates to itself divine titles (the "blasphemous names upon its heads" [13:1] will in the Roman case include "divus Augustus" and "dominus ac deus" [compare and contrast John 20:28!]) and attributes to itself divine achievements (compare and contrast the *megala* of 13:5 with the *megaleia tou theou* of Acts 2:11). The beast thus rivals God and even, in the worship it attracts, outstrips God: "Who is like the beast, and who can fight against it?" (such incomparability is reserved in the Scriptures for the Lord God: Exodus 15:11; Psalm 35:10; Isa. 45).

Second, the beast not only speaks, it acts: it wages war against "the saints" (13:7a). Those whose "dwelling is in heaven," themselves the "tent" of God (*skēnē* v. 6), are "metaphysically the archenemies" of the beast, which exercizes its finally impotent rage upon them (12:12). It will fail to gain the worship of those whose name has been written in the Lamb's book of life (13:8). In face of persecution, the saints are meanwhile called to "patience and faith" (Rev. 13:10).

Third, the beast is allowed "power over every tribe and people and tongue and nation" (v.7). In the Roman case, the emperor is called "potens terrarum dominus," "terrarum gloria" (cf. Matt. 4:8–9 = Lk. 4:5–6!). "In the beast the historical cosmos finds its unity" (Schlier, p.24). Here, "all differences are finally removed," and yet "the peoples never become, as they innocently dream, 'free'." There is Another to whom "all authority in heaven and on earth has been given" (Matt. 28:18). "On earth" this is still a matter of faith. There is a choice: "Entweder ist Christus der Herr im gegleiderten und geordneteten Leibe der Kirche aus allen Völkern, oder der Antichrist im entarteten, tierische Leibe seines Imperiums aus allen Nationen" (Schlier, p.24).

The manifestation of Satan is not yet done. In Revelation 13:11–18 a "second beast" arises "from the earth" to join the dragon and the first beast in what Jung-Stilling called "a satanic trinity." The origin of the second beast, says Schlier, is Asia Minor, the land of prophets and cults, and in particular of "apotheoses of the emperor." Lamb-like (v.11), this beast apes *the* Lamb.[34] He is, says Schlier, the false prophet, the propagandist priest (cf. 16:13; 19:20; 20:10). The sacral power in the service of the administrative, his function is to lead people to worship the first beast (13:12). He employs three tricks: he performs miracles (v.13), arousing misplaced faith (contrast Matt. 4:3–6 = Lk. 4:2–4,9–11); he builds up a deceitful "image" of the "immortal" beast (vv.14–15);[35] and makes worship of it a test of religio-political loyalty (the "crimen laesae Romanae religionis" was a "crimen laesae maiestatis," and that was the "dolus" needed for the condemnation of Christians, the "atheists" who did not deserve to live in such a religious Empire): for, finally, the priestly propagandist of the Antichrist's power makes religious belief a matter of permanent public control, stamping the worshippers of the beast with its mark (vv.16–17, a "reappropriation" of the (invisible) seal of baptism.

Let me now briefly, independently of Schlier, come to a fundamental systematic reflection upon worship of the State. My inspiration this time is a Catholic who turned Lutheran, namely "Dr. Martin" himself. "That to which your heart clings and entrusts itself is," says Luther, "really your god."[36] In that sense, worship is a phenomenon universal to humanity. The grounds of its universality reside in the fact that humankind was created in the image of God, for reverential communion with its Maker ("to glorify God and to enjoy him for ever"). If we do not worship the Creator, we shall inevitably worship the creature (cf. Rom. 1:18–32). And the creature most "like" God is, of course, the human being. Idol-worship

[34]The worship of the beast is "a usurpation of the worship due to God alone in a terrible hellish imitation of the *proskynesis* before God and the Lamb" (J. Horst, *Proskynein,* Gütersloh: Bertelsmann, 1932, p. 263—264).

[35]An inscription from an imperial statue read: *Autokratori theōi Domitianōi Kaisari Sebastōi.*

[36]Luther, Large Catechism, on the first commandment.

is ultimately worship of self. The *homo in se incurvatus* determines its own supreme values.

Idolatry of the State has to be seen in the perspective of the *imago dei.* One theme in traditional Christian interpretations of the creation of humankind in God's image concerns the political task of humanity. By analogy with the custom of ancient near eastern rulers to erect statues of themselves in distant provinces in order to assert their claim to sovereignty over the country, humankind is considered as God's viceroy upon the earth.[37] If the introduction of the monarchy into Israel was controversial, the danger lay in the risk that a single ruler might more easily usurp the primary place of Yahweh. Good kings, in the subsequent history of Israel, were those who ruled by the divine values of justice and mercy and kept the nation faithful to the Lord. In the New Testament we have seen that even "secular" rulers have the divine ministry at least to promote what is right and good, while restraining what is evil. At least as long as they do that, Christians are to obey them.

The need to hold evil in check is a recognition of the Fall. So radical and pervasive is human fallenness, however, that no exemption can in fact be made for the institutions of government, administered as they are by human beings. *Quis custodiet ipsos custodes?* (Juvenal) "Power tends to corrupt, and absolute power corrupts absolutely" (Lord Acton). "Those who are supposed to rule over the Gentiles lord it over them . . ." (Mk. 10:42). Whether it need be so among the followers of Jesus is a question that became delicate with the developments outlined in the next paragraph. But meanwhile we pick up again the note from Revelation 13, that even the badly ruled may unfortunately but willingly comply with the evil rulers: "for people imagine that life is better under the rule of the beast than under the rule of Christ" (Schlier, p.25). That is the measure of perversion in fallen humanity. That is why God's Kingdom is such a saving alternative. Those who belong to God's Kingdom will refuse to acquiesce in imperial or popular idolatry.

Since the fourth century, interpreters of the New Testament have had at their disposal at the contemporary end of the hermeneutical ellipse a possibility that was not envisaged by the apostolic writers nor seriously contemplated by the immediately intervening generations. Perhaps the most unlikely event in the history of Christianity was the "conversion of Constantine." For Tertullian (in part, perhaps, on account of his understanding of the restraining role of the Roman Empire in the eschatological drama), the conversion of an Emperor had been *institutionally* unthinkable: Pontius Pilate, a "Christian in his own conscience" (cf. perhaps Jn. 19:22), sent word to Tiberius, "and the Caesars too would have believed on Christ, if either the Caesars had not been necessary for the world, or if Christians could have been Caesars."[38] Alistair Kee has revived the thesis, more commonly found in minority churches than in the Church of Scotland, that what took place in the early fourth century was in fact Constatine's *sub*version of Christianity: "Why it has been previously thought that Constantine was a Christian is not because what he believed was Christian but because what he believed came to be called Christian."[39] In particular, says Kee, Con-

[37]See G. von Rad, *Das erste Buch Mose* (Das Alte Testament deutsch), ad Gen. 1:26–28.

[38]Tertullian, Apology, 21 (PL 1, 461). The grounds Tertullian advances in *De idololatria,* 18 for the impossibility of a Christian Caesar are more radical and render potentially malign the eschatological role of the Roman Empire: Christ's rejection of an earthly kingdom showed that "all secular powers and dignities are not merely alien from, but hostile to, God" (PL 1, 766–767).

[39]A. Kee, *Constatine versus Christ,* London: SCM Press, 1982: "It is not true that Constatine gave up all idea of an imperial cult in favour of Christianity. Rather, a transformed Christianity became the imperial cult by any other name . . . Constantine thus not only defeated the Church, which his predecessors had fialed to do, but enlisted the aid of the Church in unifying the Empire. And to add insult to injury, when Constantine reconstructed the imperial cult by which the wisdom of the world and the ambition of one man were given the absolute status of divine law, the Church actually pronounced this cult to be Christianity! . . . Did the Empire become a Christian state? No: Christianity sold its birthright for a pension and became the state religion" (pp. 158–159).

stantine overturned the notions of power that go with a servant Messiah. Yet the Church *did* hail Constantine as "the equal of the apostles" and a "great" emperor. For the fifteen or sixteen centuries of Christendom, theocracy became both an ideal and a temptation, sometimes in a more caesaropapist shape, sometimes in a more papocaesarist.

For post-Constantinian interpreters of the "political" texts of the New Testament, the full range of Niebuhr's "types" of relation between "Christ and culture" is available for bringing to the reading.[40] The extreme attitude of "Christ against culture" will be attracted by Revelation 13 and find confirmation there of the perennially demonic character of the State. The extreme "Christ of culture" attitude will have to maximize the positive correspondence between the Petrine "fearing God" and "honoring the king" and emphasize the new possibilities that became historically present through the acceptance of Christianity by rulers and nations. The moderate "dualist" or "synthetist" will be encouraged by the exhortation in *1 Timothy* to pray for the civil authorities, so that at the least they may secure a civil peace that allows free course to the gospel (so the dualist), or even (on a synthetic understanding) so that the civil authorites may promote religious and ethical values that the grace of God can perfect rather than destroy. Niebuhr's "'transformationist" will remember "'the washing of regeneration and renewal in the Holy Spirit" of *Titus* and look for signs of the baptismal life in the community of believers in whom conversion to God's Kingdom has begun.

## VI

We were asked in this symposium to examine the assigned New Testament texts in the perspective of our own discipline. I am a (Methodist) systematic theologian who holds that Christian faith begins and ends in worship, which is therefore a constant reference-point for theology.[41] The tendencies of my approach to the texts were gently indicated at the outset and will have emerged at various points along the way, and in return several "messages" from the texts have been picked up as we went along. What, then, with the aid of expert and sympathetic exegetes, have I seen, and perhaps helped the reader to see, in our texts when they are read in a systematic perspective colored by the liturgy? Briefly, I return from my reading this time with the following picture:

1) Humankind is a worshipping animal. The only and all-important question is whether it glorifies and enjoys the living God—or rather idolizes itself and finally dies.

2) In Christ God has provided means for the salvation of all. That is a cause for thanksgiving and a source of hope.

3) Civil rulers have a divine commission at least (a) to mitigate the ravages of sin sufficiently to preserve a social order while the gospel can be preached; perhaps also (b) to further, or at least protect, a natural or civic piety and virtue that grace can come to perfect; and maybe even (c) to function still for believers in terms of the "third use" of the law that Calvin and Wesley allowed, in order to exhort and encourage Christians in the way of sanctification.

4) Perversely, civil leaders are in perpetual danger of coming to embody that very will to "self-rule" in which rebellion against God consists. They are then apt to attract the worship of a compliant populace, which may indeed have cast their leaders in that role in the first place. Even under persecution, the New Testament writers—perhaps because success was

[40] H. Richard Neibuhr, *Christ and Culture,* New York: Harper & Row, 1951.

[41] Questions of Christianity and politics received some treatment in my *Doxology,* especially chapters XI (Culture) and XII (Ethics), and in *The Ecumenical Moment* (Grand Rapids: Eerdmans, 1983), especially chapter IX (Revolution and Quietism).

historically inconceivable—offer no advice to Christians on active resistance to authorities who have apparently ceased to carry out the minimal divine commission to rule according to right and wrong. Calvin concluded that "no command has been given us except to obey and suffer"—and even to suffer all the more, if obedience to God entails, in extreme cases, disobedience to the king.[42] It seems equally beyond the historical horizon of the New Testament writers that Christians or the Church should have any participatory influence upon "public policy."[43]

5) The Church is the company of those who have been reconciled in the love of God. It adumbrates and anticipates the final salvation in God's Kingdom. Drawing its life from that future, this Church is by word and deed, in its liturgy, its proclamation, and its conduct, a sign to the world of what is promised to all who, by the power of the Holy Spirit, come to believe in the God and Father of our Lord Jesus Christ. It prays and hopes for all as the objects of God's love. It prays for civil rulers in the official execution of their God-given responsibilities. It should pray for them as human beings also, to whom salvation is offered as to all.

[42]Institutes IV. 20, 31–32. Calvin did allow that other agents might *unwittingly* do God's work in overthrowing wicked rulers (IV. 20, 30).

[43]Where the State is at least open to the Church and to the Christian faith, the best account of the proper relation of the Christian community to the civil community is to be found along the lines of Karl Barth's "analogy," whereby the Christian witness seeks to promote in society the values of God's kingdom, although this will be in an "exterior" and "provisional" form, whereas faith knows in an "interior" and "definitive" way those same realities of freedom, justice, peace, humanity, and the like (*Christengemeinde und Bürgergemeinde,* Munich: Kaiser, 1946; English translation in *Against the Stream,* New York: Philosophical Library, 1954). When a society or a government is not open to the Christian faith, the question of whence it draws even minimal standards of right and wrong raises the difficult theological theme for which "natural law" and "general revelation" stand as pointers. Further: whether it be a matter of minimal notions of right and wrong or of the more profiled values of God's kingdom, the complexities of human affairs are such that it seems there must always be room on our side for considerable variety of judgment in practical implementation and casuistical application.

# THE CONTRIBUTORS

JAMES D. G. DUNN, Professor of Divinity, Department of Theology, University of Durham, Durham, England.

RICHARD K. FENN, Professor of Christianity and Society, Princeton Theological Seminary, Princeton, New Jersey.

REGINALD H. FULLER, Professor of New Testament, Emeritus, The Protestant Episcopal Theological Seminary in Virginia, Alexandria, Virginia.

THOMAS W. GILLESPIE, President and Professor of New Testament, Princeton Theological Seminary, Princeton, New Jersey. Editor, EX AUDITU.

SEAN E. McEVENUE, Acting Chairman, Department of Theological Studies, Concordia University, Montreal, Quebec, Canada.

ULRICH W. MAUSER, Dean and Professor of New Testament, Pittsburgh Theological Seminary, Pittsburgh, Pennsylvania.

BEN F. MEYER, Professor of Religious Studies, McMaster University, Hamilton, Ontario, Canada.

PATRICK D. MILLER, JR., Professor of Old Testament, Princeton Theological Seminary, Princeton, New Jersey.

DAVID C. STEINMETZ, Professor of Church History and Doctrine, Divinity School, Duke University, Durham, North Carolina.

PETER STUHLMACHER, Professor of New Testament, Tübingen University, West Germany.

ROBERT D. TAYLOR, Professor of Law, School of Law, Duquesne University, Pittsburgh, Pennsylvania.

GEOFFREY WAINWRIGHT, Professor of Theology, Divinity School, Duke University, Durham, North Carolina.

# NEUMANN SYMPOSIUM ATTENDANTS

FRED E. CASSELL
J. CHRISTIAAN BEKER
CRAIG D. BOWMAN
JAMES A. CHARLESWORTH
JAMES T. CLEMONS
MR. AND MRS. JAMES D. G. DUNN
RICHARD K. FENN
REGINALD H. FULLER
THOMAS W. GILLESPIE
ROBERT A. GUELICH
DIKRAN Y. HADIDIAN
DANIEL C. HARLOW
MARK HOLLINGSWORTH
TRAUGOTT HOLTZ
MERWYN S. JOHNSON
MR. AND MRS. W. GERALD KENDRICK
NANCY J. LAMMERS
MR. AND MRS. ULRICH MAUSER
SEAN E. McEVENUE
DONALD G. MILLER
PATRICK D. MILLER, JR.
JOHN S. MUNDAY
EDITH NEUMANN
BARCLAY M. NEWMAN
HAROLD P. SCANLIN
MR. AND MRS. DANIEL A. SCHWAN
BRUCE E. SHIELDS
DAVID C. STEINMETZ
DAVID A. STEVENS
PETER STUHLMACHER
WALTER C. SUTTON
ROBERT D. TAYLOR
KRIJN A. VAN DER JAGT
GEOFFREY WAINWRIGHT
GORDON E. WHITNEY

# EX AUDITU

Subscription Rates (for one year)

Individuals (includes membership of the Symposium)

| | |
|---|---|
| ☐ USA | $15.00 |
| ☐ Canada (in U.S. Funds) | $12.00 |
| ☐ All other countries (in U.S Funds) | $15.00 |

Institutions and/or Libraries (includes one membership of the Symposium.)

| | |
|---|---|
| ☐ USA | $25.00 |
| ☐ Canada (in U.S. Funds) | $20.00 |
| ☐ All other countries (in U.S. Funds) | $25.00 |